D0712674

Platonism, Music and the Listener's Share

Continuum Studies in Philosophy:
Series Editor: James Fieser, University of Tennessee at Martin

Platonism, Music and the Listener's Share

Christopher Norris

continuum

Continuum International Publishing Group
The Tower Building
11 York Road
London
SE1 7NX

80 Maiden Lane, Suite 704
New York, NY 10038

British Library Cataloguing-in-Publication Data
A catalogue record for this book is available from the British Library.

ISBN: 0826491782 (hardback)

Typeset by Fakenham Photosetting Limited, Fakenham, Norfolk
Printed and bound in Great Britain by Biddles Ltd, Kings Lynn, Norfolk

Contents

For David Hume (1946–)

Introduction and Acknowledgements

What is a musical work? What are its identity-conditions and the criteria (if any) that these establish for a competent, intelligent and musically perceptive act of performance or audition? Should the work-concept henceforth be dissolved – as some 'New Musicologists' would have it – into the various, ever-changing sociocultural or ideological contexts that make up its reception-history to date? Can music be thought of as possessing certain attributes, structural features or intrinsically valuable qualities that are response-transcendent, i.e., that might always elude or surpass our present-best, even future-best-attainable, consensus of informed opinion? If so, should music be conceived – in Platonist terms – as inhabiting a realm of absolute ideal objectivity along with those other abstract items (like numbers, sets, classes or propositions) which make up the putative object-domain of mathematics, logic and the formal sciences? Or should it rather be conceived as one among many cultural practices or forms of life which acquire meaning and value only in so far as they give voice to some given range of (maybe conflicting) ideological interests? These are some of the questions that this book raises by way of a sustained critical engagement with the New Musicology and other debates in recent philosophy of music. It puts the case for a 'qualified Platonist' approach that would respect the relative autonomy of musical works as objects of more or less adequate understanding, appreciation and evaluative judgement. (I should note that this phrase is also used by Jerrold Levinson in his 1990 book *Music, Art and Metaphysics,* though with different philosophical ends and priorities in view.) At the same time this approach would leave room for the 'listener's share' – or the phenomenology of musical experience – in so far as those works necessarily depend for their continuance and repeated realization from one performance or audition to the next upon certain subjectively salient modalities of human perceptual and cognitive response.

In particular I reject the fashionable claim that criticism should sever its ties with 'old-style' music analysis, since the latter is irredeemably in hock to notions of organic form, thematic integration or long-range structural development which betray the hold of an 'aesthetic ideology' with politically dubious (chauvinistic, ultra-nationalist, even protofascist) implications. I therefore come out strongly in defence of analysis – of its role in our better understanding and appreciation of music – through a detailed critique of this sweeping claim and its sources in a highly selective reading of texts by Jacques Derrida and Paul de Man. What is needed is a more philosophically and musically informed treatment of these issues that combines the best insights of the analytic and the 'continental' (i.e., mainland-European) traditions of thought. Above all, it would seek to accommodate two (as they might seem) sharply conflicting theses: that musical works are response-dependent in various phenomenologically salient ways whilst also possessing certain formal properties that may have intrinsic value and yet go unrecognized (or undervalued) by any individual listener or within any given cultural context of reception. In the former respect musical works involve an irreducible appeal to dimensions of humanly significant experience which cannot be captured by a purely formalist approach to music criticism nor by a purely Platonist approach to philosophy of music. In the latter respect, musical works can be thought of as ontologically comparable to the objects of the formal sciences, though always with sufficient allowance for our different (perceptually mediated) mode of access to them.

I have tried to reflect this dual orientation by taking a lead from Adorno and stressing the ways in which music – through its vivid particularities of sensuous form – holds out against the lures of conceptual abstraction and thus poses a peculiarly intimate challenge to philosophic thought. Some philosophers, Kant among them, can be seen to have reacted by downgrading music *vis-à-vis* literature and the visual arts, the former since it is arguably more amenable to treatment in terms of its conceptual content, the latter since its representational qualities (in some cases at least) may also give a hold for such treatment. Others – like Schopenhauer, Nietzsche and Adorno, in their different ways – have valued music precisely on account of its resistance to conceptualization and yet (as Mendelssohn famously remarked) its seeming to communicate certain kinds of thought and feeling more precisely than could ever be achieved by verbal language. So this is partly a book about the relationship between philosophy and music, and partly – I should admit – a book about one listener's efforts to get some order into his philosophic thinking about issues in musical aesthetics, criticism and theory. Those efforts again divide roughly along personal *versus* academic or 'professional' lines, some taking rise from nearly four decades of immensely rewarding though sometimes puzzling and recalcitrant experience of music while others have emerged more as a response to developments in current thinking about music which I find unhelpful or wrongheaded in various ways.

I should acknowledge that the latter (theoretically oriented) kinds of argument occupy a large amount of space, a fact that some readers may find symptomatic of my own unfortunate tendency to replicate just those predominant modes of specialized and overly academic discourse on music which I am apt to deplore elsewhere. My defence, briefly put, is that certain trends in the more 'advanced' quarters of the New Musicology – theories that reject (among other things) the concept of the musical work as a proper object of evaluative judgement and the idea of analysis as a means toward better, more adequate musical appreciation – are in truth nothing like as progressive or liberating as their proponents would wish to claim. Rather, they are examples of the odd predilection for throwing out the baby along with the bathwater, or finding reason to discredit various modes of perceptive and intelligent response by way of an attack on 'organic form', 'aesthetic ideology', 'structural listening' or other symptoms of the lingering attachment to elitist (canonical) values. Thus I criticize various aspects of the New Musicology, in particular its somewhat promiscuous deployment of ideas from other fields such as literary theory and cultural studies. These cross-disciplinary ventures all too often run the risk of ignoring or devaluing what is specific to the experience of music: that is, its uniquely effective capacity for combining sensory-perceptual with analytically informed and sociopolitically aware modes of listener-response. However, any power it may possess to challenge our acculturated (ideological) preconceptions can be realized only through better, more acutely trained musical perceptions, along with a willingness *not* to take refuge in doctrinaire theories that would leave no room for concepts such as those of thematic integration, tonal development or long-range structural grasp. I also make reference to recent ideas in cognitive psychology as a counter to the textualist bias of 'deconstructive' music theory which risks losing touch with whatever is most distinctive and potentially transformative in our experience of music.

As will soon become clear, I do quite enjoy these theoretical debates and would otherwise scarcely have devoted so much time and effort to pursuing them. Still the pleasures and rewards of musical experience go so far beyond the pleasure to be taken in that kind of strictly second-order pursuit that any leaning in the opposite direction should properly be thought of as a bad case of academic psychopathology. Since browsers might come away with just that impression from a sampling of the pages that follow – or from a glance at the index and endnotes – I should say straight away that this book has been written out of a longstanding passionate involvement with music which I hope can be felt to inform its arguments at every stage, even where they go by way of various (on the face of it) more remotely 'philosophical' concerns. Also it is the product of a strong conviction that music sets the terms for any theoretical approach rather than providing just a handy pretext for theorists to treat it in accordance with their own metaphysical, ontological or – most often nowadays – sociocultural–political views. What has characterized the thinking of those philosophers who have had the most keenly perceptive and illuminating things to say about music is precisely this sense of its ultimate irreducibility to system, method or creed. On the other hand, what has typified the work of those who come to it in search of ratification for some preconceived doctrine or theoretical *parti pris* is, naturally enough, a tendency to find their ideas confirmed wherever they look. This is mainly because their arguments are pitched at such a level of methodological abstraction or remoteness from the work itself – that is, from any genuine engagement with it through awareness of its structural and phenomenological qualities – that the music becomes just a sounding-board for those fixed preconceptions.

Of course one would expect music theorists and philosophers (especially those with a strong metaphysical, sociopolitical or other such argumentative bent) to bring along with them a range of standing commitments that are apt to influence their judgement in this or that case, and even to affect their perceptual responses in so far as perception is always to some extent theoretically informed. Certainly this applies to the above-mentioned three thinkers – Schopenhauer, Nietzsche and Adorno – each of whom approached music from his own, decidedly idiosyncratic standpoint, and all of whom (despite their otherwise huge differences of view) may be said to have constructed a system within which it played a crucial, philosophically load-bearing role. Yet one should also remark – by way of contrast with present-day trends – that they each had such respect for the autonomy and uniqueness of musical experience that it figured, for Schopenhauer and Nietzsche, as a touchstone or test-case against which to measure their own and every other system of thought, and for Adorno as a constant (often problematic) point of reference for his treatment of social, political and philosophic issues. Indeed, it is very often when writing about music – or when seeking to articulate those other concerns with his musical philosophy – that Adorno's intensely demanding mode of self-reflexive or negative-dialectical thought presses closest to the limits of conceptual intelligibility. This sense of music as a challenge and a provocation – all the more so for its strangely intimate yet elusive relationship to philosophic thought – is just what one misses in a good deal of present-day 'advanced' music theory, especially where the latter takes its cue from other disciplines (such as literary criticism or the sociology of culture) whose methods and priorities may differ greatly from its own. Thus I argue that the sorts of claim advanced by (some, not all) New Musicologists would have the unfortunate effect, if carried across into our actual listening practices, of producing a drastically impoverished mode of musical experience.

The same issue is raised between two philosophers, Peter Kivy and Jerrold Levinson, when the former protests against the latter's thesis (in his book *Music in the Moment*) that analysis is a largely futile and misconceived enterprise since listeners possess a limited attention-span and simply can't take in the kinds of long-range thematic, tonal or structural relationship that analysts typically purport to discover. Here I would want to say, with Kivy, that there is a great deal more to be had from music than finds room in Levinson's highly deflationist (and somewhat listener-demeaning) account. Also I would suggest – with an eye to the New Musicology – that notions of thematic development, formal integrity, 'structural listening', and so forth, need not always (even if they do on occasion, as notoriously in Schenker's case) bear witness to a deep-laid aesthetic ideology with its roots in the politically suspect notion of a privileged (i.e., Austro-German) line of musical descent. What needs defending here is the claim that musical works have at least a degree of formal autonomy, and that this gives a hold for analyses, structural descriptions and value-judgements that are not just the products of some self-deluding organicist creed or some ideologically motivated will to discover the marks of 'organic' unity where no such unity exists. More than that: I shall argue – in Platonist vein – that any well-formed descriptive or evaluative claims put forward in this regard are truth-apt in the strong (objectivist) sense that they are rendered true or false by certain features of the work which might always elude or surpass the best judgement of any individual listener or musical community.

Some of this argument has to do with current philosophical debate regarding other areas of discourse – such as mathematics, logic and the formal sciences – where truth may conceived either in realist (recognition-transcendent) terms or as 'epistemically constrained' within the limits of attainable verification, knowledge or proof. Elsewhere I have a good deal to say about the idea of response-dependent (or response-dispositional) properties and other such attempts by analytic philosophers to find some alternative, less problematical middle-ground account which avoids coming out categorically on one or the other side. This takes me into regions of epistemological enquiry that might seem pretty remote from any first-hand experience of music or even any direct concern with the issues that it raises for reflective, theoretically minded or philosophically engaged listeners. However, it is a central plank in my argument that those issues do have a genuine bearing on our attitudes toward that experience and also on the way that we encounter, interpret and evaluate various works. Thus, for instance, the question with regard to truth in matters of musical perception and judgement – whether or not it makes sense to claim that there exist standards of adequate response beyond the appeal to personal taste or to best opinion amongst those deemed fittest to judge – is within reach of any doubts we may feel concerning our own (or other people's) capacity to understand and appreciate some music at its true worth. This has been a frequent experience for me and, I guess, for most seasoned listeners to music: that is, the nagging sense that some particular work holds out possibilities of a fuller, richer, more complex and rewarding response than anything that one has so far been able to achieve. It may be felt to come about either through some present responsive deficit that might be rectifiable by further, more attentive listening, or else through the kind of perceptual-appreciative shortfall – the basic lack of attunement – which probably no amount of patient effort could do very much to remedy.

My point is that this feeling is not (or not always) just a vague intimation of insights, understandings or pleasures to be had if only we could open our ears or minds a bit more. Rather – I suggest – it is a widely shared intuitive grasp of the Platonist claim that music, like the formal sciences though in a different way, makes demands and offers possibilities of adequate knowledge and appreciation that may or may not be met by any given response on the part of some individual listener or even some standing consensus of expert (musically informed) judgement. Where the difference shows up *vis-à-vis* the formal sciences is through the obvious fact that music involves a phenomenological dimension – an appeal to the modalities of human sensuous, perceptual and cognitive experience – which clearly has no place in any realist (or objectivist) understanding of mathematics and logic. A large part of my book is concerned with establishing just how far a Platonist approach has to be adapted or qualified if it is to capture this salient distinction. That is to say, any plausible account will need to draw a definite line between truth conceived as absolutely and categorically recognition-transcendent and truth conceived – in the musical case – as likewise potentially surpassing our best powers of appreciative grasp yet also as depending for its pertinence and content on the repertoire of human responsive capacities. It seems to me that these issues of ontology and epistemology, although fairly technical in nature, don't belong solely to the realm of abstruse philosophic debate but are apt to arise for any reflective listener who has experienced that worrisome sense of a gap between actual, potential and somehow just-beyond-reach modes of understanding or enjoyment. Thus there is no sharp distinction, or so I would hope, between what I have to say on the 'personal' side about music and my own experience of it and what I have to say about the kinds of discussion that occupy music theorists, aestheticians and those in other branches of philosophy – such as epistemological realists and anti-realists – whose concerns touch closely on these matters.

The same applies to the current debate around analysis and the claim advanced by some on the cultural 'left' of the New Musicology that, for all its quasi-objectivist rhetoric, analysis serves merely to uphold the canon of established great works and thereby to keep itself (not to mention the concert-promoters and sundry conservative ideologues) safely in business. Here again I make the adversary case – a defence against this often indiscriminate blanket charge – partly through reflection on the way that my own musical experience has been deepened and extended by reading the work of various music analysts, and partly through a more philosophical critique of the arguments involved. Still I would want to claim that the two approaches are complementary, indeed inseparable, since analysis can only work – only carry conviction with the listener – in so far as its results (e.g., its pointing-out of thematic connections, tonal relationships, long-range structural features, and so forth) are such as to strike that listener with a force of intuitive rightness. That is to say, it works either by making more consciously available what had hitherto been a matter of largely unconscious, even if musically salient response or – with a greater sense of revelatory power – by drawing our attention to details or formal structures that had previously not registered even in such a subliminal way.

Philosophers of logic have had much to say about the so-called 'paradox of analysis': that is, the idea that conceptual analysis cannot have anything to teach or to tell us since it is a prior condition of analytic statements, in the strict sense, that their conclusion must contain nothing that wasn't already contained in their premises, or their predicate nothing that wasn't already contained in their subject-term. One line of argument pursued in this book is that a great deal of present-day philosophic work in the broadly 'analytic' tradition – including the above-mentioned debate about realism, anti-realism and response-dependence – is still hung up on this problem in various forms, especially in the wake of Quine's 1951 essay 'Two Dogmas of Empiricism', which conducted a full-scale demolition job on the concept of analyticity. However the paradox gets no purchase in the case of music analysis since here it is not a question of statements purporting to be self-evidently true or valid in virtue of their logical form, but rather of statements whose validity (or otherwise) is a matter of their managing (or failing) to specify just those distinctive features of the music that evoke some particular, likewise distinctive response. This is why I include a lengthy discussion of the complex, in some ways antagonistic, relationship between structuralism and phenomenology, deploying those terms not only with reference to two fairly recent and culture-specific movements of thought but also as descriptive of two much wider and longer-term philosophic tendencies. Thus on the one hand there has developed, from Aristotle down, a formalist approach that aims toward standards of objective (or at any rate methodological) rigour, while on the other there has emerged a way of thinking about music, language and human culture in general that lays more stress on their creative–expressive than their formal–structural aspects. Here I take a route via Jacques Derrida's early, intensive studies of Husserl – studies positioned very much at that critical juncture – by way of pursuing my general case for a philosophy of music that would accommodate both our responsive dispositions as evoked by this or that work and our ability at least to conceive the idea of their having fallen short in some decisive respect. Again, I take this as good reason to believe that analysis – perceptive and intelligent analysis – has a large role to play in our better understanding and appreciation of music, rather than a merely accessory or downright collusive role in maintaining the cultural–ideological status quo.

I had now better give some more detailed indications of the way my argument proceeds. In Chapter 1 I put the case for a qualified Platonist approach to issues of musical ontology. The qualifications have to do with (1) the range of works (not all) that lend themselves properly to such an approach; (2) the need that it be tempered by a due allowance for the 'listener's share', or the phenomenological dimension of musical experience; and (3), closely connected with this, the requirement that Platonism not be confused with a high-formalist conception which takes insufficient account of music's sensuous or bodily-perceptual aspect. By way of introduction I briefly describe the history of philosophy's complex and ambivalent relationship to music from Kant, via Schopenhauer and Nietzsche to Adorno, again with primary reference to this topic of musical Platonism. After that I suggest some ways in which philosophy of music might offer an insight into various issues in present-day epistemology and philosophy of mind, especially the debate between realists and anti-realists. My conclusion is that anti-realist arguments are unconvincing in this context and that Platonism is still very much in the field, albeit subject to the above-mentioned qualifications.

In Chapter 2 I further suggest that certain ways of thinking about music – about the ontology of musical works, the nature of musical response and the issue of validity in musical judgement – can offer useful guidance in other regions of philosophical enquiry. More specifically, such thinking can help to clarify the sorts of dispute that often arise in areas such as philosophy of mathematics, logic and the formal sciences. Thus, for instance, it brings out the problems with any compromise stance – such as that adopted by response-dependence theorists – which stops short of an objectivist, (i.e., recognition-transcendent) conception of truth and appeals to the assent of well-placed, competent subjects under normal, standard or (at the limit) ideal epistemic conditions. Here I maintain that philosophy of music has to negotiate a path between two seemingly opposed but jointly indispensable modes of thought. On the one hand is the Platonist conception of musical works as objectively existent (though abstract or suprasensuous) entities whose structures, properties and salient features fix the truth-value of our various statements and judgements concerning them. On the other is the basically phenomenological (rather than downright subjectivist) approach that makes due allowance for the involvement of human perceptual and cognitive responses in any properly musical experience. Thus I take music as a highly problematic but (for just that reason) revealing test-case with regard to the current debate as to whether truth can be conceived as always potentially transcending the scope and limits of attainable knowledge or accredited best judgement.

Chapter 3 makes the case that analytic (i.e., mainstream Anglophone) approaches to philosophy of music have much to gain from a deeper acquaintance with developments in post-1900 'continental' (mainland-European) thought. In particular, the issue of Platonism *vis-à-vis* musical works and their mode of existence might be brought more sharply into focus by taking stock of the encounter between phenomenology and structuralism in the work of thinkers such as Merleau-Ponty and Derrida. That encounter is strikingly prefigured – as Derrida shows – in Husserl's writings on mathematics, logic and the formal sciences. I develop this case through a running comparison between the kinds of debate that have so far characterized each tradition of thought. Thus analytic philosophy is chiefly concerned to clarify the logical grammar of our various (e.g., musical) modes of descriptive/evaluative talk, while 'continental' thinkers often proceed via a phenomenological account of our various modes of experience, knowledge and judgement. Here I claim that this approach goes further toward explaining how music can be seen to share certain properties with the abstract objects of the formal sciences but also to involve a phenomenological dimension that sets clear limits to any such analogy. By reflecting on those limits philosophers may achieve a more nuanced awareness of how the issue between realism, anti-realism and response-dependence works out in other areas of discourse.

Chapter 4 seeks to resist what I see as the excessive reaction, among some 'New Musicologists', against any notion of the musical work as an autonomous entity with certain perduring (e.g., formal, tonal, developmental or likewise intrinsic and distinctive) properties. Very often this attack goes along with a suspicion of values like structural unity or organic form, taken as indicative of the way that music analysis works to promote the canon of accepted 'great works' and thus falls in with a strain of deep-laid 'aesthetic ideology' which these theorists aim to deconstruct. My chief purpose here is to rebut that blanket charge by offering an extended critique of its various philosophic, historical and sociopolitical commitments. In particular I question its somewhat indiscriminate use of deconstructive motifs – drawn from the work of Jacques Derrida and Paul de Man – in a context (that of music theory and criticism) where they have only limited relevance since their primary application is to verbal (i.e., philosophical and literary) texts. Moreover, it tends to ignore the complex interplay in Derrida's thought between the twin legacies of structuralism and phenomenology, the former tending toward a Platonist conception of form, structure and meaning, while the latter attaches greatest significance to language or art in their creative–expressive aspect. I suggest that this tension cannot be resolved straightforwardly in either direction but that it constitutes the single most challenging issue in philosophy of music.

Beyond that, its implications extend to other areas of discourse – such as epistemology and philosophy of mathematics, logic and the formal sciences – which have lately been the subject of much debate between realists and anti-realists. I conclude by calling Adorno to witness on the need for an approach that does justice to the truth-content of musical works, conceived in objective (or response-transcendent) terms, while none the less avoiding those reified notions of musical form and meaning that merely reflect certain dominant modes of acculturated taste and judgement. Also relevant here is the widespread loss of critical nerve or confidence in powers of evaluative judgement that has led to the acceptance of so much bad (derivative, simplistic, banal, pretentious, regressive, pseudo-profound, emotionally self-indulgent) music as meriting respectful attention from presumably well-qualified commentators. Having ridden this particular high horse elsewhere I shall not go into further details now save to say that a great deal of what currently goes under the minimalist – or 'holy minimalist' – label is such as to merit some or all of the above descriptions. Sufficient to say that there is a close relation between such laxity of critical judgement and the kinds of theoretical outlook that persuade postmodern–deconstructive musicologists to deplore the idea of 'structural listening' – or long-range thematic and developmental grasp – as merely a product of elitist prejudice or ideological collusion.

Chapter 5 looks in more detail at various aspects of the 'New Musicology' and their relation to work in other disciplines such as literary theory, cultural studies and cognitive psychology. It focuses on the claims of deconstructive musicologists to have thought their way through and beyond such presumptively discredited notions as 'organic form' or the musical work as possessing any kind of structural autonomy. Along with this goes a widespread scepticism as regards the legitimacy of value-judgements, the role of analysis as a means toward better musical understanding, and the existence of 'great works' whose canonical status – so the argument runs – is merely a product of entrenched ideological prejudice backed up by the claims of analysis to locate and explain wherein that greatness resides. I concede that the New Musicology has produced some valid and worthwhile interpretative insights, but argue that it risks becoming just another kind of iron-cast critical orthodoxy when pushed in these overly generalized, prescriptive and theory-driven directions. In particular I question the tendency to import ideas from other fields – such as the deconstructive approach in philosophy or literary criticism – without taking adequate account of those features that distinguish musical experience from the activity of reading and interpreting verbal texts. Very often this results in a failure to engage with precisely those aspects of music that could put up a genuine – rather than abstract or notional – resistance to orthodox (ideologically inflected) ways of listening.

In support of this claim I adduce certain arguments from the field of cognitive psychology which might help to explain how music achieves that effect through our jointly perceptual and theoretically informed modes of response. For the same reason I defend Adorno's conception of 'structural listening', (i.e., the attentiveness to long-range features of thematic, harmonic and tonal organization) as against the attack on this (supposedly) elitist idea mounted by proponents of a deconstructive (for which read 'postmodernist') musicology. Such approaches not only sell theory short by precluding its active dialectical engagement with specific details of musical form but also go along – as Adorno would surely have been quick to remark – with the increasing commodification of music as just another object of passive, uncritical consumption. Thus my aim is not so much to discredit the New Musicology as to shift it from a stance of embattled opposition to 'old-style' musical analysis and encourage a more productive relationship between these currently antagonistic but, on their own terms, equally valid modes of critical discourse. Above all I reject the doctrinaire claim that analysis is always – and by its very nature – complicit with the values of a dominant culture and a musical canon that, naturally enough, reflects and perpetuates those same hegemonic values. On the contrary, I argue: analytically informed listening (and performance) can combine with historically and socioculturally aware music scholarship to produce a very effective challenge to routine, entrenched or sedimented habits of response.

It remains to say that this book has benefited greatly from discussions with (among others) Ken Gloag, Rob Stradling and my colleagues and postgraduate students in the Philosophy Section at Cardiff University. I am more than grateful to Alison Scott-Baumann (along with Gideon Calder, Clive Cazeaux and David Webster) for organizing a conference at Gregynog which covered many aspects of my work to date, including some of the topics discussed here. The occasion was distinguished and enlivened not only by a range of excellent papers but also by some wonderful music-making, for which I thank my South African friends Nicol and Martina Viljoen, along with self-taught jazz pianist *extraordinaire* David Roden. Wendy Lewis, Ray Davies and my comrades in Cor Cochion Caerdydd (the Cardiff Reds' Choir) have offered much inspiration and a constant reminder of music's power to revitalize the sources of political will at a time of widespread apathy and cynicism. As commissioning editor at Continuum, Sarah Douglas provided the initial spur and thereafter did much to help the work along, while Andrea Stavri and Slav Todorov were unfailingly ready with practical help and advice.

Like so many others, I felt a great sense of loss at the news of Jacques Derrida's untimely death in 2004, both on account of his pre-eminent status as the most perceptive, intelligent and original of contemporary philosophers and because he had shown me such exceptional kindness and generosity over the years. This book owes much to Derrida's encouragement and personal example, as well as to those aspects of his thinking – especially his classic early essays on the encounter between structuralism and phenomenology – that provide a main point of reference in several chapters. That he never wrote directly on the subject of music (although his commentary on Rousseau in *Of Grammatology* has some singularly penetrating things to say in that connection) is perhaps one reason why the New Musicologists have been able to promote so partial and reductive a view of what 'deconstruction' amounts to in their own disciplinary context. Finally, for reasons too many and varied to recount, let me send best wishes and greetings to Manuel Barbeito, Brian and Eileen Coates, Reg Coates, David Edwards, Terry Hawkes, Dave Hildrup,

Dave Hume, Dick James, Dan Latimer, Radmila Nastic, Scott Newton, Marianna Papastephanou, Basil Smith and Robin Wood.

Chapters 2, 4 and 5 are revised versions of essays previously published in *The Richmond Journal of Philosophy, Journal of the British Society for Phenomenology* and *Musicological Annual* (Ljubljana). I am grateful to the editors and publishers concerned for their permission to reprint this material.

(Note: I have not provided notes or bibliographical data for the various authors and works mentioned here since they are all discussed at greater length in what follows and readers can easily track down the relevant details via the index and endnotes.)

Platonism, Music and the 'Listener's Share'

I

In this chapter – and in various ways throughout this book – I shall seek to defend a qualified version of Platonism with respect to musical works. Platonism I take (conventionally enough) to involve the claim that there exist sundry objects, properties, and states of affairs – along with the truth-value of statements, theories or hypotheses concerning them – which might always potentially elude our present-best or even our utmost attainable capacities of perceptual or conceptual grasp.[1] My argument is 'qualified' not in the sense that it stops safely short of any fully fledged ontological commitment but rather in so far as it applies to some works only and enters no claim with regard to many others which may well have genuine and distinctive merits of their own but which don't qualify in this particular respect.[2] That is to say, there are kinds of music and modes of musical appreciation to which a Platonist approach is either irrelevant or largely off-the-point as concerns even the most expert or discriminating listener. Nor would I wish to be taken as suggesting that works which fall into this category – or the sorts of pleasure they provide – are *ipso facto* less rewarding or enjoyable than those that may strike us (for reasons yet to be specified) as candidates for assessment on qualified Platonist terms. Still it would be idle to pretend that I am not making evaluative claims or at least putting forward certain criteria of musical worth – and hence of truth or validity in musical judgement – which I take to hold good quite apart from any purely subjective or response-dependent account.[3]

However, this sort of argument is apt to produce some pretty cock-eyed opinions if pushed too hard or applied in the wrong way. Such is the case, for example, when Karl Popper opines that J. S. Bach's music marked the highpoint of the Western post-Renaissance tradition on account of its perfectly achieved objectivity and rigour, values that were soon thereafter exposed to the creeping malaise of an increasingly rampant or unbridled subjectivism.[4] That Popper cites Beethoven by way of contrast with Bach – i.e., as symptomatic of much that had gone wrong with music in the interim – is a sure indication, rather, that something has gone wrong with Popper's evaluative system. More specifically, it shows how an over-readiness to extrapolate directly from one to another discipline or subject-area – in this case, from philosophy of mathematics and the natural sciences to philosophy of music – can work to enforce a rigidly dogmatic and misapplied Platonist creed. Popper is on firm ground, mathematically or scientifically speaking, when he holds that our sundry well-formed statements, theories or hypotheses possess an objective truth-value that we aspire to grasp through various (e.g., empirical or formal) methods of investigation but which might yet in principle transcend our best efforts to verify or falsify their content.[5] While this case would no doubt be strongly disputed by anti-realists, constructivists or cultural relativists it does at least capture what is centrally at issue in current debate on these topics.[6] Still the argument lacks any semblance of plausibility when transposed from a scientific or mathematical to a musical-evaluative context. Thus it is one thing – a perfectly legitimate (if nowadays fiercely contested) claim – to argue that works should be assessed according to criteria of formal coherence, structural development, or long-range thematic and tonal integration. But it is quite another – and a dubious move in philosophical as well as musical terms – to suppose that unless such features are manifest in works of a (seemingly) objective, impersonal, or Bach-like rather than a Beethovenian 'subjective' or expressively charged character then the music in question must fall short of the highest aesthetic value. That is to say, this involves a kind of category-mistake whereby an ontological thesis with regard to the mode of existence of musical works is deployed as an evaluative yardstick for ranking or comparing such works.

My point is that Platonism must take different forms as applied on the one hand to formal disciplines – such as mathematics or logic – where it requires that any eligible (truth-apt) statement be conceived as objectively true or false quite apart from our present-best means of ascertainment, and on the other to fields (such as philosophy of music) where ontological objectivism can and should go along with an adequate allowance for the role of human responsive powers and capacities. Otherwise the Platonist will end up by adopting a narrowly prescriptive theory which confuses the basic philosophical issue as to whether works have a mode of existence above and beyond their realization in this or that performance, reception-history, individual hearing, etc., with the issue as to how those works should be valued in musical-aesthetic terms. Indeed, it is largely in reaction to such thinking – whether amongst advocates of a pure-bred Platonist approach or hardline formalists such as Schenker – that many musicologists have lately swung across to the opposite extreme of a cultural-relativist or social-constructivist outlook which dismisses all talk of musical value as a product of elitist bias or 'aesthetic ideology'.[7] (See Chapters 4 and 5 for more detailed arguments to this effect.) So my version of Platonism is not put forward as an absolute standard or infallible touchstone of musical worth. Quite simply, there are too many good reasons – doctrinal adherence apart – for counting music among the most important, emotionally rewarding and (beyond that) intellectually and ethically significant components of a life well lived. After all, philosophers of otherwise diverse persuasion – from Schopenhauer and Nietzsche to Adorno – have regarded music as in some sense the ultimate challenge to philosophical reflection, on the one hand intimating truths of the deepest import while on the other teasing rational-discursive thought to a point where it encounters the utmost limits of conceptual understanding. Then again, there have been those who devalued music either because, like Plato, they acknowledged its extraordinary powers in this regard or because, like Kant, they were (so far as one can tell) very largely unresponsive to it and hence unwilling to concede that it might have something more to offer than mere sensuous gratification.

Thus the music–philosophy relationship has been marked by a curious dialectic of mutual attraction and repulsion, or – less dramatically – of shared interests mixed with a certain degree of reciprocal mistrust. On the musical side this latter response is most often a product of the inverse suspicion that whatever philosophers might value in music could only have to do with its formal properties or with concepts at the furthest possible remove from the register of sensuous experience. Such was of course Nietzsche's mythical idea – in *The Birth of Tragedy out of the Spirit of Music* – that the destiny of art since the ancient Greeks had itself been played out between the twin poles of an 'Apollonian' drive toward formal perfection or classical restraint and a Dionysian appeal to the realm of unfettered instinctual drives.[8] Here he was taking a lead from Schopenhauer who had likewise – albeit from a different metaphysical perspective – treated music as the art which alone gave us direct access to the Will in its ceaseless, inchoate striving, as opposed to those other forms of aesthetic experience (i.e., the visual, plastic and literary arts) which operated always at a certain remove of conceptual 'representation'.[9] Where Nietzsche transvalued this Schopenhauerian outlook was in rejecting its deeply pessimistic conception of our ultimate servitude to Will as a kind of perpetual torment from which there was no escape except in those occasional, fleeting moments of contemplative withdrawal or aesthetic detachment when 'the wheel of Ixion stands still' and we are released from 'the penal servitude of willing'. After all, there would appear to be a flat contradiction between, on the one hand, Schopenhauer's idea of music as the highest, most authentic mode of aesthetic experience in virtue of its directly expressing (rather than merely representing) the insatiable character of Will and, on the other, his belief that the greatest attainable human good was to be found in those brief periods of respite offered by aesthetic contemplation. Hence Nietzsche's affirmative recasting of Schopenhauerian themes whereby it became the world-historical destiny of German music – more specifically, of Wagnerian music-drama – to resurrect the spirit of ancient Greek tragedy through the achievement of a new-found creative fusion between Apollonian form and Dionysian energy. Only thus, he asserted, could European culture overcome its present state of epochal decline and music regain its pre-eminent role as an expression of the deepest, most tragic but also most authentically life-enhancing values.

Whatever their differences in this regard, Schopenhauer and Nietzsche are united in opposing any Platonist conception that would locate music – or musical value – in a realm of absolute, ideal objectivity beyond the vicissitudes of human emotion or passional response. Indeed, the term 'Platonism' might seem grossly inappropriate here since, for Plato, it was just this aspect of music (i.e., its power to evoke such responses beyond the governance of reason) that led him to place strict limits on the range of socially and ethically acceptable melodic-harmonic modes. For Kant, likewise, what provoked a negative judgement on music in comparison to other, supposedly more elevated forms of art was first its sheer immediacy – its seeming to present an intensive manifold of sensuous experience resistant to formal analysis – and second its lack of any definite, conceptually determinate content which might offer a hold for philosophical discussion.[10] Yet in truth this deficit was no such thing, according to Kant's own criteria, since the chief distinguishing mark of aesthetic judgement on his account was precisely its *not* conforming to the rule whereby, in all matters of determinate knowledge, intuitions should be 'brought under' adequate concepts and thus subject to jointly rational and empirical justification. That is to say, aesthetic judgements were strictly *sui generis* in so far as they involved the 'free play' of imagination and understanding (in the case of the beautiful) or imagination and reason (in the case of the sublime), and could thus be referred to a faculty whose remit – or whose proper sphere of application – was ideally unconstrained by the standards incumbent on knowledge or conceptual understanding. Yet there could then be no reason in principle why music (as the mode of aesthetic experience furthest removed from such constraints) should occupy the role of a poor relation *vis-à-vis* literature and the visual or plastic arts, or indeed why it should not rate highest among them on just those Kantian grounds. And indeed, the history of post-Kantian aesthetics bears ample witness to this dawning realization, not least as regards the emergence of music – or a certain maximally content-free or 'absolute' conception of music – as that to which those other arts should henceforth aspire in their striving for formal perfection.[11]

This development has been well documented in recent studies from a range of philosophic, musicological, literary-critical and cross-disciplinary viewpoints.[12] Where they converge is on the claim that, as music assumed this prominent role in aesthetic speculation, so it became ever more closely associated with those aspects of Kantian thought – or of its subsequent reception-history – that privileged the sublime over the beautiful in so far as the former was taken to evoke modes of aesthetic experience that transcended any possible accounting in terms of programmatic or representational content. Thus the rise to public favour of new genres like the classical symphony and string quartet went along with a cognate shift in aesthetic valuation whereby, on the one hand, literature asserted its break with the classical idea of *ut pictura poesis* (that poetry should imitate the visual arts) while, on the other, music disclaimed its hitherto largely subservient role as an expressive vehicle for religious or secular texts.[13] At the same time music was able to enjoy not only this new-found spirit of autonomy in relation to the other arts but also – most notably in the case of a composer like Beethoven – a strengthened sense of ethical purpose which came of its close link to the Kantian sublime, whatever Kant's lack of appreciation in that particular respect. The end-result of these various interlocking developments was a set of ideas or beliefs about music that are still very much with us, though currently subject to vigorous challenge from a range of quarters. They include the doctrine of musical autonomy, the commitment to formal or structural analysis as the primary mode of serious, properly qualified engagement with music, the belief that any talk of 'content' (or 'meaning') can be justified only as the outcome of such analysis, and – above all – the idea of musical value as intrinsic to the work and in no sense a product of 'extraneous', (i.e., cultural–historical or sociopolitical) factors.[14]

As I said, these assumptions have lately come under attack with the emergence of a strong counter-movement – handily if roughly labelled the 'New Musicology' – which rejects each of them on much the same grounds, that is, on account of their subscribing to a form of deep-laid 'aesthetic ideology' whose effect is to conceal its own, highly conservative value-judgements behind a spurious rhetoric of objectivity, analytic rigour and fidelity to 'the work'.[15] Thus, from one (often hostile) point of view, what the New Musicology really amounts to is a point-for-point retraction or repudiation of all those values that accrued to music in consequence of its finally breaking free from the constraints once imposed by enforced subjection to various religious and secular powers.[16] Indeed, there is a sense in which it does return to a programmatic or content-based mode of criticism, albeit one informed by various (e.g. Marxist, feminist, cultural-materialist or psychoanalytically oriented) theories that yield very different ideas of what counts as the 'content' of any given piece. Moreover, here, as with earlier kinds of programmatic approach, the level of discussion ranges all the way from complex, subtle and sophisticated treatments which manage to make their point while respecting the 'relative autonomy' of music to reductive or caricatural accounts which purport to read off a composer's conflicts of class allegiance or psychosexual leaning from this or that passage in their work.[17] What they share is the basic conviction that musical formalism has long exerted a powerful and ideologically suspect (not to say pernicious) grip on the mindset of a great many critics, analysts and even those music scholars who feel obliged to offer occasional chunks of set-piece formal analysis by way of supporting their broader historical or sociocultural claims. This idea is often pushed to a reactive extreme, so that various counter-hegemonic agendas appear to displace any real interest in the music, or at least any serious desire to make sense of it in other than their own doctrinally partisan or ideologically driven terms. Still, one cannot wholly deny the force of some recent critiques in this vein which have shown up the kinds of predisposed bias – chiefly the taken-for-granted conceptions of structural unity or large-scale organic form – that characterize 'analysis' as practised not only by hardline Schenkerians but also by critics whose general approach is nothing like so dogmatic and inflexible.[18] So there is a case to answer by the upholders of musical formalism, even if that case has sometimes leaned over into a new anti-formalist orthodoxy with its own very definite ideological axe to grind.

II

So we now have to ask: what can remain of a Platonist conception of music if that conception entails a commitment to certain formalist-objectivist principles and values that must at least be subject to qualification in response to the kinds of challenge outlined above?

Briefly stated, musical Platonism as I understand it involves subscribing to all or most of the following six premises, each of which finds its equivalent – or near-equivalent – in other fields of enquiry where the issue is engaged between defenders and opponents of the case.[19] (1) Musical works can best, most properly be thought of as enjoying an objective mode of existence quite apart from the vicissitudes of cultural context and reception-history or the vagaries of individual listener-response. (2) Such works are not so much invented as discovered, or 'invented' more in the early (e.g., the classical rhetoricians') sense of the term *inventio*, that is, derived from some standing though perhaps hitherto unrealized set of expressive and formal possibilities. (3) Those possibilities also have to do with the phenomenology of musical understanding, i.e., its affordance of certain highly complex perceptual and to this extent subjective (or inter-subjective) modes of apprehension which characterize the nature of a full and adequate response. From which it follows (4) that musical Platonism cannot be treated entirely on a par with Platonist conceptions of logic, mathematics and the formal sciences, since it must – inescapably – involve some reference to the way that music does (or should) register with a duly attentive or musically responsive listener. On the other hand (5) this need not be taken to entail such a large and damaging concession to the value-sphere of subjective judgement or taste as to leave the Platonist thesis devoid of substantive content. For it can still accommodate the argument (6) that musical responses and evaluative claims are justified not merely as a matter of individual or communal warrant but rather as the products of an interaction between work and listener whereby such responses may be held accountable to standards which always potentially transcend any *de facto* consensus of judgement among those deemed fit to judge.[20] That is to say, what the Platonist needs to uphold – without giving rise to a strictly insoluble antinomy – is a position that makes due allowance for the role of normalized (or optimized) response while none the less maintaining an objectivist outlook with regard to musical works, their structures, attributes and hence their capacity for justifying various statements about them.

Where the problem lies, here as in the case of mathematical, natural-scientific, historical, moral and other (arguably) truth-apt modes of discourse, is with the standard anti-realist rejoinder: that if truth is indeed objective or verification-transcendent then it must, *ex hypothesi*, exceed or surpass our utmost powers of cognitive grasp.[21] Thus the Platonist is faced with the task of explaining how we could possibly claim access to truths that in principle had nothing whatsoever to do with our epistemic warrant for asserting them or our cognitive grounds for accepting them on the best, most reliable sources of evidence. Such has been the main challenge addressed to Platonists about mathematics and realists across the entire gamut of the natural, social and human sciences. After all, so it is said, what sense can be made of the realist (or Platonist) claim to *know* as a matter of self-evident or apodictic warrant that there are certain statements whose truth-value outruns our utmost capacities of proof or verification? Hence the conclusion of some sceptically inclined philosophers of mathematics: that one can *either* have the notion of objective, recognition-transcendent truth (which thus by very definition cannot be known) *or* the possibility of humanly attainable knowledge (which likewise by very definition falls short of fully fledged objectivist truth), but surely not both unless by fudging the issue. And again, as concerns moral values: *either* they exist in some realm of absolute ideal objectivity which places them forever beyond our human, all-too-human grasp *or* they must be thought of as knowable by us and hence as epistemically constrained, at whatever stretch of normalized (or idealized) human judgement.[22] Thus, quite simply, *tertium non datur* – no room for any middle-way solution – if one accepts this anti-realist logic whereby any thought of objective truth-values or of statements whose truth or falsehood is fixed by the way things stand in reality quite apart from our best available proof-procedures or sources of evidence is a thought that can only open the way to some form of global scepticism. For it is here, anti-realists argue, that the sceptic is able to insinuate doubt concerning the very possibility that human knowledge might ever make contact with objective truths or with anything beyond its own (perhaps utterly deluded) range of sense-impressions, a priori concepts, mathematical theorems, scientific hypotheses, and so forth. Only by closing the gap between truth and knowledge – restricting the scope of truth-apt statements to those for which we possess some adequate means of proof or verification – can this dilemma be resolved and scepticism held at bay. Otherwise it is always on the cards, epistemologically speaking, that truth and knowledge will come apart as indeed they very often must, on the realist's account, but – so the sceptic will insist – in a way that leaves no room to conceive how they could possibly be brought back together.[23]

Of course one may conclude that, if this argument goes through, then anti-realism is a small price to pay for finally defeating the sceptic at his own game. That is, there would seem to be every advantage for the moderate, non-'metaphysical' realist in conceding that 'truth' so far as we can know it is by very definition epistemically constrained, but turning this argument around – *contra* the sceptic – to show that such anxieties are surely misplaced since they result from nothing more than the failure to accept this straightforward, unproblematical fact about the human epistemic situation. In recent debate there have been numerous variations on this middle-way theme, all of them seeking to defuse the sceptical challenge whilst not pressing so far in an anti-realist direction as effectively to let the case go by default. They range from

Hilary Putnam's idea of 'internal' (or framework-relative) realism, via Crispin Wright's just-short-of-realist ideas such as 'superassertibility' and 'cognitive command', to theories of response-dependence that count properties real or statements concerning them veridical just in case they would evoke the affirmative response of a normally equipped perceiver/ knower under specified (maximally truth-conducive) epistemic conditions.[24] Nevertheless, as I have argued elsewhere, these proposals all run up against the same sceptically induced dilemma, that is, the choice between a realist outlook that dare not quite speak its name yet still falls prey to the standard counter-arguments and an anti-realism that manages to deflect or forestall those arguments but only at the cost of reducing truth to the compass of human understanding.[25] They all try to get around the sceptic's challenge by tailoring truth-conditions to some current-best or – perhaps more plausibly – some best-attainable state of knowledge amongst those deemed fittest to know. Only thus, so it is claimed, can philosophy hope to steer a path between the rock of an objectivist realism that places truth beyond epistemic reach and the hard place of a thoroughgoing verificationist approach that flouts our most basic realist intuitions by denying that any statement we could make might be objectively yet undetectably (i.e., unknowably) true or false. Still it is difficult to see how the picture is improved by adopting one or other of those compromise positions which do not so much resolve as evade the issue by redefining truth in terms that are either vacuous and trivially self-confirming (where truth is equated with 'best opinion' on the part of ideally placed respondents) or else come down to just another, however elaborately qualified, version of the anti-realist case.

Thus, far from offering the best of both worlds, these alternatives leave us altogether worse off by renouncing the *prima-facie* highly plausible idea that there *just are* a great number of undetectably true (or false) statements while also rejecting the assurance that comes – at any rate for some anti-realists such as Michael Dummett – from conceiving truth as epistemically constrained and hence as proof against sceptical attack.[26] This predicament is nicely captured by Wright – although not (one suspects) in quite the way he intends – through a comparison with Plato's *Euthyphro* where discussion turns on whether acts should be accounted virtuous because they are approved by the gods (whose judgement is of course infallible) or whether, on the contrary, such acts are objectively, intrinsically good and hence sure to gain the gods' approval on account of their divine omniscience or nonpareil truth-tracking power.[27] In a sense this is a distinction without a real difference since, as Wright says, the class of pious acts is extensionally equivalent in both cases, that whereby the gods determine what is right through their own sovereign or stipulative power and that wherein their judgement is effectively constrained (just in virtue of its infallibility) by truth-conditions that transcend the limits of any, even godlike adjudicative gift. All the same he thinks the analogy useful since it brings out the main point at issue between those of an anti-realist persuasion who view moral realism as opening the door to various kinds of far-gone sceptical or cultural-relativist thinking, and those in the realist camp who view anti-realism as a line of least resistance which ends up by yielding crucial ground in just that regard. And it might seem equally attractive to philosophers of music since here also there is a need to be clear about just how and where the issue arises between objectivists about musical form or structure, on the one hand, and on the other hand those who maintain – from a phenomenological or response-dispositional standpoint – that such notions are wholly out of place in this context.

Yet one could argue that Wright's use of the *Euthyphro* contrast in order to make this point itself suggests strongly that the whole debate amongst advocates of a 'third-way' approach – whether leaning toward the realist or the anti-realist side – has become little more than a notional (semantic) dispute over different ways of redefining the truth-predicate so as to head off the sceptical threat. That is to say, all parties accept that if truth is conceived in objectivist or Platonist (recognition-transcendent) terms then this threat looms large over every attempt to vindicate or justify our claims to knowledge in whatever field of enquiry. Yet, just as surely, it still shadows these attempts to specify what should count as veridical knowledge in a range of alternative (e.g., internal-realist, framework-relativist, or response-dispositional) terms. For this leaves the way wide open for the sceptic to remark that if knowledge amounts to no more than that – to a matter of conformity with our current-best (or even best-attainable) truth-claims, theories, conceptual schemes, inves-tigative methods, sources of epistemic warrant, etc. – then the emperor has no clothes and had much better graciously retire from the scene. As with the *Euthyphro* contrast, so here: *either* the claim cashes out as a mere tautology ('statement *x* is true/false if and only if *x* would be affirmed/denied by a subject well placed to judge of its truth or falsity'), thus simply collapsing the distinction between knowledge and truth, *or* it renders truth dependent on/relative to/decided by whatever is taken to constitute best judgement or optimal response at any given time. Or again, this dilemma might better be viewed as a trilemma, with the third (equally problematic) horn involving some such limit-point conception of truth as Putnam's 'that upon which all rational enquirers would converge when all the evidence was in', or – to much the same effect – Wright's epistemically beefed-up ideas of 'superassertibility' and 'cognitive command'. For the sceptic will hardly be stuck for an answer, pointing out as he can that his opponent gains nothing – and indeed loses everything – by adopting this ever more circumspect, scaled-down, or elaborately qualified view of what it takes to be a 'realist' in the face of his (the sceptic's) well-practised counter-arguments. These redefinitions of truth as in some respect or to some degree epistemically constrained will always invite the standard charge – from realist and sceptic alike – that they just cannot capture what it is for a statement to be properly (objectively) true or false, as distinct from verifiable or falsifiable by our best means of ascertainment. One is reminded of a well-known atheist's phrase about the 'death by a thousand qualifications' that Christian theology was bound to suffer once its defenders started to yield ground under pressure from various moral and logical objections.[28]

Nevertheless we can get some useful bearings on the issue about musical ontology from this current debate about response-dependence as an answer to the challenge of global scepticism and a putative solution to other longstanding philosophical problems. One reason why such claims are less than convincing in that particular context (i.e., as part of the mainstream analytic agenda) is that they lack the kind of substantive *phenomenological* content that comes from a close and detailed engagement with actual processes of sensory-cognitive and structural-conceptual grasp.[29] Thus the whole debate about response-dependence has typically been conducted through an analysis of concepts or validity-conditions which are taken to apply only at a large and philosophically damaging remove from the first-order business of describing and accounting for what goes on at that phenomenological level. Hence, I would suggest, the striking prominence of Plato and Locke – two otherwise improbable bedfellows – in discussions of how this approach might deliver a solution to various epistemological quandaries. Plato's contribution is to offer (through the *Euthyphro* contrast) a means of setting up the debate in such a way as to make it appear *both* that there is a genuine, philosophically significant issue between objectivist and response-dispositional accounts of moral virtue *and* that, since the two accounts are in accord with respect to the class of virtuous acts, that issue must be capable of resolution on mutually acceptable terms.[30] Locke's is to provide, through his notion of secondary qualities, a way of thinking about the realism/anti-realism issue which likewise promises to resolve this seemingly deadlocked dispute without leaning too far in either direction. That is, we should treat the various modes of sensory discrimination – what it means correctly to identify red objects as red, bitter-tasting substances as bitter, loud or discordant sounds as loud or discordant, etc. – in terms of a formula that spells out the normative criteria for accurate (i.e., communally warranted or non-deviant) perception and thereby captures the validity-conditions for any statement or judgement of the relevant type.[31]

However, the trouble with both these analogues – Plato on morals and Locke on sensory uptake – is that they fail to make good on that promise since the middle-ground stance for which they are recruited amounts to no more than another variation on the same old epistemological dilemma. When transposed to this present-day context of debate they work out *either* as a purely tautological claim, one that reduces to a trivial equation of truth with optimized (infallibly truth-tracking) response or idealized rational warrant, *or else* as a more elaborately specified version of the projectivist approach that would assimilate truth in such matters to the scope and limits of actual, i.e., received or *de facto* best judgement. In neither case can it offer much help with the epistemological issue as to how we might reconcile a realist commitment to the existence of recognition/verification-transcendent truths with the surely not unreasonable demand that some – though of course not all – such truths should be accessible to human enquiry or investigation. For if realism is to carry genuine weight and not come down to just another self-evident since purely circular truth of definition or just another pseudo-solution to the problem on compromise terms then it will need to keep both these requirements squarely in view. In other words, it will have to find some way of upholding the strong ontological-realist thesis while explaining why this doesn't – *pace* Dummett and company – create insuperable problems for a realist epistemology by placing truth forever and in principle beyond the utmost bounds of human knowledge.

III

My point so far is that objectivist realism – or Platonism with respect to abstract entities or the objects of the formal sciences – still merits serious philosophic attention and has not been played off the field by these latest, no matter how refined and conceptually resourceful efforts to come up with a workable middle-way solution. I shall now address the question of how this relates to issues in philosophy of music and, more specifically, the question raised in my opening paragraph as concerns the possibility of a 'qualified Platonism' that would meet the above-mentioned desiderata. That is, it would maintain an objectivist conception of musical works whilst also allowing for the vital role of human perceptual, responsive and (not least) imaginative capacities in transforming those works from an abstract-potential to a fully realized mode of existence.

To be sure, my choice of music as a test-case here may well strike many philosophers – including some whose ideas I have been discussing up to now – as curious or even as manifestly begging the question with regard to the issue between realism and anti-realism, whether approached primarily in terms of its ontological or epistemological aspects. After all, the realist might say, musical works must surely be taken to occupy a rather special ontological domain quite distinct from that realm of absolute ideal objectivity wherein are to be found the abstract entities of logic, mathematics and the formal sciences and also from the physical object-domain which includes the whole range of mind-independent realia (on every scale from quarks to galaxies) along with their various properties, structures, dispositions, causal powers, and so forth. Thus the issue as to music's mode of existence is one that falls within the remit of disciplines – such as aesthetics, phenomenology and perhaps the cultural sociology of taste – whose claims can at most be thought of as possessing an intersubjective or communally warranted (rather than properly objective) order of validity and truth. Meanwhile the anti-realist might also complain that music fails to pose the right sort of question – or to pose it in an adequately clear-cut way – since the issue of 'truth' with respect to our statements concerning musical meaning, structure, ontology or value is one which cannot be specified with anything like the degree of conceptual precision that is required in order to get such debate off the ground. That is to say, any claims advanced in this respect must appeal to a register of more or less competent, qualified or sensitive listener response whose validity-conditions – no matter how strongly backed up by techniques of formal or thematic analysis – are inherently such as to elude formulation in realist *or* anti-realist terms.

Thus the relevant criteria here have to do with what might hopefully be agreed upon by various parties with a fair claim to subjective (even if widely shared) competence in matters of musical judgement. This seems to rule out the appeal to any set of normalized standards or validity-conditions such as those which apply, say, to the veridical perception of coloured objects under average-to-good lighting conditions or of acoustic phenomena (such as pitch relationships or volume/intensity gradients) whose character lends itself to specification in physical as well as response-dispositional terms. In the latter sorts of case, so the argument goes, one can always construct a quantified and duly provisoed biconditional formula so as to capture what it takes for such perceptions – or for statements concerning them – to count as 'true' (or at any rate as warranted according to best judgement among those competent to judge).[32] Thus, for instance, "*x* is red" if and only if *x* appears red to any observer with properly functioning visual apparatus when viewed at noon under favourable (not-too-bright) weather conditions and in the absence of any proximate light-source or cause of interference that might have a disturbing effect on her otherwise normal powers of perception'. Or again: 'sound *y* is higher-pitched/louder/more *staccato* than sound *z* if and only if perceived as such by a listener with properly functioning auditory apparatus in a reasonably quiet (maybe not wholly anacoustic) setting and in the absence of any proximate sound-sources that might mask or distort its character'. So the validity of statements like these – statements with regard to Lockean 'secondary qualities' – can be treated as determinate enough for all practical, normative-judgemental purposes. At the same time this approach avoids both the problem faced by hardline objectivists for whom truth in such matters must be thought of as always potentially lying beyond our utmost capacities of recognition or verification and the problem faced by advocates of a purely subjectivist or projectivist approach that leaves no room for even such a scaled-down standard of veridical perception.

However, the thesis becomes less plausible if extended from the case of auditory response (where the biconditional can be so constructed as to build in all the requisite, domain-specific provisos and qualifications) to that of musical response, where any normative claims are felt to possess nothing like such a high degree of invariance as between different listeners or respondents. For we then have to reckon with a great range of other factors – such as cultural background, historical context, breadth and depth of musical experience, not to mention the various (strictly unreckonable) idiosyncrasies of taste and judgement – for which there is no possible means of accounting on the basis of the standard biconditional formula, however elaborately specified. That is to say, there is something inherently wrong (either circular and hence trivial or manifestly question-begging) about any such attempt to specify the normative criteria which need to be met in order for a musical response to count as veridical, competent or indeed properly 'musical'. On one reading the right-hand portion of the quantified biconditional – the part containing the various provisos – works out as a claim to the empty (tautologous) effect that getting it right, musically speaking, *just is* a matter of normalized or optimized response, which in turn *just is* what all competent parties would assent to if listening with due care and attention and in the absence of any obtrusive extra-musical sounds. (Here 'competent' functions as a place-holder term which in effect means simply 'fill out as required' or 'whatever it takes' to satisfy the normative requirement.) Otherwise, one might seek to avoid this nugatory outcome by demanding that the right-hand formula should specify some truly substantive, informative or at least non-trivial set of criteria which define what such competence actually entails, rather than simply equating it *per definiens* with just those criteria that figure on the left-hand side of the biconditional. However, one is then up against the equally intract-able problem that this specification will have to include a proviso for every possible appreciative deficit and for every conceivable source of interference – whether ambient noise or the effect of irrelevant musical expectations or sociocultural factors – that might detract from a full and adequate response. Which is also to say that this alternative to the purely formal (i.e., redundant or trivializing) version of the claim is one that would require an indefinitely long, detailed and complex specification in order to interpret the theory in terms that offered an adequate account of musical aptitude or competence. It would then defeat the very purpose of a response-dispositional account by effectively renouncing any plausible claim to capture what we mean by validity in musical judgement through an equation – the quantified biconditional – that is supposed to hold good as a matter of plain definitional self-evidence and thus provide a basis for ascriptions of normative warrant that yield no hostages to sceptical fortune.

That is, one can *either* have an adequately filled-out, substantively specified right-hand clause that goes beyond anything amenable to treatment, analysis or justification on these a priori (hence strictly uninformative) terms *or* a formula that meets the latter condition whilst thereby inherently depriving itself of any such substantive content. So it looks very much as if we are here faced with a *tertium non datur* of much the same type that epistemological sceptics are fond of invoking when they argue that realists can't have it both ways – objectivist truth plus attainable knowledge – and that there is simply no escape from this predicament save that which leads to some kind of anti-realist or response-dispositional approach. My point is that any purported 'solution' along these lines is one that faces its own inescapable dilemma – as between a trivially self-confirming and an over-specified (since non-true-by-definition) variant of the claim – but that this need not be taken, in sceptical fashion, to exclude any possible alternative approach with stronger realist credentials. Indeed, to the extent that thinkers like Wright see a need to avoid the twin nemeses of scepticism and Dummett-type, doctrinally committed anti-realism, yet fail to make their case in other than trivial or question-begging terms, one is led to conclude that there must be some such viable alternative which avoids this particular dilemma. Thus, at risk of excessive tortuosity: if *tertium non datur* on the sceptical or anti-realist account then the *tertium* required is more likely to involve some variant of the realist case which rejects this very notion that we need to make a flat, dilemma-inducing choice between objectivist truth and humanly attainable knowledge. Why not rather adopt the less problematic, more commonsensical but by no means naïve or simplistic view that belief can always fall short of veridical knowledge and the extent of our knowledge always fall short of truth in some particular respect but that this gives absolutely no reason to conclude that knowledge or truth must always be indexed to the scope and limits of epistemic warrant? Thus *of course* there exist all manner of truths that exceed our best powers of proof, ascertainment or verification and a vast potential range of well-formed statements whose truth-value is none the less objective for our being unable to discover or detect it. Yet *of course* this doesn't prevent us from having an adequate grasp of what it takes for our beliefs in this or that regard to count as genuine, veridical knowledge, as likewise for our best state of knowledge at any given time to be under certain epistemic constraints that render it partial or inadequate even if – from a long-run perspective – basically on the right track.

Such is the realist's cardinal claim: that only by endorsing these crucial distinctions along with the correct order of priority between truth, knowledge and (more or less warranted) belief can we make sense of the progress of science to date or of even our everyday, routine processes of knowledge-acquisition. Thus realism stands up as a matter of inference to the best, most rational explanation with regard not only to the conduct of enquiry in the physical sciences but also to the way we set about various practical-investigative tasks.[33] Moreover, so its advocates will argue, this case can be extended even to those formal disciplines of thought (such as mathematics and logic) whose indispensable role in the growth of scientific knowledge would otherwise have to be regarded as sheerly miraculous.[34] No doubt there are deep philosophical puzzles as to why or how – by what extraordinary 'gift' to the advancement of human knowledge – those disciplines should have turned out to yield such a wealth of empiri-cally tested descriptive, predictive and causal-explanatory data. Eugene Wigner memorably voiced this sense of amazement when he referred, in a well-known essay, to the 'unreasonable effectiveness' of post-Galilean mathematics as a source of knowledge concerning objects and events in the physical world.[35] Of course there have been as many answers – or attempted answers – to this question as there have been philosophical schools of thought as regards the realism/anti-realism issue. These have ranged from an outlook of unqualified Platonism whereby entities such as numbers, sets and classes are conceived as existing in a realm of absolute ideal objectivity to which we somehow (inexplicably, the anti-realist would say) have epistemic access, via middle-ground theories of a framework-relativist or response-dispositional type, to full-fledged constructivist, intuitionist, or fictionalist approaches that count mathematical 'reality' a world well lost for the sake of explaining how we actually gain or produce mathematical knowledge.[36]

Thus, for instance, Dummett takes the latter (anti-realist) view when he argues against Frege's objectivist idea that the process of 'discovery' in mathematics, logic and the formal sciences can best be thought of by analogy with that of geographical exploration, or of trekking across some *terra incognita* and noting the location of its various lakes, forests, mountains, and so forth.[37] Rather, we should think of it as more like what the artist (whether painter, novelist, or composer) does when she 'discovers' some new range of expressive or formal possibilities which can then – with sufficient skill and creative resource – be brought to fruition in a work of hitherto unrealized imaginative power. That is to say, mathematical proofs have this much in common with works of art: that they are *constructed* out of the best, most intuitively promising means at our disposal and also that their 'truth' is primarily a matter of their carrying conviction with those who are able to follow them. For the only alternative, Dummett thinks, is an objectivist (or Platonist) conception of the formal sciences which places truth beyond the furthest reach of knowledge and knowledge beyond what is humanly attainable in terms of probative warrant. To which opponents typically respond that this is a false dilemma, that mathematical realism is in no such sorry plight, and that the problem has been mischievously foisted on them through the anti-realist's tendentious charge that they (the realists) are claiming some kind of quasi-perceptual epistemic access to a realm of purely abstract entities which by very definition cannot be accessed in that or in any remotely similar way.[38]

IV

Meanwhile there are others – response-dispositionalists or adherents to an outlook of 'humanized Platonism' – who maintain that this debate is wholly misconceived since one can have all the objectivity one needs without going for a 'sublimated' notion of truth or a 'super-rigid-rail' conception of what counts as correctly following a rule such as those for arithmetical calculation or valid deductive reasoning.[39] Rather, we should see that this hankering for truths that transcend the best capacities of human grasp – or whose objective status precludes their being subject to any kind of epistemic constraint – is itself just a product of that misplaced desire to escape our human, all-too-human cognitive limits and achieve a god's-eye view from nowhere that the sceptic can easily denounce as just a figment of the realist's deluded imagining. Much better – so thinkers like John McDowell argue – to accept those limits but also understand (with help from a naturalized or de-transcendentalized reading of Kant, as well as from the later Wittgenstein) that they are enabling rather than disabling constraints, or capacities whose scope and limits are precisely the condition for all knowledge and experience.[40]

Alex Miller puts the case for a 'humanized Platonist' approach to mathematical truth in a passage that will bear quoting at length since it raises these issues in a pointed way and also deploys a musical analogy which, however fanciful, takes on a certain added relevance in the present context of discussion. 'In our pre-theoretic, pre-philosophical thinking', he writes,

> we have a perfectly healthy desire for a degree of independence between our judgements and the facts which those judgements are capable of tracking. When we do philosophy, this healthy desire becomes sublimated into an unhealthy philosophical conception of what this independence has to consist in. So just as Gustav Mahler's perfectly healthy respect for women becomes sublimated into an unhealthy syndrome known as the Virgin Mary complex, our own perfectly healthy desire for a measure of independence between the knower and what is known becomes sublimated into the idea that the properties which the judgements of the knower cognitively access have to be conceptually unstructured.[41]

Miller basically follows McDowell in making the case that all the big, unresolved problems in epistemology result from a false conception of knowledge that involves the idea of an 'interface' between subject and object, mind and world, or Kantian 'concepts of understanding' and the sensuous or phenomenal intuitions to which those concepts somehow apply.[42] McDowell's proposal is thus to ignore all that deeply problematical (and scepticism-inducing) Kantian talk about 'concepts' and 'intuitions'. Rather, he suggests, we should take a lead from the other pair of terms – 'spontaneity' and 'receptivity' – whereby Kant seeks to close the epistemological rift and thus restore mind and world to their proper relationship, that is, one of intimate codependence or reciprocal interinvolvement. As McDowell puts it:

> what we find in Kant is precisely the picture I have been recommending: a picture in which reality is not located outside a boundary that encloses

the conceptual sphere ... The fact that experience involves receptivity ensures the required constraint from outside thinking and judging. But since the deliverances of receptivity already draw on capacities that belong to spontaneity, we can coherently suppose that the constraint is rational; that is how the picture avoids the pitfall of the Given.[43]

However, one might guess from McDowell's tortuous phrasing – in particular the Chinese-box-like grammatical and logical structure of the first sentence here – that the argument is encountering a certain resistance and that it is not, after all, so easy to derive a genuine and working resolution of the mind/world or subject/object dichotomy from Kant's gestures in that direction.

I have discussed these complications at length elsewhere and will here just remark that they seem to reproduce – albeit (one suspects) to a large extent unwittingly – the whole range of unresolved dilemmas that have marked the history of post-Kantian epistemological debate, from Fichte's subjective versus Schelling's objective idealism to present-day disputes around realism, anti-realism and their various middle-ground (e.g., response-dispositional) alternatives.[44] Hence McDowell's problem in trying to explain how receptivity can exert the 'required constraint from outside thinking and judging' even though 'reality is not located outside a boundary that encloses the conceptual sphere'. Unpack that sentence however you like and it will still end up – on any logical account – by placing 'reality' *inside* the 'conceptual sphere' (i.e., the 'space of reasons as McDowell calls it, borrowing the phrase from Wilfrid Sellars).[45] But in that case it can scarcely leave room for any kind of 'constraint' save that brought to bear by a notion of 'receptivity' which already – in distinctly Hegelian manner – takes for granted a limit-point conception of truth where, quite simply, 'the real is the rational'. Indeed, this whole recent chapter of developments in post-Quinean philosophy of knowledge and mind is one that typically swings right across – often with putative warrant from Sellars on the 'myth of the given' – to a position much further out toward the rationalist (or anti-empiricist) end of the scale than anything that Kant would have wished to condone. Hence perhaps the current revival of interest in Hegel – and in Hegel, moreover, as a follow-up and useful corrective to the revival of interest in Kant – amongst thinkers (such as Robert Brandom) who share McDowell's sense of the need for an escape-route from the deep-laid dilemmas of logical empiricism but who also share the conviction of Kant's immediate successors that no sheerly a priori approach to these problems is likely to be of much use.[46]

What is centrally at issue here is again the question as to whether, or precisely how, we can hope to reconcile the claims of objectivist (recognition-transcendent) truth with the claims of humanly attainable knowledge under specified epistemic conditions. From an anti-realist (Dummettian) standpoint this is not merely a tall order but one that cannot possibly be met except through some philosophic sleight of hand which yields to the sceptic's perennial challenge once subject to the slightest pressure of counter-argument. For the advocate of a middle-ground (e.g., response-dispositional) approach, it is a false dilemma that could never have arisen were it not for the unfortunate grip on our minds of what Miller calls a 'sublimated' realist conception, that is, an all-or-nothing objectivist outlook that rejects any move to accommodate truth to the compass of normalized (even optimized) human perceptual, cognitive or epistemic grasp. To a realist way of thinking, conversely, anything less than objective truth in matters ontological and knowledge as justified true belief in matters epistemological is either, like Dummettian anti-realism, a product of sheer metaphysical prejudice or, like those various compromise approaches, an evasion of this clear-cut philosophic issue most likely induced by over-respect for the purported logic of the anti-realist case.

Thus – again – the realist is frankly unimpressed by that version of the *tertium non datur* argument according to which she cannot but choose between, on the one hand, a notion of truth that places it beyond our utmost epistemic reach and, on the other, an account of knowledge that forgoes objectivist truth for the sake of humanly attainable knowledge. To accept it on anything like those terms is to fall in with the same sort of thinking that has bedevilled so many otherwise laudable attempts to defend realism against the sceptic by meeting the latter on his own chosen, i.e., primarily epistemological ground. What very often results from such attempts – especially when mounted, as now, in the face of a widespread anti-realist trend with strong metaphysical leanings – is that the realist finds herself driven to adopt some kind of compromise solution (or scaled-down, epistemically constrained notion of truth) whereby to head off that current challenge while also answering the more familiar kinds of sceptical argument. And from here it is no great distance to the root confusion that typifies so many strains of anti-realist thought, that is to say, the epistemic fallacy according to which there is simply no raising the issue of truth except by way of those other issues concerning the scope and limits (along with the methods, procedures and validating grounds) of knowledge. For once launched on this slippery path it is hard – if not impossible – to stop short of the wholesale anti-realist conclusion that truth *just is* reducible to knowledge, knowledge to a matter of epistemic or assertoric warrant, and warrant to whatever counts as such by our best communal lights.

Still it may be asked: what has all this to do with music, given the fact (as mentioned above) that its relevance to the realist/anti-realist dispute is likely to be challenged by both parties on account of its belonging to an ill-defined region somewhere in the border-zone between ontology, epistemology and phenomenology where the terms of that dispute can scarcely get a hold. However, this is just my point: that the issue is best raised by considering cases where it is *really* an issue, rather than by focusing on set-piece instances – like the Lockean debate around 'secondary qualities' or the Platonic (Euthyphronist) debate about moral judgement – where it tends to work out as a flat choice between trivial self-evidence and other, more substantive claims that run aground on the failure to justify their own purportedly self-evident character. For if one thing has emerged throughout the history of philosophical reflection on music it is the problem of producing any workable account that would reconcile the depth, complexity and (as many would assert) the intimately personal nature of our musical responses with the need for those responses to have some justification – some more than *merely* personal warrant – in the work itself.

Post-Kantian debate on this topic has typically swung back and forth between various polarized viewpoints – objective versus subjective, formalist versus programmatic or content-based, analytic versus appreciative, autonomist versus cultural–historical–sociological, etc. – which closely resemble those on the agenda of current metaphysics, epistemology and philosophy of language. Thus the options can likewise be placed on a scale that extends from the idea of musical works as belonging to a realm of absolute ideal objectivity beyond the mere vagaries of culturally influenced thinking, taste or response to a standpoint (like that of the 'New Musicology') which utterly rejects such objectivist notions, along with any concept of the musical 'work' as somehow transcending the contingencies of its reception-history to date.[47] And somewhere between these poles can be found a whole range of compromise positions that seek to maintain some measure of objective truth – or at least some reasonably strong notion of intersubjective validity – for statements with regard to musical form, structure or content, while none the less making adequate allowance for the role of acculturated listener-response when it comes to assessing such statements.[48] Thus the options here are very much like those that have figured in recent epistemological debate concerning the relation between truth and knowledge, or the extent to which claims for the existence of objectivist (recognition-transcendent) truth can be squared with claims for the possibility of humanly attainable knowledge. Where the cases differ – and crucially so, I shall argue – is in the fact that musical responses (unlike perceptions of colour, smell, taste, [non-musical] sound and other such Lockean 'secondary qualities') must be seen to raise questions of normative warrant that cannot be reduced either to a trivial product of semantic definition nor yet to a vague, since largely subjective account of what constitutes good judgement. That is, by taking music as a test-case one can sharpen the issue not only with regard to matters of aesthetic valuation but also with regard to those disciplines (like the formal and physical sciences) where objectivist truth might plausibly be thought of as the default option, as well as those others – like the social or human sciences – where different criteria are commonly taken to apply.

Of course this debate has been running for a long time now and produced a great many different approaches or attempts to achieve a workable *modus vivendi* between the two modes of truth-seeking endeavour. Starting out with nineteenth-century discussions of the distinctive role of hermeneutic (i.e., depth-interpretative) understanding as a needful supplement to the methods of the natural sciences, it has cropped up again under various descriptions – 'nomothetic'/'ideographic', 'structural'/'phenomenological', or (in current philosophic parlance) 'analytic'/'continental' – whenever there has occurred a fresh outbreak of the 'two cultures' debate or a new-found desire, amongst those in the broadly hermeneutic camp, to offer some principled justification for their own distinctive methods and procedures.[49] Thus the differences have tended to be played down by social scientists and others with an interest in combining some degree of methodological rigour with the claims of a more subject-centred, humanistic or meaning-oriented approach. Meanwhile, conversely, they have tended to be played up on the one hand by hard-headed scientific realists or likeminded philosophers who reject such hermeneutic alternatives outright, and on the other by 'strong' sociologists, cultural theorists or Rortian neo-pragmatists according to whom the old science-first paradigm had best be abandoned in favour of the claim that meaning or interpretation go 'all the way down'.[50] Here again – as with the realist/anti-realist debate – the result is very often something of a *dialogue des sourdes* where the opposing parties have such different ideas of what constitutes a sound, valid or remotely plausible philosophic argument that their claims and counter-claims seem scarcely to mesh.

Hence, to repeat, my point about music: that it offers a highly instructive case of such conflicting views, not only amongst professional musicologists, theorists and aesthetic philosophers but also – I would guess – amongst a good many lay listeners who have reflected on the mode of existence of musical works or on the source and nature of the value-judgements to which they give rise. Such listeners may feel themselves torn between an objectivist belief in those works as transcending the vicissitudes of cultural reception, performance history or individual taste and something more akin to the anti-realist (or social-constructivist) position whereby that belief comes to seem just a product of the values enshrined in certain habits of acquired (i.e., 'classically' acculturated) listener-response. Or they might adopt the more moderate view – one, as we have seen, with its analogue in current epistemological debate – which attempts to steer a path between these extremes by acknowledging the listener's role along with that of the various, historically changing communities within which music is performed and conserved while none the less maintaining an outlook of qualified ontological realism. Then again, some listeners may decide that realism in the strong (Platonist) sense applies to just a certain class of works, those that strike us – on sufficiently deep acquaintance – as having been discovered, rather than created, in so far as they seem to realize a set of pre-existent or standing possibilities such that every detail is just as it must be in order to achieve that degree of formal perfection. Clearly this is an evaluative stance and, if the argument succeeds, an adequate reason for ranking some works higher than others, or for thinking that we ought to value them just to the extent that they succeed or fail in meeting so exalted a requirement. So it is that many people are strongly attached to certain works which they wouldn't rate anything like that high but which none the less exert a powerful and lasting appeal, while (if truth be told) deriving little pleasure or sense of involvement from others which they all the same regard – not merely out of deference to expert opinion – as among the very greatest of their kind.

In the latter sort of case what is happening, I think, is that they recognise something in the music that transcends any issue of cultural bias, personal taste or idiosyncratic response, and which thus makes it the listener's task to come up to the required standard of appreciative grasp, rather than a test of the work's merit that it should manage to evoke such a judgement. In other words, it is not just cultural snobbery that leads some people to profess admiration for music which they don't much enjoy or, conversely, to enter a note of self-deprecation by confessing to musical enjoyments of the deepest, most intimately personal kind which none the less they are unable or unwilling to defend on principled evaluative grounds. Of course this split between pleasure and principle might have to do with a snobbish desire for the gain in real or imagined cultural capital which results from a display of the 'right' sorts of musical taste, in which case it is more a topic for sociologists than philosophers or music theorists.[51] Nevertheless, as I have said, it is a matter of fairly common experience amongst listeners afflicted by no such pathology, or with no such need to make a good impression on friends, colleagues, examiners, or whoever. That is, they may find themselves deeply engaged by music that doesn't (as they will more or less readily concede) strike them as belonging to the category 'great work' and may fail to register anything like the same degree of intense involvement with music that does so strike them.

In the latter case this seems to come about not only on account of the work's canonical status according to the best authorities but also – oddly enough – as a matter of genuine (i.e., first-person and authentically 'felt') response. Then again, in the event of disagreement over the value of this or that musical work between parties who respect each others' judgement but are now, for once, sharply at odds the discussion may conclude with them both taking a subjectivist line and saying: 'Well, each to her own', '*De gustibus non est disputandum*', or 'Let's just agree to differ.' On the other hand they may feel that more is at stake, both in terms of intrinsic musical worth and (no less) of their own fitness to judge or pronounce on such issues. In which case the debate will most likely continue for quite some time, with one attempting to ground her judgement in features of the work that presumptively warrant a high valuation, while the other denies that it exhibits any such features, or else – shifting to a different tack – that possessing them is truly a mark of the highest musical worth. At any rate neither will wish to let go at that basic, unreflective stage of discussion where the issue comes down to a mere exchange of personal likes and dislikes. To this extent – whatever his own responsive short-comings with regard to music – Kant must be thought to have got it right: that in matters of aesthetic judgement, as distinct from merely sensuous gratification, there is far more involved than could ever be accounted for through any such appeal to the vagaries of individual taste.

V

The various scenarios that I have sketched above by no means exhaust all the possible ways in which musical pleasure, enjoyment and evaluation can at times come apart or exhibit a striking degree of non-alignment. Such instances call out for some means of resolution, whether they occur between different listeners or – less often but more problematically – within the same listener who has somehow to square them without undue psychological or conceptual strain. Thus it sometimes happens (speaking for myself but also, I think, for a good many others) that one has not yet managed to explain in adequate (i.e., analytically cogent or communicable) terms what makes a particular piece so utterly compelling despite the strong sense that this case can and should be made in a way that lifts it above the sphere of subjective or personal taste. Then the usual response is either to listen more carefully, maybe with a score in hand, or to see what the best, most reliable or trusted critics and commentators have had to say in the hope that one's own, as yet largely inchoate responses will find support or validation through a more detailed analysis.

I doubt that this process could often (or ever) have an opposite effect, or that one might be persuaded *not* to find genuine pleasure in a piece that one had hitherto greatly enjoyed but which then turned out to be the subject of an essay that sought to demonstrate its formal weaknesses, thematic incoherence, tonal or structural predictability, etc. All the same that exposure to a negative estimate – so long as one found the analysis cogent and borne out by repeated, more critically attentive or perhaps less self-indulgent hearings – might well result in the kind of dissociated mindset described above. Thus it might produce or reinforce the conviction that there exist certain standards of musical judgement and correlative aspects of musical form, thematic inventiveness, tonal development, or harmonic resource which the music in question demonstrably fails to meet, despite one's continuing enjoyment of it for reasons that belong more to the realm of personal or idiosyncratic response. In which case one is likely to conclude not so much that this enjoyment is downright wrong – just a product of bad taste or deficient musical education – but rather that it springs from emotional, cultural, or private-associative sources which simply don't give an adequate hold for assessment in critical-evaluative terms.

This is what I mean by a 'qualified Platonist' approach to issues of musical ontology and value-judgement. Ontologically speaking, it is one that finds room for a concept of the work (i.e., its identity-conditions or mode of being) above and beyond its reception-history, cultural role, differing styles of rendition or persistence in the minds and memories of various listeners, past and present. From an evaluative standpoint it is one that maintains a similar commitment to standards of truth – or of adequate (musically informed) judgement – which likewise transcend any merely *de facto* consensus of opinion among those presumed expert in such matters or any appeal to the subjective responses of this or that individual. What makes it a *qualified* version of Platonism is my point that it applies to certain works only, that is to say, those works whose particular virtue or distinguishing feature is to render any difference of views concerning them an issue that calls for further discussion on principled (analytic and evaluative) grounds, rather than a mere exchange of personal reactions. Or again, in negative terms: these works are such as to justify the claim that any failure to perceive and appreciate their merits on the listener's part is itself *purely and simply* a matter of subjective response and *not at all* an issue touching their intrinsic worth.

This is why we might sometimes feel justified in claiming that someone whose estimate differed sharply from our own with regard to, say, the greatness of Bach's *B Minor Mass*, or any number of Haydn string quartets from Op. 20 on, or Mozart's '*Jupiter*' Symphony, or Beethoven's late piano sonatas, or ... (continue as you see fit) is thereby revealing a shortfall in their powers of musical perception and understanding, rather than the fact of their just not happening to like this or that piece. Here again, any charge of arrogance in this regard – any risk of setting up our own, presumptively superior standards as a touchstone of absolute value – can best be countered by an honest acceptance that we are sometimes in the same unfortunate position. Thus we may find ourselves compelled to acknowledge on the one hand that some particular work (or even some composer's entire œuvre) is doubtless among the very greatest of its kind and yet, on the other, that it leaves us curiously uninvolved and incapable of any response save that of a detached, though in its own way genuine, admiration. Conversely, as I have said, there is the common experience – common at least among those who know and enjoy a wide range of music – that one's powers of discriminative judgement may sometimes be called into question by music that one greatly enjoys, even counts amongst one's most cherished works, even while having to concede (if pressed) that it falls well short of the highest standards.

I suppose that most readers will have their own candidates for inclusion in each of these categories, so that any poll would throw up some widely varying ideas of where and how the relevant distinctions might be drawn. Of course it follows from what I have said that disagreements with regard to this higher-level issue (i.e., the question as to what, if anything, could or should constitute a relevant criterion) are not just matters of subjective response but matters on which any judgement is accountable to standards of validity and truth beyond the sphere of personal taste or even the tribunal of widely accredited best judgement. So to offer pertinent examples from one's own experience – instances of how judgement and enjoyment can get more-or-less out of kilter – invites the charge of purporting to argue an objectivist case while in fact just parading an assortment of subjective responses. All the more so, it might be said, for this misconceived Platonist idea that such responses can somehow be ranked on a scale extending from the most to the least truthful, or from those that find warrant in the work 'itself' to those that concern nothing more than the listener's idiosyncratic way of reacting to this or that musical experience. However, it is just my point that any listener who has progressed beyond the stage where this is indeed the case – where their reactions are wholly or very largely determined by subjective, perhaps temperamental, or even (as it might be) neurologically rooted habits of response – will *for that very reason* have acquired the capacity to make the kinds of distinction mooted above. In which case it might after all be worth airing a few examples of my own, so as to put phenomenological flesh on the rather dry and abstract bones of my argument up to this point. At the same time I shall hope to show how the qualified-Platonist approach works out as a matter of actually listening to music with an ear to as-yet unrealized possibilities of heightened understanding and also in the knowledge that even one's best, most intelligent or acutely perceptive response might always be deficient in some respect or degree. For it is the virtue of that approach – *contra* those who routinely denounce it as just another high-handed technique for promoting 'the canon' and its self-authorized guardians – that it leaves room for anyone (promoters included) to be wrong in their musical judgements, whether through attaching inordinate value to works which don't warrant it or insufficient value to works that do.

So here are a few of my own dilemmas, the result (I should add) of some 40 years' sustained and at times concentrated listening to a range of mainly 'classical' (i.e., European post-Renaissance) musical genres that has extended pretty far beyond the standard concert repertoire but would no doubt strike some 'world music' adepts as absurdly narrow and parochial. There are works that I admire but don't much enjoy while none the less feeling – even knowing, in some hard-to-specify sense of that term – that this lack of intellectual and emotional involvement is down to a responsive shortcoming on my part rather than to any kind of defect in the music. Among them are a good few of Mozart's mature works including some of the piano concertos, although (I am glad to say) none of the symphonies after No. 25 or the string quartets and quintets; Beethoven's Ninth Symphony (the final movement at any rate) and much of the *Missa Solemnis*; all of Verdi's operas except *Falstaff* and *Othello* and all of Wagner's except *Meistersinger* and some parts of *Tristan* (occasionally *Parsifal*, when I manage to ignore its ethos of cloying and portentous religiosity); Mahler's Eighth Symphony and parts of the Second (*Resurrection*), which I find rhetorically overblown; Sibelius's Third and Seventh, at least as compared with what seem to me the consummate achievements of his Fourth, Fifth, and Sixth; much of Schoenberg, excepting his earliest and least representative (i.e., high-Romantic and tonally based music); the string quartets and orchestral scores of Elliott Carter (which it pains me to confess because I can hear all sorts of complex, intriguing, yet to me musically inaccessible things going on); and sundry other works that have failed to yield their secrets or, more to the point, whose secrets I have failed to unlock despite repeated hearings and a strong sense of my own inability to respond as the music properly requires. In each case – some more than others but always to similar, disturbing effect – there is a sense of non-alignment (of 'cognitive dissonance', as psychologists might put it) between what one thinks, even feels to be 'there' as a matter of relatively abstract conviction and what is *there* as a matter of genuine, jointly intellectual and sensuous involvement.

Then again, there is the question how to account for works that one finds uniquely powerful, compelling, evocative or – the phrase seems appropriate – close to one's heart even though, if pressed by somebody who took a very different view, one might just conceivably be willing to accept that they were not, after all, works of the very highest stature. Here it is more difficult to offer examples for the obvious reason that this betrays doubts not only with regard to the music's real (as opposed to merely private or subjective) value but also with regard to one's own capacity for discerning what it is about particular works that offers a sufficient (i.e., a musically and even, one might hope, philosophically adequate) basis for making that distinction. Still I would hazard a few composers and works that, for me, fall into this problematic category, such as (in no particular order): Franz Berwald, Arthur Honegger (especially his Third Symphony, the *Liturgique*), Frank Martin, Arnold Bax, Herbert Howells, Karl Amadeus Hartmann, E. J. Moeran (the G Minor Symphony and *Sinfonietta*), Alan Rawsthorne, most (not all) of Martinu's music and Roy Harris's splendid Third Symphony. Let me be clear: these are works that I greatly enjoy and admire, and in support of which – as well as in defence of my own musical judgement – I'd be willing to stake a good deal by way of descriptive, phenomenological and even – so far as my competence goes – thematic and structural analysis. Indeed I might well be driven to make that case with more vigour and passionate conviction than when talking about other, widely acknowledged canonical works which, doubtless through some failure on my part, evoked nothing like so strong a subjective or personal response and which anyway stood in no need of such elaborate defence. Yet there is still, I think, a distinction worth drawing between the kind of music (or musical response) that leaves this sense of a case to be made – and, if necessary, backed up with further, more detailed analysis – in order to vindicate one's judgement and, on the other hand, the kind of music (whatever the degree of one's subjective involvement or personal responsiveness to it) that makes any such dispute seem largely otiose or off-the-point.

If these examples are all bunched very much at the modern end of the temporal scale then no doubt this reflects the relative lack of security that goes along with most attempts to form a balanced, judicious estimate of music which is either unfamiliar or lacking the contextual-evaluative background that comes of a longer historical view. However, it also has something to do with the fact that my attachment to these works is subjective, even idiosyncratic, in so far as it involves a heightened sensitivity to certain likewise idiosyncratic features – harmonic traits, modal inflections, rhythmic patterns, tonal ambiguities or melodic turns of phrase – which happen to evoke a particularly charged and intense emotional response. In other cases – such as that of Hanns Eisler – I'd incline more to say, on critical-evaluative but also on historical and sociocultural grounds, that their work has been massively underrated as a consequence of certain musically extraneous but none the less relevant factors. Eisler was a Schoenberg student who very much went his own way, continued to compose music of an 'advanced' though never less than approachable character, yet was also much involved in the communist movement and other left-wing political and cultural activities during the 1930s.[52] He took refuge in the USA when Hitler assumed power, maintained a strongly dissident or left-oppositional stance, and then – as a result of his defiant response to the McCarthy inquisition – was deported to East Germany where he worked closely with Brecht on various projects and became, in effect, composer-laureate of the GDR. Given these circumstances – and, I would claim, the extraordinary range, inventiveness and originality of Eisler's music – it does seem reasonable (rather than just another half-baked paranoid conspiracy-theory) to suppose that all this had a great deal to do with the near-complete absence of his work from US and Western-European concert programmes, broadcasting schedules and record catalogues right up until the collapse of Soviet communism and the end of Cold War cultural politics.

Yet of course it is primarily the quality of Eisler's music that justifies one's offering such likely explanations for its lack of due recognition in the West, rather than those explanations somehow serving – through a kind of special-case allowance – to augment or enhance one's sense of its value. That is to say, the music is itself more than able, having now at last emerged from beneath that blanket of strictly 'unofficial' but none the less effective censorship, to make its own case with eloquent force and thus throw a sharply revealing light on the cultural politics of its postwar reception-history, rather than the other way around. Moreover, one could enter a similar claim for those British composers – among them Alan Bush and Bernard Stevens – whose communist allegiance can be seen to have worked strongly against the diffusion of their music through the various channels of publication, performance and broadcasting where censorship of this kind was more second nature to those with the relevant decision-making power than a matter of overt policy.[53] Even so, any argument to this effect would need to acknowledge the priority of musical-evaluative over ideological or sociocultural–historical considerations. Hence the importance of distinguishing (say) Bush's best, most expressive and strongly wrought compositions – like his string quartet *Dialectic* and Violin Concerto – from other works whose express political content clearly had much to do with their receiving so few performances in this country, but where the question of their musical value is perhaps more open to debate.

V

Given time, space and exceptional fortitude on the reader's part I could go into more detail with respect to each of the above-mentioned instances and attempt to explain – in subjective or phenomenological terms – just why and how these works manage to exert such a powerful effect. More than that, I could probably make a fair shot at linking my response to certain analytically but also subjectively salient characteristics, such as, in Martinu's case, the interplay of duple and triple metres and the constant major/minor transitions that hold – for me – a hard-to-describe yet none the less potent emotional charge. Indeed, I could take any one of the above examples and, perhaps with some help from the analysts, put up a case for regarding my response as *not* just the product of some deep-laid subjective disposition but rather as correlated with – and to that extent warranted by – certain features of the work in question. Yet this would scarcely constitute a good, musically or philosophically cogent justification for making the further claim that it showed those particular features (along with my correlative response) to possess a stronger, more adequately grounded kind of evaluative warrant. For there is no legitimate inference from the mere fact of my experiencing pleasure in this or that analytically describable feature of the work to a judgement that directly equates such pleasure with a value transcending any merely subjective or idiosyncratic response. After all, it might be that the reason for (or perhaps, more precisely, the cause of) my particular attachment to certain works or passages is a kind of affective disposition which has more to do with peculiarities of a strictly personal kind – a complex of cultural or private-associative traits – than with anything remotely pertaining to the music's intrinsic worth. I suspect that this is very often the case – more often than we might care to admit – with music that tends to haunt the memory and evoke our most intimate or powerful responses. On the other hand I would also suggest that this feeling may consort with a strong countervailing suspicion, or conviction, that our judgements here are less than reliable since there is always the possibility of those responses having come apart from any properly warranted assessment of the work or passage in question. That is, it might always be the case that the sheer strength of our identificatory or emotional reactions misled us into attaching a higher value to the music than we – or even the sharpest-eared, most perceptive and intelligent analyst – could possibly make good.

Of course this is not to adopt some kind of perversely ascetic or self-denying ordinance and deny the value of any music which affords genuine pleasure just so long as it is exempted from the rigours of analysis or not held to more elevated standards of formal perfection. Such an attitude would indeed fall prey to the charge that Miller brings against what he sees as a kind of extreme or reactive objectivism, namely – to repeat – that 'just as Gustav Mahler's perfectly healthy respect for women becomes sublimated into an unhealthy syndrome known as the Virgin Mary complex', so likewise 'our own perfectly healthy desire for a measure of independence between the knower and what is known becomes sublimated into the idea that the properties which the judgements of the knower cognitively access have to be conceptually unstructured'.[54] That is to say, it would press the case for a Platonist conception of musical works and the values they embody to a point where it completely lost touch with the character of human perceptual, phenomenological and musically informed response. However, one should bear in mind that Miller's rather fanciful analogy here has to do with music only by way of colourful illustration, since his argument is centrally concerned with the debate between realists, anti-realists and advocates of various third-way (e.g., response-dispositional) approaches to problems in epistemology or theory of knowledge. Thus the fact that it carries conviction when applied to issues in the musical domain – since, after all, it is hard to conceive how we could 'cognitively access' a work of music unless that work was in some sense 'conceptually structured', or subject to phenomenological uptake by a suitably responsive listener – doesn't have quite the knock-down philosophical force that Miller here claims for it. On the 'sublimated Platonist' account, he remarks, 'we can think of our judgements about the instantiation of a property as capable in principle of tracking or cognitively accessing the facts about its instantiation only if the property in question is conceptually unstructured'. On the 'humanized Platonist' account, conversely, we can 'think of ourselves as tracking or cognitively accessing the facts about the instantiation of conceptually *structured* properties', since this approach entails no such rigid dichotomy between objective (mind-independent) features of a real-world ontological domain and subjective (humanly constituted) features of our knowledge and experience of it.[55] In which case we should see that the 'problem of knowledge' is by no means so deep or intractable as is often claimed, since we need not accept the false dilemma exploited by sceptics – and nowadays by Dummettian anti-realists – which trades on that supposedly unbridgeable gulf between objectivist truth and whatever counts as knowledge by our best perceptual, cognitive or epistemic lights.

I have argued that compromise 'solutions' of this sort simply cannot come up with the philosophic goods because they work out *either* as a trivial thesis to the effect that 'truth just is what all parties would agree on under ideal epistemic conditions' *or* as a roundabout, elaborately qualified version of anti-realism which offers a more substantive (adequately specified) account of those conditions but thereby reduces truth to the compass of human epistemic or assertoric warrant. This applies just as much to Miller's 'humanized Platonism' as to Wright's notions of 'superassertibility' and 'cognitive command', and likewise to the various proposals put forward by the advocates of response-dependence as an answer to all our epistemological woes. However, as I have said, these ideas do have a bearing on the issue about musical works, their mode of existence and the status or validity-conditions of our various judgements or evaluative claims regarding them. For in this context there is always some reference, overt or implied, to the register of human responsive capacities and to the fact that any plausible ontology of musical works has to make allowance for normative standards – of perceptual acuity, harmonic grasp, structural comprehension, and so forth – in the absence of which our auditory experience would simply not count as an experience of the music. That is to say, it is a kind of 'humanized' (or qualified) Platonism in so far as it involves this strictly irreducible appeal to the phenomenology of musical response while none the less holding that works may possess certain attributes, qualities or structural dimensions that transcend the limits of any particular, no matter how refined or perceptive audition. It seems to me that such an outlook best makes sense of both our musical experience – especially its more complex, demanding, or elusive aspects – and the various ways in which music acts as a stimulus and challenge to philosophic thought. In Chapter 2 I shall have more to say about the issue of judgement or evaluation, and how a duly qualified Platonist approach might help to resolve some of the more intractable problems of musical aesthetics.

On Knowing What We Like: 'Best Opinion' and Evaluative Warrant

I

What I want to explore in this chapter is the notion of response-dependence – or of response-dispositional attributes and qualities – as applied to our experience, knowledge and judgement of musical works. I go on to develop the case for a qualified Platonist approach to philosophy of music which I think does better justice to our standing intuitions in this regard and also faces up more squarely to the very real problems involved rather than taking refuge in any such attempted compromise or middle-ground position. Moreover, I suggest, this approach has significant implications for our thinking about wider issues in ontology, epistemology and philosophy of mind.

Up until now the debate around response-dependence in the analytic (i.e., mainstream Anglo-American philosophical) literature has been focused chiefly on issues in these areas.[1] It has sought to provide the conceptual groundwork for a theory of knowledge that would somehow avoid both the Scylla of fully fledged anti-realism, or a conception of truth as always epistemically constrained, and the Charybdis of a hardline (objectivist) realism which – so it is argued – ends up by placing truth beyond our utmost epistemic reach and hence falling prey to the ravages of sceptical doubt. This it claims to do, in brief, through adopting a sensibly moderate approach whereby the criteria for certain kinds of statement can be specified in terms of whether or not those statements would normally elicit assent from well-placed respondents with properly functioning sensory equipment or cognitive faculties when exposed to the relevant kinds of stimulus under the right sorts of ambient condition. On this account, so advocates claim, one can have both an adequate measure of objectivity – adequate for any but the hardline realist or his shadow self, the hardline sceptic – and a decent, even 'realistic' allowance for those various factors that promote or hinder the quest for knowledge and truth. It then becomes a matter of testing just how far the theory might extend beyond its paradigm case, i.e., that of sensory perception as regards the Lockean 'secondary qualities' of colour, sound, taste and smell to other, on the face of it less amenable (since more objective), areas of discourse such as mathematics, the natural sciences or – arguably – morals.[2]

In these latter instances there is much disagreement concerning the relevance or applicability of a response-dispositional approach to statements whose truth-conditions would appear to demand a more robustly realist (non-epistemic or recognition-transcendent) mode of specification. Still it is often held that the approach can be tweaked – suitably adapted or adjusted – by building in various further refinements or provisos so as to stop short of outright objectivism about truth while meeting the realist more than half-way on the need to explain why those other discourses cannot be response-dependent to the same degree or in quite the same way. Crispin Wright has done most to promote this adaptive strategy through his introduction of epistemically beefed-up terms such as 'cognitive command' and 'superassertibility' as a kind of last-ditch anti-realist concession to the weight of realist counter-arguments.[3] These are intended to capture – or at least to accommodate – our stubborn realist intuitions with respect to certain areas of discourse which seem to demand such treatment without, in the process, going so far as to embrace an outlook of full-strength ontological realism and thereby invite (as the anti-realist would have it) the standard sceptical riposte. However, and to just this extent, they fail to meet the realist's main objection: that unless we endorse her conception of truth as objective, recognition-transcendent, or epistemically unconstrained we shall have no means of accounting for the possibility of error and hence, by the same token, no means of explaining or justifying our knowledge of the growth of knowledge.[4] For once truth is conceived as subject to the scope and limits of human cognitive grasp – whether on the strict anti-realist view or the more flexible kinds of approach adopted by Wright and the response-dependence theorists – it then becomes impossible to square the circle by restoring that dimension of objectivity that realism takes as the *sine qua non* of knowledge as distinct from certainty or epistemically warranted belief. In which case these purported third-way alternatives fail to offer an escape-route from the realist/anti-realist dispute or the chronic oscillation between objectivism and scepticism that anti-realists are fond of remarking – justifiably or not – in their opponents' position.

All the same the response-dependence thesis does have a certain prima-facie plausibility when applied to issues on its original home ground, i.e., those having to do with the criteria for correct ascription of sensory attributes or Lockean 'secondary qualities'. Thus, for instance, in the case of colour-perception one can truly assert that an object is red just so long as that assertion would be borne out by the response of any observer whose eyesight was unimpaired, whose optical cortex was likewise in good working order, and who viewed the object clearly during daylight hours in the absence of any proximate light-source which might exert a distorting effect on their powers of accurate perception. More technically: one can always construct a quantified biconditional statement to the effect: '"x is red" is true if and only if x is reliably perceived as red by any normal observer under normal conditions', where what counts as 'normal' in both respects is given a substantive rather than a vague or all-purpose, 'whatever-it-takes' specification. Yet its proponents also claim – problematically, I would argue – that this approach comes up with an answer to the realism/anti-realism issue by combining that substantive specification with a force of a priori self-evidence which derives from the impossibility of doubting the truth of the duly provisoed and quantified biconditional. That is to say, we must take it as intrinsic to the very nature of colour-perception – and likewise for the other secondary qualities – that what counts as an accurate description, response or statement concerning them *just is* what any normal and well-placed perceiver would assent to, or again, that the validity-conditions for such reports just *cannot come apart* from the consensus of judgement amongst those best qualified to judge. However, as I have said, there is a problem here in so far as the theorist can't have it both ways, on the one hand claiming the kind of a priori warrant that could only apply to analytic statements or tautologous truths-of-definition, while on the other purporting to fill out the biconditional with a range of informative or non-trivial specifications. Indeed what seems to operate here is a kind of inverse-proportional relationship whereby the formula gains such content only at the cost of losing its a priori status while retaining that status of logical self-evidence only at the cost of foregoing any claim to genuine, substantive content.

II

I shall now put the case that a suitably modified version of the response-dependence thesis has more to offer when applied to issues in philosophy of music than it does when applied – as by most of its present-day advocates – to issues concerning the truth-conditions or standards of assertoric warrant for statements about basic, that is, purely sensory modes of cognition. In the latter case, to repeat, the argument works out as a trivial thesis to the effect that, for any given area of discourse, those standards equate with the deliverance of best judgement or optimized response under ideal epistemic conditions and discounting for any localized sources of perceptual interference. In the case of music, conversely, any adequate statement of just what is required in order for some given work to warrant a certain kind of response or for some given mode of response to be warranted in relation to this or that work will need to provide much more by way of detailed specification. A bare-bones response-dispositional account might perhaps take the form: 'work *x* has property or quality *y* if and only if that judgement is such as would gain the assent of any subject with sufficiently acute and well-developed musical responses, when listening under suitable (non-distracting or attention-conducive) conditions, and in the absence of any psychological or cultural factors that might create interference'. However, this tells us precisely nothing about what constitutes *either* the property/quality in question *or* the particular kind of responsiveness, that is, the aptitude or proven capacity for sensitive listening and musically informed judgement that qualifies some (and not other) subjects as authorities in this regard. That is to say, the biconditional amounts to just a roundabout or needlessly complicated way of asserting the empty (tautological) claim that property *x* is correctly attributed to work *y* just so long as it would be so attributed by someone ideally (or infallibly) placed to pronounce on the matter.

Such is at any rate the standard take on the Lockean topos of secondary qualities amongst those – chiefly the response-dependence theorists – who would claim to derive a more general lesson as regards other areas of discourse, such as morals or even mathematics, where the realist versus anti-realist dispute has run into something of a brick wall.[5] It is also the conclusion reached by some of these same thinkers on the basis of Plato's '*Euthyphro* contrast': that is to say, the issue as to whether certain acts are pious by virtue of the gods deeming them so, or whether the gods are constrained so to deem them on account of their own, infallibly truth-tracking powers of moral judgement.[6] Here again the advocates of response-dependence think that there is some insight to be had – or epistemological mileage to be gained – by remarking that the class of pious acts is coextensive or numerically identical in each case. There is no difference, in this regard at least, between the realist account which takes best judgement as *responsive to* what is truly and objectively virtuous and the response-dependent account according to which best judgement is in some sense *constitutive of* what counts as a virtuous act. Thus the Lockean and Platonist analogies serve as a handy way of putting the case for this proposed *via media* between the two scepticism-inducing extremes of a realist conception that places truth forever beyond epistemic reach and – in stark reaction to that – a Dummett-type anti-realist approach that reduces truth to the compass of human evidential, epistemic or assertoric warrant.[7] However, as we have seen, this is a 'solution' that in fact solves nothing, since it works out either as a straightforward (truth-preserving but vacuous) tautology or else as a more substantive (more adequately specified) set of provisos on the right-hand of the quantified biconditional which *for that very reason* carries nothing like the requisite force of a priori self-evidence.

My point is that this whole debate around response-dependence has been slung between the poles of a drastic dichotomy whose terms are dictated by the fixed idea that one cannot have *both* objectivist (i.e., recognition-transcendent) truth *and* humanly attainable knowledge, at least on any definition of 'knowledge' that meets the classical specification of justified true belief. Hence what will seem, on the face of it, an odd or even quite absurd suggestion: that taking music as a test-case instance (rather than colour-perception or the other standard Lockean topoi) might help to point the way through and beyond these epistemological perplexities. After all, could one seriously wish to maintain that such deep-laid problems might find their answer in an area of discourse where value-judgements are as prone to dispute – or to the vagaries of subjective response – as is often the case with musical appreciation, or even with the more technical varieties of music analysis? Or again: why abandon the (relatively) safe ground of those widely shared basic perceptual responses – the Lockean secondary qualities of colour, sound, taste and smell – only to venture much farther afield into areas of phenomenological enquiry that offer no such reliable hold for normative standards of epistemic warrant or widespread consensual judgement? However, this is just my point: that by raising these issues in a different, more problematical context, but one less prone to various kinds of reductive or trivializing approach, we may then be placed to address them more productively in other (standard or familiar) contexts of debate.

Thus the question with regard to music, its ontological status or mode of existence *vis-à-vis* the register of normalized or optimized listener-response is one that strongly resists any treatment purporting to resolve it in any of the three main directions (realist, anti-realist or response-dispositional) which currently dominate the philosophic field. Rather, it requires that these issues be tested *both* against our given musical intuitions *and* against our standing philosophical concepts, not only as regards their applicability to the case in hand but also – crucially – as regards their pertinence (or lack of it) to other areas of discourse. What the instance of music brings out to particularly striking effect is the necessity of drawing a clear-cut distinction between areas such as mathematics, logic and the formal sciences where an objectivist (even Platonist) account is at any rate a plausible contender and areas such as the human and social sciences where it applies, if at all, only when subject to certain crucial provisos and qualifications.[8] At the same time it may sharpen the debate by avoiding the sorts of fuzzy compromise 'solutions' – such as the response-dependence thesis in its more generalized, less discriminate forms – that purport to achieve a *modus vivendi* between realism and anti-realism by extending those provisos and qualifications well beyond their appropriate sphere.[9] Thus music, or the discourse on music, would seem a prima-facie eligible candidate for treatment in response-dispositional terms in so far as it self-evidently does involve certain modes of more-or-less sensitive, refined or competent listener-response. Yet it also leaves room – arguably at least – for the Platonist claim that there exist certain intrinsically valuable modes of musical experience and certain correlative features, structures or attributes of the musical work that might always transcend or elude the grasp of even the most responsive, well-equipped listener.[10]

The special interest of music in this regard is that it offers useful grounds for comparison with other topics or areas of discourse that either lay a stronger claim to treatment in realist (objectivist) terms or else give no adequate hold for such treatment. So, for instance, it might strain the case for musical Platonism if one pressed too hard on the analogy between music and mathematics and argued – perhaps with Bach primarily in mind – that the greatest works should be thought of as discovered, not created, since they exhibit a kind of formal autonomy or structural objectivity that is otherwise found only in the realm of mathematical truth. As concerns Bach, this notion has been most power-fully challenged by Adorno, who sees in it not only a failure to grasp the music's dynamic and expressive qualities but also another melancholy sign of the reifying grip exerted on its present-day reception through the near-universal dominance of late-capitalist commodity culture.[11] Still it would be wrong – a reactive swing in the opposite, so to speak 'consumerist' (or subjectivist) direction – to deny that Bach's music does gain much of that same expressive power from its extraordinary sense of formal perfection and the quasi-mathematical working-out of possibilities somehow latent or inherent in its basic thematic material.

What gives the analogy an added force is the fact that anti-realists are apt to put their case in terms of the metaphorical contrast between knowledge conceived as resulting from the exploration of hitherto uncharted but none the less real or topographically objective terrain and knowledge as the outcome of a process which, more like the artist, shapes or refashions a landscape in accordance with certain creative–imaginative ends. Thus, on Dummett's account, any talk of 'discovery' in connection (say) with some new mathematical proof or some striking development in number-theory should be abandoned in favour of the anti-realist (or intuitionist) view that mathematical 'truths' exist only in so far as we are able to specify their formal validity-conditions.[12] Rather than conceive such truths as awaiting discovery in a timeless Platonist or Fregean realm of absolute ideal objectivity we should think of them as subject to a constant process of invention or creative elaboration which may indeed involve the highest standards of formal rigour, but only in so far as those standards are set by the proof-procedures in question. So it is wrong – just the product of a misconceived ontology – to take mathematics as a paradigm instance of the realist/objectivist claim that truth can always come apart from knowledge, or again (more precisely) that veridical knowledge can always come apart from the deliverance of present-best or even future-best-possible judgement. For this is to assert (nonsensically, Dummett believes) that we can somehow have legitimate or rational grounds for claiming that a certain class of statements – the 'disputed class' – can be known to possess an objective truth-value despite our lacking any adequate proof-procedure or means of resolving the issue either way. Such is the realist's basic supposition that well-formed yet unproven theorems (such as Goldbach's conjecture that every even number greater than 2 is the sum of two primes) are either true or false – objectively so – even though we don't yet, and indeed might never, be able to supply the requisite formal proof. On the contrary, Dummett maintains: it is strictly unintelligible that truth-values should exceed our best capacities of proof or verification since *ex hypothesi* we should then be in no position to acquire, manifest or recognize the truth-conditions for any statement, conjecture or theorem concerning them.

It is on these grounds that Dummett prefers the analogy between mathematics and painting (or the creative arts in general) to that between mathematical discovery and the explorer who ventures into unknown country and notes the location of various lakes, mountains, forests, and other such objective topographical features. For the realist, conversely, Dummett's line of argument runs up against insuperable problems, among them – not least – its failure to explain how longstanding issues (such as the truth or falsehood of Fermat's Last Theorem, or the possibility/impossibility of its ever being proved) may at last gain a passport out of the 'disputed class' through some dramatic new advance in the scope and methods of formal proof.[13] Besides, so the realist will claim, there is something highly counter-intuitive – even absurd – about any

theory which limits the other (i.e., truth/falsehood-apt) class of statements to those in respect of which there happens to exist some humanly
achievable means of ascertainment. Such a claim can only strike the
realist as a straightforward instance of the anthropocentric fallacy, one
that equates the limits of truth with the limits of attainable knowledge,
and these in turn with the highly restricted range statements that are
plausibly up for verification by our best epistemic, conceptual or investi-
gative lights.[14]

My main interest here – with a view to its bearing on issues of musical
ontology – is in Dummett's anti-realist approach to mathematics, logic
and the formal sciences. However, it is worth noting that he extends this
approach to empirically based disciplines or areas of discourse such as
that of historiography where it works out as a flat denial that we could ever
have grounds for asserting the objective truth or falsehood of statements
that we – or the community of expert historians – are in no position to
verify or falsify. Thus any 'gaps in our knowledge' must also be thought
of as 'gaps in reality', regions whose *epistemically* inaccessible character
deprives them of any determinate features onto which our statements or
hypotheses could possibly latch, and thereby consigns them to a limbo
of unreal (since to us unknowable) 'facts' or 'events'.[15] The same applies
to well-formed though unverifiable scientific conjectures – such as 'there
exists a solar system with a planet inhabited by organic life-forms in some
remote (radio-telescopically invisible) region of the expanding universe'
– which must likewise be viewed as failing to meet the standard for
meaningful, truth-apt or warrantable statements and hence as revealing
not only a lacuna in our knowledge but also a 'gap in reality'.[16] That is
to say, if one accepts the logic of Dummett's anti-realist case then there
is simply no escaping the ultimate conclusion (as realists would have it:
the ultimate *reductio ad absurdum*) that the scope and limits of human
knowledge are also, and by very definition, the scope and limits of truth
as concerns every aspect of physical reality.

III

It is here precisely that philosophical reflection on music – on its mode of
existence *vis-à-vis* the capacities of human perceptual and cognitive grasp
– might offer some help in sorting out these epistemological issues. On
the one hand there is clearly a whole dimension of musical experience
that belongs to the phenomenology of human responsive powers and
capacities, and which therefore finds no place in any purely objectivist
(response-independent) ontology of musical works. Hence the disanalogy
– the sense of a false or misleading comparison – between music and

mathematics, or the sense of 'invention' that would seem most aptly to describe what occurs in the process of musical composition and the sense of that term which applies to mathematical proof-procedures or other such formal, no matter how 'inventive' (i.e., resourceful and conceptually ground-breaking) modes of thought. On the other hand this comparison does have a certain force, especially when set against the prevailing wisdom in various circles of present-day 'advanced' musicological theory. Such is the claim that any talk of musical value – or even of 'the work' as somehow existing quite apart from the various ups and downs of its cultural reception-history – is best explained (or explained away) entirely in terms of that same history.[17] My point is that we sell music short *either* by espousing a pure-bred Platonist (or formalist) doctrine that would lift it clear of any involvement with the contingencies of culturally inflected listener-response *or* by adopting one of those current (e.g., deconstructive or New Historicist) approaches that would treat music as nothing more than a product of certain ideologically determined 'discourses' or mindsets.[18]

The tendency to swing between drastically opposed positions of this sort is a prominent feature of much recent thought across a range of disciplines, from epistemology and cognitive science to philosophy of language and logic. It is most pronounced in those areas of philosophic thought where the problems with old-style logical empiricism – especially in the wake of Quine's celebrated attack – gave rise to various, equally problematic attempts to close the gap between concepts and sensuous intuitions, or logical structure and empirical content.[19] The latest such attempts very often involve a 'naturalized' version of Kantianism which claims to deliver the epistemological goods – i.e., to explain how knowledge comes about or how precisely that gap might be closed – without any appeal to the transcendental subject and other such 'metaphysical' excrescences.[20] Response-dependence theory is very much a product of this same conjuncture: one that seeks salvation more directly from the Lockean empiricist than the Kantian idealist quarter, but which none the less draws (in company with thinkers like John McDowell) on the notion of a *via media* between all the vexing dualisms of subject and object, mind and world, or internalist and externalist accounts of knowledge-acquisition.[21] It is here, to repeat, that philosophical reflection on music – on its distinctive ontology as well as its epistemological aspects – might well have something of importance to contribute. More specifically, it raises the issue as to just where music stands in relation to those other 'areas of discourse' that have figured centrally in recent debate. What sets music decisively apart from mathematics on the one hand and the vagaries of purely subjective experience on the other is the fact that any adequate theory of music involves an irreducibly phenomenological component – an appeal to the register of normalized (or maybe optimized) listener-response – but also, beyond that, a presumed grounding in formal or structural features of the work which cannot be reduced without remainder to any purely response-dependent account.

Thus music provides the most striking since hard-to-categorize instance of an ontological domain whose very elusiveness requires that we define just how and where it differs from those other object-domains or areas of discourse. All the more so, I would suggest, since the sorts of confusion which often arise in that particular case are closely akin to the sorts that arise elsewhere in the philosophic literature. This is evident when Dummett recommends, in keeping with his anti-realist outlook, that we should change our view of so-called mathematical 'discoveries' and treat them as something more closely analogous to the process of artistic creation than to that of geographical exploration. One possible line of response to Dummett is that artworks themselves have an aspect of discovery – of 'invention' in the other, etymological sense of the term – which renders his comparison doubly problematic. That is, it can be seen both to overestimate the kinship between mathematics and art, taken (as Dummett clearly intends) by way of a riposte to the claims of mathematical realism, and at the same time to underestimate the strength of art's claim – albeit in a different way – to discover certain kinds of hitherto unrecognized formal, structural or expressive possibility. The difference here of course has to do with the last of these aspects: that is, the expressive dimension of art and its relation to those formal structures with which it is closely bound up at every level but which tend very often to elude the grasp of analysis in formal or structural terms. This issue has been central to aesthetic debate since Plato and Aristotle, and has lately been pressed to most striking effect by those – Derrida among them – who find it re-enacted in the conflict of priorities between phenomenology and structuralism. Thus, according to Derrida, what is here being played out is an issue of the utmost consequence not only for aesthetics but also for epistemology and the philosophy of logic, mathematics and language.

This is not the place for a detailed exposition of Derrida's remarkably subtle and acute early readings of Husserl where he pursues the various deep-laid aporias that emerge through the latter's intensive engagement with foundational issues in each of these disciplines.[22] Suffice it to say that they result from the strict impossibility of resolving those issues and from the fact that any rigorous enquiring-back – such as Husserl undertakes – into the grounds and history of the formal sciences will always, at some point, encounter this aporetic moment. With respect to mathematics (and, in particular, to Husserl's late text on 'The Origin of Geometry') it takes the form of a constant oscillation between the claims of a priori knowledge or 'absolute ideal objectivity' on the one hand and, on the other, those of a genetic account that would make room for the progressive unfolding of geometrical thought through its various historical stages of development.[23] Hence the antinomy of 'structure' and 'genesis' that Derrida finds everywhere present in Husserl's project, and which he treats not so much as a defect or failing but rather as a sure sign of the analytic rigour – the exemplary willingness to think these issues through with the greatest conceptual precision – that Husserl brings to bear in the course of his logico-mathematical investigations.

At this point I should like to cite two rather lengthy passages from Derrida's essay '"Genesis and Structure" and Phenomenology', since they bring out not only the aspects of Husserl's thinking that Derrida wishes to emphasize but also the precise character of his (Derrida's) critical engagement and – beyond that – their bearing on those issues in analytic philosophy of logic, mathematics and language that have been my main focus of discussion so far. Thus:

> [i]f Husserl gives up the psychological route when confronted by all the difficulties of accounting for a structure of ideal meaning on the basis of a factual genesis, he no less rejects the logicizing conclusion with which his critics wished to corner him. Whether in the then current Platonic or Kantian style, this logicism was preoccupied above all with the autonomy of logical ideality as concerns all consciousness in general, or all concrete and non-formal consciousness. Husserl, for his part, seeks to maintain simultaneously the normative autonomy of logical or mathematical ideality as concerns all factual consciousness, and its original dependence in relation to a subjectivity in general; in general, but concretely. Thus he had to navigate between the Scylla and Charybdis of logicizing structuralism and psychologistic genet-icism (even in the subtle and pernicious form of the 'transcendental psychologism' attributed to Kant). He had to open up a new direction of philosophical attention and permit the discovery of a concrete, but nonempirical, intentionality, a 'transcendental experience' which would be 'constitutive', that is, like all intentionality, simultaneously productive and revelatory, active and passive ... Husserl will attempt to prepare an access to this common radicality through the diverse 'reductions', which are presented initially as neutralizations of psycho-logical genesis and even of every factual genesis in general.

The first phase of phenomenology, in its style and its objects, is structuralist, because first and foremost it seeks to stay clear of psychologism
and historicism. But it is not genetic description in general which
is disqualified, but only the genetic description which borrows its
schemas from naturalism and causalism, and depends upon a science
of 'facts' and therefore on an empiricism; and therefore, concludes
Husserl, depends upon a relativism incapable of insuring its own truth;
therefore, on a scepticism. The transition to the phenomenological
attitude is made necessary, thus, by the impotence or philosophical
fragility of geneticism when the latter, by means of a positivism which
does not understand itself, believes itself capable of enclosure by a
'science-of-facts', whether this be a natural science or a science of the
mind. The expression 'worldly genesis' covers the domain of these
sciences.[24]

I must forego any detailed commentary on this passage and content
myself with just a few remarks concerning its relevance to the topic in
hand. Perhaps most striking – apropos the realism/anti-realism debate
– is Derrida's insistence (following Husserl, though pressing somewhat
harder on the various antinomies here opened up) that one cannot
resolve the structure/genesis problem by straightforwardly endorsing one
approach and declaring the other irrelevant, unworkable, or philosophically off-limits. Thus a twin necessity imposes itself: that of acknowledging
(*contra* anti-realists like Dummett) the claims of mathematics, logic
and the formal sciences to be concerned with a realm of objective,
verification-transcendent truth quite aside from the various episodes that
have marked their development to date, while none the less allowing that
those disciplines *do* have a history – a 'genetic' aspect – which cannot be
ignored or bracketed out since it constitutes the very condition of possibility for grasping that development along with its latest (present-day)
stage of advance.

The second passage from 'Genesis and Structure' may help to clarify
what is involved here. Thus, as Derrida reads Husserl:

an eidetic descriptive science, such as phenomenology, may be rigorous,
but it is necessarily inexact – I would rather say 'anexact' – due to no
failure on its part. Exactitude is always a product derived from an
operation of 'idealisation' and 'transition to the limit' which can only
concern an abstract moment, an abstract eidetic element (spatiality, for
example) of a thing materially determined as an objective body, setting
aside, precisely, the other eidetic elements of a body in general. This

is why geometry is a 'material' and 'abstract' science. It follows that a 'geometry of experience', a 'mathematics of phenomena' is impossible: this is an 'attempt doomed to miscarry'. This means in particular, for what concerns us here, that the essences of consciousness, and therefore the essences of 'phenomena' in general, cannot belong to a structure or 'multiplicity' of the mathematical type. Now what is it that characterizes such a multiplicity for Husserl, and at this time? In a word, the possibility of closure ... What Husserl seeks to underline by means of this comparison between an exact and a morphological science, and what we must retain here, is the principled, essential, and structural impossibility of closing a structural phenomenology.[25]

It should be evident that Derrida is here broaching, by way of Husserl, a range of ontological, epistemological and (not least) metaphysical issues that have likewise preoccupied philosophers in the analytic tradition from Frege and Russell to the present day. Chief among them is the issue – most provocatively raised by Dummett – as to whether certain statements belonging to the 'disputed class', i.e., statements that are well-formed and (apparently) meaningful, yet for which we possess no formal proof-procedure or means of empirical verification, can none the less be thought of as true or false (objectively so) just by virtue of the way things stand in reality and quite aside from any such epistemic considerations. For the realist about truth the answer is plainly 'yes'; for the Dummettian anti-realist it is 'no', perhaps hedged about by some qualifying clauses with respect to how far the verification-principle might be stretched to accommodate various conceivable but so far unachieved methods of proof; and for the stakers-out of a middle-ground (e.g., response-dispositional) approach it is a suitably provisoed 'yes/no' according to the area of discourse in question and its presumed degree of truth-aptitude.[26]

Then again, for a Kantian revisionist such as McDowell – one who proposes a 'naturalized' reading of Kant shorn of the whole transcendental apparatus but retaining the idea of an active reciprocity between mind and world or knowledge and the objects of knowledge – the answer would seem to be another 'yes/no', but more to the effect that this problem simply doesn't arise so long as we refuse to mount the dualist seesaw.[27] However, it is scarcely resolved by McDowell's claim that we can best avoid the residual dualism in Kant's talk of sensuous intuitions that must somehow be 'brought under' concepts of understanding through the simple expedient of switching to Kant's alternative idiom of 'receptivity' and 'spontaneity', these latter envisaged as powers of mind whose mutual and inextricable inter-involvement prevents any such false dichotomy from getting a hold. For it is clear from the problems that McDowell has in striving to maintain this position – from the often tortuous phraseology and signs of extreme conceptual strain – that the switch is more a matter of cosmetic appearance than a genuine working solution.[28]

IV

The point of my above brief detour via Derrida on Husserl was to signal the existence of another approach to the realism/anti-realism issue that avoids the kinds of unproductive deadlock or evasive middle-ground solution produced by a great deal of current analytical (or 'post-analytical') debate. What Derrida brings out most forcefully in his readings of Husserl is the necessity of thinking these issues through to the point where 'a certain structuralism' can be seen as 'philosophy's most spontaneous gesture', while none the less acknowledging that this project meets its limit in 'the principled, essential, and structural impossibility of closing a structural phenomenology'.[29]

It would not be hard to show, given time, that analytical debate on these matters has been hobbled by the turn it took through Frege's rejection of Husserlian phenomenology as just another species of thinly disguised psychologism.[30] This view was further reinforced by Gilbert Ryle's dramatic change of mind – from a well-developed interest in Husserl's work to a dismissal of it on similar grounds – and again (most recently) by Dummett's rather grudging concession that there might be something of interest in Husserl though only to the extent that his thinking bore limited comparison with Frege's altogether more adequate approach.[31] The result has been precisely that drastic polarization of views according to which one can either espouse a notion of objective and recognition-transcendent (hence unknowable) truth or else make do with a scaled-down conception of Dummettian warranted assertibility or 'truth' as epistemically constrained. What Derrida's readings of Husserl hold out is the prospect of steering a critical course between these poles that would neither accept the terms of that putative dilemma nor seek to defuse it by adopting some middle-ground approach which finally reduces to the trivial thesis whereby truth equates with whatever counts as such according to normalized or optimized best judgement. The above-cited passages should make it clear that Derrida is far from rejecting the Platonist view, that is, the basic realist premise that there exists a vast range of unproven or perhaps unprovable statements and theorems in mathematics, logic and the formal sciences that must be thought of as objectively true or false despite our inability to settle the issue either way. Yet at the same time Derrida is keenly aware – like Husserl before him – of the need to take account of those various epochal stages of advancement or knowledge-acquisition that constitute not only the background history but (in some sense) the enabling context and prior condition of possibility for any further such advances.

Other commentators – Føllesdal and Mohanty among them – have argued that the problems confronted by post-Fregean philosophy of mathematics and logic, in particular its having given rise to these intractable dilemmas, might well have been avoided were it not for that unfortunate parting-of-the-ways between the two traditions.[32] More specifically: it might not have witnessed the emergence of a strongly reactive movement of thought which took the problems with Fregean objectivism (i.e., its purportedly placing truth beyond the utmost reach of attainable knowledge) as a pretext for adopting the kinds of extreme or more moderate anti-realist approach exemplified by Dummett and the advocates of response-dependence. To be sure, Dummett never goes quite so far as L. E. J. Brouwer, the most influential philosopher of mathematics to have espoused an intuitionist approach that rejects the idea of objective (recognition-transcendent) truth in favour of equating truth with knowledge, knowledge with provability and the latter with just those sorts of construction that strike the enquirer as possessing intuitive conviction or plausibility. Thus, according to Brouwer, it is wrong to suppose that 'mathematics, when it is made less formal, will pay for it by a loss of "exactness", i.e., of mathematical "truth"'. On the contrary, '[f]or me, "truth" is a general emotional phenomenon, which by way of "Begleiterscheinung" [accompanying phenomenon] can be coupled or not with the formalistic study of mathematics'.[33] Yet Dummett is well within hailing distance of this *echt*-intuitionist approach – albeit treated with a decent measure of British reserve as regards such extravagant talk – if one considers his clearly stated preference for the analogy between mathematical thought and artistic creativity as against the Platonist/Fregean analogy between mathematics and the exploration of a pre-existent (i.e., objective or mind-independent) conceptual domain.[34]

What is most characteristic of these debates is a curious loss of ontological bearings, a tendency to confuse 'areas of discourse' – or the kinds of criteria that properly apply in this or that area – so that even mathematical truth seems in danger of floating off into some realm of ultimate unknowability unless brought back within human grasp through a response-dependent or 'humanized Platonist' approach.[35] Hence the idea that any progress in these matters will have to start out by conceding the logic of the anti-realist case – that objectivist truth and attainable knowledge simply don't mix – and then work out some viable or face-saving solution along just such conciliatory lines. Hence also, I would suggest, the strange way in which discourses like those of mathematics, logic or the formal sciences that would appear prime candidates for treatment in Platonist (or verification-transcendent) terms are subject to a kind of analogical transfer or metaphoric displacement whereby such treatment is made to seem inappropriate, misconceived or philosophically downright absurd. Thus when Dummett invites us to consider the business of proving a mathematical theorem as more like an act of artistic creation than a geographical discovery – or when Alex Miller proposes his 'humanized Platonism' as a reasonable middle-ground stance – it is clear that, for many present-day thinkers, anti-realism is the default option and realism one for which the best, perhaps only, credible line of defence is a fallback to some such quasi-realist or compromise solution.[36]

No doubt this situation has come about very largely in consequence of various problems in mathematics and philosophy of mathematics over the past century and more. These will be familiar enough to most readers and require only a brief rehearsal here. Among them are the advent of non-Euclidean geometries which dealt a sizeable blow to the Kantian idea of synthetic a priori knowledge and to aprioristic truth-claims of whatever kind; the later emergence of non-classical (i.e., many-valued or 'deviant') logics; the paradoxes of classical set-theory as first revealed by Russell; Gödel's incompleteness theorem, along with its wider, likewise unsettling implications for mathematics, logic and the formal sciences; and the various problems with regard to our knowledge of a (supposedly) objective real-world domain thrown up by quantum mechanics on the orthodox (Copenhagen) interpretation.[37] Yet if one thing is equally clear it is the fact that mathematics has long served *both* as the paradigm instance of objective, recognition-transcendent truth *and* – from the time of Galileo up to and including the quantum revolution – as a chief source of knowledge or better understanding as regards physical reality. So it is very much a case of putting the philosophic cart before the scientific horse when sceptical or anti-realist doctrines purport to show that these beliefs are ungrounded or that truth and knowledge cannot both be had except on pain of manifest self-contradiction.[38]

Thus, as David Lewis pointedly remarks, '[i]t's too bad for epistemologists if mathematics in its present form baffles them, but it would be hubris to take that as any reason to reform mathematics ... Our knowledge of mathematics is ever so much more secure than our knowledge of the epistemology that seeks to cast doubt on mathematics'.[39] And again: '[c]ausal accounts of knowledge are all very well in their place, but if they are put forward as general theories, then mathematics refutes them'.[40] What Lewis here has in mind is the sort of 'reliabilist' or causally based epistemology which requires that all legitimate claims to knowledge be grounded either in perceptual acquaintance with the objects or states of affairs concerned or else in some unbroken and reliably informative chain of transmission with a good (i.e., truth-preserving) pedigree. By these lights any Platonist (or realist) philosophy of mathematics, logic or the formal sciences is *ipso facto* a non-starter since it cannot explain how we could ever have the right kind of causal contact with abstract entities such as numbers, sets, truth-functions, propositional contents, and so forth. To which Lewis responds, once again, that in that case we had better junk the causal theory of knowledge-acquisition at least with regard to those areas of discourse – chief among them mathematics and logic – where it clearly doesn't apply. No doubt there are deep, philosophically recalcitrant questions as to why and how such abstract entities should have proved to possess so impressive a degree of descriptive, predictive and even explanatory power in the development of the physical sciences. Hence Eugene Wigner's expression of wondering puzzlement at the 'unreasonable effectiveness' of mathematics as a strictly indispensable source of knowledge concerning real-world objects and events on every micro- to macro-physical scale.[41] However, there is something distinctly perverse about raising that puzzlement to a high point of doctrine and then declaring either, like the anti-realists, that we are faced with a flat, non-negotiable choice between mathematical truth and mathematical knowledge or else – the currently favoured line – that the only way out of this impasse is to opt for some middle-ground (e.g., response-dependent or 'humanized Platonist') approach.

Jerrold Katz puts the case for mathematical realism in a passage that will bear citing *in extenso* for its clarity and force:

> [t]he entire idea that our knowledge of abstract objects might be based on perceptual contact is misguided, since, even if we had contact with abstract objects, the information we could obtain from such contact wouldn't help us in trying to justify our beliefs about them ... In virtue of being a perfect number, six must be a perfect number; in virtue of being the only even prime, two must be the only even prime. Since the epistemic role of contact is to provide us with the information needed to select among the different ways something might be, and since perceptual contact cannot provide information about how something must be, contact has no point in relation to abstract objects. It cannot ground beliefs about them [42]

The importance of getting things right with regard to such ontological distinctions may be gauged from some of the more *outré* consequences when this kind of realism as applied to abstract entities or the object-domain of mathematics and the formal sciences is carried across into other, very different, areas of discourse. Thus Lewis has a larger quarry in view when he argues that the objectivity of mathematical truth – and the security of our knowledge concerning it – will always trump any challenge brought by the sceptic or the advocate of a causal-reliabilist approach to epistemology. In brief, his purpose is to put the case for an outlook of uncompromising realism with respect to all those 'possible worlds' or counterfactual scenarios that modal logicians are wont to invoke as a matter of descriptive or explanatory convenience, but which Lewis holds to be fully as *real* as those which we inhabit in our everyday lives, only non-actual in so far as they occupy some other (to us epistemically inaccessible) region of the modal multiverse.[43] So, for instance, when historians or scientists routinely deploy counterfactual-conditional modes of reasoning – 'had event *x* not occurred, then neither would event *y*' – in order to explain why event *y* did in fact occur, they had better accept his modal-realist account since otherwise they are trading on a false licence and have no right to draw such often far-reaching explanatory consequences from merely suppositious or fictive premises. Moreover, should it be objected by exponents of a this-world (actualist) or causal-realist approach that Lewis has created a wildly profligate ontology replete with objects and events that must, by very definition, lie utterly beyond our epistemic ken, he can always come back – as in the above-cited passages – with the argument-by-analogy from mathematics.

Thus Lewis's trump-card is again to remark that abstract entities such as numbers, sets and classes are likewise both causally inert and beyond any means of sensory-perceptual acquaintance and yet – perhaps for that very reason – have a strong claim to count among our surest items of a priori knowledge. In which case, he concludes, actualists about modal logic – those who take possible-worlds talk as just that, a convenient *façon de parler* for explicating notions of possibility and necessity – are merely trying to have their cake and eat it.[44] Were it not for their perverse refusal to accept the logic of their own arguments they would perforce come to see that it entailed the reality (i.e., the non-actual but objective existence) of all those counterfactual situations, or might-have-been-otherwise turns of event, which alone give genuine explanatory content to talk about causes, necessary conditions, decisive historical conjunctures, and so forth. Yet clearly this involves a pretty massive conflation of distinct ontological domains, among them – crucially – the transworld necessary truths of logic and mathematics and the various contingent or world-relative, whether actual or unactualized states of affairs that concern historians and (arguably) most if not all physical scientists. Thus it is hard to conceive how Lewis can extract his mind-boggling range of 'really' existent possibilia from the analogy with a discourse – that of mathematics – whose object-domain on the realist (Platonist) view is defined precisely by its abstract nature, its character of absolute ideal objectivity, and therefore its utter remoteness from any such contingent order of events.

Hence the widespread resistance to Lewis's ideas, not only amongst thinkers who stress the relevance of modal logic to issues in epistemology and philosophy of science, but also amongst philosophers of mathematics who acknowledge – like Katz in the passage cited above – that any adequate account of mathematical truth will need to respect its autonomy as well as its singular effectiveness in physics and the other sciences. After all, this is the only plausible answer to proponents of a hardline causal epistemology who argue that since we cannot have perceptual contact with intangible 'objects' such as numbers and sets, therefore those objects must either be thought of as inherently unknowable or else brought back within the compass of knowledge by treating them as so many constructs out of our various methods of proof or well-established formal procedures.[45] Thus Katz might seem in agreement with Lewis as regards the basic modal-realist claim that there exists a vast range of objective though abstract realia whose properties – along with the truth-value of any statement concerning them – have nothing whatever to do with our state of knowledge, let alone with our somehow (impossibly) being able to access them via some kind of perceptual 'contact'. However, this agreement runs out at the point where Katz makes his cardinal claim: that what distinguishes logic, mathematics and the formal sciences from other (say historical, natural-scientific or everyday-investigative) fields of enquiry is their concern with an order of necessary truths whose character of absolute ideal objectivity places them forever and intrinsic- ally beyond reach of empirical disconfirmation. That is to say, *contra* Lewis, they cannot provide a legitimate basis for arguments concerning the reality of alternative, non-actual 'possible worlds' since these must surely be similar to our own, at least in so far as they contain all manner of strictly contingent (i.e., transworld variable) happenings, histories and turns of event, as well as a great range of likewise contingent physical objects along with their various world-relative properties, dispositions, causal powers, and so forth. Indeed, it is the point most forcefully made by 'this-world' realists such as Saul Kripke and Hilary Putnam that modal logic is a useful means of picking out just those essential properties – e.g., subatomic, molecular or genetic-chromosomal structure – that distinguish various intramundane natural kinds like 'gold', 'acid', 'water' or 'tiger'.

Such was the aim of Putnam's famous series of 'twin-earth' thought experiments, designed to bring out its crucial relevance to issues in metaphysics and epistemology as well as in philosophy of logic and philosophical semantics.[46] Thus if twin-earth 'gold' looked and behaved very much like its earthian counterpart but turned out *not* to be the metal with atomic number 79, or if twin-earth 'acids' were not proton-donors, or if twin-earth 'water' had the molecular composition XYZ rather than H_2O, or if twin-earth 'tigers' were found to have an entirely different genetic constitution then any visitor from earth, when confronted with the evidence, would surely conclude that these were *not* in fact genuine (as opposed to like-seeming) samples of the kind in question. Moreover, the process of finding this out would involve the same sorts of investigation or the same techniques for looking beyond surface appearances that have typified the conduct of this-world scientific enquiry, such as that which led from 'gold = yellow, ductile metal soluble in *aqua regia*' (thus failing to distinguish it from 'fool's gold', or iron pyrites) to 'gold = metallic element with atomic number 79', and likewise *mutatis mutandis* for my other examples. What Kripke and Putnam deduce from all this is that such discoveries have to do with an order of *a posteriori* necessary truths, that is to say, truths which are clearly not a priori (self-evident to reason) but which none the less obtain as a matter of necessity in this world and all other close-by possible worlds whose constituent kinds are compatible with ours in the relevant physical (e.g., microstructural or genetic-chromosomal) respects.[47] As I have said, this puts them squarely at odds with that other, ontologically profligate form of modal realism propounded by Lewis according to which it is merely a sign of parochial prejudice to treat the world that we 'actually' inhabit as any more 'real' than the numberless counterpart worlds wherein things have worked out differently across the entire range of alternative (logically conceivable) possibilities. For there could then be no arguing, in Kripke/Putnam mode, from certain distinctive features of the way that our language picks out natural kinds along with their essential properties, structures or attributes to a metaphysical-realist worldview wherein they set the truth-conditions for our various statements, theories or hypotheses concerning them.[48]

Thus 'actualism' is not so much the product of some drastically restricted ontological purview as a necessary means of drawing the line between issues properly amenable to treatment from a philosophical or scientific standpoint and issues that belong more to the realm of science fiction or the possible worlds of a writer such as Jorge Luis Borges. This is the sort of objection to Lewis's argument that is apt to count strongly with the realist about matters of empirical fact or natural-scientific truth. However, there is a kindred objection to be raised from the mathematical-realist quarter since a further consequence of that argument is to blur the ontological distinction between transworld necessary truths (those that pertain to logic, mathematics and the formal sciences) and the kinds of contingent truth that pertain in our own and other (to us non-actual but to their denizens actual and in any case equally real) possible worlds. That is to say, Lewis's case for his ontologically extravagant variety of modal realism is one that involves a confusion of properly distinct ontological domains, and which hence falls plump within the sights of a sceptical or anti-realist approach. For, as we have seen, a chief plank in many such arguments is the claim that truth cannot possibly exceed the bounds of attainable knowledge while this must involve some kind of perceptual or quasi-perceptual contact between knower and known. Katz once again provides a succinct explanation of why this idea is philosophically so wide of the mark. Thus:

> [t]he epistemological function of perceptual contact is to provide infor-
> mation about which possibilities are actualities. Perceptual contact
> thus has a point in the case of empirical propositions. Because natural
> objects can be otherwise than they actually are (*non obstante* their
> essential properties), contact is necessary in order to discover how
> they actually are ... Not so with abstract objects. They could not be
> otherwise than they are ... Hence there is no question of which math-
> ematical possibilities are actual possibilities.[49]

All of which suggests that getting straight about these modal distinctions – as between the actual, the possible and the necessary – is important not only for philosophy of language, mathematics and science but also for other disciplines where ontological issues have a real bearing on our sense of what counts as a defensible truth-claim or evaluative judgement.

V

Now it is time – well past time, the reader may be thinking – to bring these various lines of argument together and explain just how they might relate to questions of musical ontology. I propose to put the case for a 'qualified Platonist' approach that would treat some (not all) musical works as being comparable in some (not all) respects to the kinds of abstract entity such as numbers, sets, propositions, logical functions, and so forth, that make up the object-domain of the formal sciences. Where this comparison hits the mark, I suggest, is in the sense that these works are best thought of as discovered rather than created, or at least as involving more in the way of access to certain standing possibilities of musical expression, form and development than finds any room on commonly received – especially Romantic and post-Romantic – accounts.

This is not to say that all music aspires to the condition of mathematics, or that the best music is the kind – prototypically that of J. S. Bach – which most readily lends itself to quasi-mathematical or ultra-formalist ideas of structure and development. For one thing, that conception ignores the most basic difference between music and mathematics: that whereas mathematics, at least on the Platonist view, has to do with abstract or ideal entities that inherently elude the utmost reach of human perceptual grasp, music must by its very nature involve our sensory-perceptual responses before we can make a start with the business of formal or structural analysis. Thus any such analysis will have to meet the test of matching (even if it also deepens and refines) the intuitions of a competent listener, just as – in a different though related field – any theory of grammar, no matter how technically advanced, will have to chime with the standing intuitions of competent native speakers. In the case of music that requirement is all the more difficult to satisfy since musical responses are subject to a far greater range of variation from one listener to the next, so that what counts as 'competence' in this regard – as providing the relevant standard for assessment – is that much harder to specify. This is another reason why any Platonist approach to issues of musical ontology and value has to be qualified by the caveat that it cannot do more than approximate the sorts of truth-condition that apply to statements about mathematics, logic, or the formal sciences. Still the qualification need not involve falling back to some equivocal midway stance, such as that adopted by the theorists of response-dependence, or by the advocates of a scaled-down 'humanized' Platonism, which amounts to much the same thing under a different, more robust-sounding description.[50] Rather it is just to acknowledge – as can scarcely be denied – that whatever statements we make about music in the hope, belief or presumption of their holding good will have to do not only with certain salient features of the work itself but also with our competent (musically informed) perception of them or the kinds of response that they *can and should* evoke in a sufficiently keen-eared listener.

Still it may asked: what is the difference between this kind of qualified Platonist approach in the case of music and the kinds of accommodationist thinking – the various attempts to strike a compromise stance between realism and anti-realism – that I have criticized above? After all, it is hard to see how this difference could amount to very much if musical 'Platonism' is so redefined as to admit the crucial role of listener-response (no matter how perceptive and intelligent) when it comes to deciding just which elements of form, structure, thematic development, tonal progression, etc., should count as intrinsic to the work 'itself', that is to say, the work Platonically conceived as transcending any merely subjective or response-dependent dimension. Thus, here as with mathematics and the formal sciences, Platonism would seem prima facie downright incompatible with a theory that acknowledges the extent to which truth must be conceived as subject to the scope of competent, normal or optimized human judgement. Yet it is just this basic ontological distinction between music and mathematics – that the former, unlike the latter, involves an irreducible appeal to the register of human cognitive-appreciative powers – which can serve as a useful means of explaining what is wrong with any form of the response-dispositional or 'humanized Platonist' approach when extended to regions of enquiry beyond its proper remit. That is to say, it brings out both the fallacy involved in reducing mathematical or logical truth to the compass of human epistemic warrant, and the opposite fallacy of treating music – by analogy with mathematics – as *purely and simply* an affair of formal, objectively existent structures. For this is to ignore the realist case that well-formed (i.e., truth-apt) mathematical statements, theorems, or hypotheses have their truth-value fixed irrespective of whatever we may know or be able to establish concerning them. And it is also to ignore the fact that any competent, perceptive and well-informed judgement about music will involve a phenomenological aspect – an appeal to the register of normal or optimal listener-response – which cannot be discounted in the quest for objectivity or analytic rigour.

This is why, as I have suggested, the instance of music may help to clarify some of the issues that arise in other fields of enquiry, among them philosophy of mathematics, logic and the natural sciences. What it shows up by way of contrast is the fact that these latter – albeit for different, case-specific reasons – neither need nor admit any qualification of the realist-objectivist standpoint in order to make adequate room for the contribution of human perceptual responses or powers of cognitive judgement. In the former case, conversely, it is clear that analysis cannot produce any valid, musically convincing results except in so far as they fall square with the response of a competent listener under suitable conditions: that is, when exposed to a likewise competent performance of the given work and in the absence of any distorting factors (whether ambient or cultural) that might get in the way of that response. Thus the question *what counts* as a valid claim or a truth-apt statement in the context of music analysis might perhaps find an answer of the kind proposed by the response-dependence theorists, namely a quantified biconditional linking the statement to a more-or-less detailed specification of the various requirements that have to be met in order for that to be the case.

One could then come up with a wide range of such biconditional formulas, from the most basic and nearly tautologous ('piece *x* is in classical sonata-form if it would reliably be recognized as such under normal acoustic conditions by any competent, attentive listener with an adequate grasp of the relevant structural features') to other, more elaborately specified instances ('it is true that "work *y* exhibits a striking pattern of major/minor harmonic alternations together with shifts from triple to quadruple metric patterns" just so long as that statement would be endorsed by any tonally and rhythmically sensitive listener with the ability to recognize such complex interactions'). Or again, the biconditional might include certain kinds of evaluative as well as structural-descriptive predicate, always with reference to normalized or idealized listener-response as a validating ground of judgement. Thus the left-hand clause might read: 'composer *z*'s Third Symphony is the finest of his eight works in this genre since it is here that his music most fully achieves those distinctive qualities – of rhythmic drive, harmonic dynamism, sweeping tonal progression – which the others strive for but never bring off to such compelling effect'. In which case the right-hand (conditional) clause would have to specify that this claim was true, or warranted in descriptive and evaluative terms, just so long as it was such as to command the assent of listeners properly qualified to judge of its various component parts. That is to say, its truth-conditions would derive from – or depend upon – its answerability to certain well-defined standards of musical appreciation, understanding and judgement which in turn drew their adjudicative warrant from a detailed specification of the particular responsive capacities involved. So, for instance, in the two last-mentioned cases – where (as it happens) the composers I had in mind were the Czech Bohuslav Martinu and the American Roy Harris – the claims would count as veridical just on condition that the various melodic, rhythmic, tonal and dynamic attributes to which those statements refer would indeed be picked out as salient, distinctive or characteristic by any well-qualified (musically informed) listener with a good knowledge of the works in question. However, as I have argued above, the main drawback of response-dispositional 'solutions' to the realism/anti-realism issue is that they tend to work out either as merely tautologous (where the right-hand side of the biconditional amounts to a kind of all-purpose, 'whatever-it-takes' clause) or else as a more substantive and specific but *to just that extent* far from self-evident or uncontroversial specification of the relevant responsive capacities. In other words, it can look very much like a case of attempting to have one's cake and eat it but managing to do neither since the cake has crumbled away in the meantime.

It seems to me that one reason for this difficulty with response-dependent approaches to epistemology is their grounding in, and constant allusion to, the Lockean topoi of secondary qualities. On the one hand, these are clearly prime candidates for treatment in this manner since they involve a strictly irreducible reference to qualitative aspects of human sensory or perceptual experience which cannot be fully cashed out in physical-scientific terms: that is, through some putative explanation deriving (in the case of colour) from optics, reflectance theory, quantum electrodynamics, the neurophysiology of vision, etc. Such is the well-known problem of qualia – of the gap between third-person scientific and first-person phenomenological (or 'what it's like') modes of thought – which philosophers have often claimed to resolve, but which continues to divide them along various fault-lines of entrenched presupposition.[51] On the other hand, response-dependence theories pay for their ability to make this problem look misconceived – just an error brought about by seeking scientific explanations where such explanations are out of place – with their failure to provide any adequate (non-circular) account of how the truth-predicate functions when applied *either* in mathematical-scientific *or* in phenomenological contexts of debate. For in the one case they tend to collapse the idea of objective (i.e., recognition-transcendent) truth into a question of what counts as such amongst those presumptively best qualified to judge, while in the other they treat all modes of perceptual experience (or statements concerning them) as subject to assessment only in terms of an equation – the quantified biconditional – which amounts to no more than a thinly disguised or verbally spun-out tautology.

This criticism has lately been brought against the theory by Mark Johnston, one of its earlier proponents, in terms of what he calls the 'missing explanation' argument.[52] Briefly stated, it runs that response-dependent accounts of secondary qualities must always be deficient in explanatory power unless they include some causal component along with the (otherwise tautologous) formula. This would be an extra clause to the effect: 'quality x is truly perceived as such by perceiver y just so long as the requirements are met (i.e., the perceiver is up to the mark and the ambient conditions are truth-conducive) *and also* there is some adequately specified causal relation between x's perceiving y as an instance of just that quality and y's actually possessing that quality as a matter of perceiver-related but not entirely perceiver-dependent fact'. (I am paraphrasing Johnston rather freely here, but take this to capture the gist of his argument accurately enough.) The point of such objections is that any attempt to resolve or circumvent the realism/anti-realism dispute by recourse to response-dependence theory in however qualified a form can only escape a vicious (or at any rate disabling) circularity if it goes so far toward conceding the force of opposed (e.g., causal-explanatory) arguments as to leave its own thesis either redundant or downright false. That is to say, it would allow scientific realists to argue that this denouement is best regarded as a classic *reductio* not only of response-dependence theory in its current form but of any approach – from Locke on down – which has recourse to a realm of subjective (no matter how widely shared or communally warranted) perceptions and judgements.

Moreover, the same objection would apply to 'humanized Platonist' accounts of mathematics and the formal sciences, since here also – from a realist (or *echt*-Platonist) standpoint – what is lost by such concessions to the adversary camp is not merely, as Alex Miller would have it, a 'metaphysical' or 'sublimated' conception of realism but the single most basic commitment of any realism that merits the name.[53] For whatever its attractions as a middle-ground stance or a hedge against reactive sceptical doctrines, there is still a clear sense in which any proposal of this sort involves the idea of truth as epistemically constrained, i.e., as a matter of optimized assertoric warrant or of best judgement among those deemed fittest to judge. In which case it is not so much a good working compromise – one that should keep the realists happy while fending off the usual range of anti-realist objections – as a rather shuffling and evasive form of anti-realism which concedes the main point (the existence of objective, recognition-transcendent truths) and thus lets the argument go pretty much by default.

VI

This is why I have suggested that reflection on music, on its ontological status and the criteria for various kinds of judgement about it may provide a better, more helpful guide to some of these issues than reflection on the standard Lockean topos of secondary qualities. Music is a highly structured and hence – albeit in varying degrees – a cognitively more complex and articulated mode of perceptual experience which, unlike the range of everyday sonorous or acoustic phenomena, gives a hold for much subtler discriminations of normal, adequate or optimal listener-response. Thus it doesn't leave room for the kind of tautologous or blandly uninformative biconditional ('sound *x* is loud/soft/piercing/discordant, etc., if and only if perceived as such by any subject with properly functioning auditory apparatus under normal acoustic conditions') that typifies the discourse of response-dependence. Rather, it shows how trivially circular such formulas are if applied in the case of music and in the hope of establishing anything of interest with regard either to the work in question or to the question what should count as a valid, competent or musically informed judgement concerning it.

This is also to say that such judgements, if truth-apt, must be thought of as more or less responsive (and responsible) to standards of attentiveness, perceptual acuity and long-range structural grasp which *can* be spelled out in substantive terms and *cannot* be reduced to just another variant on the biconditional theme. From which it follows that there is always a further, phenomenological dimension – a reference to aspects of the work as they strike a duly perceptive and appreciative listener – that goes beyond anything accountable in terms of generalized 'best judgement'. That is, music offers a particular challenge to response-dispositional theories in so far as it involves a range of attributes (tonal, thematic, rhythmic, structural, etc.) which are not – or not solely – listener-dependent, but which also have the power to evoke certain complex and highly specific kinds of listener-response that exceed any such vague, all-purpose mode of specification. In which case there is always a question whether listeners, analysts, philosophers of music, or even those engaged – like myself at present – in a kind of metaphilosophical address to these issues have got things right or wrong (quite aside from their own or other people's best judgement) in relation to musical works. Thus the standing possibility of error must always be allowed unless it is ruled out through some such stipulative error-excluding device as the quantified biconditional which makes it, quite simply, an a priori truth that best judgement necessarily, by very definition, accords with what's there in the music. Otherwise we shall have to make terms with the fact – borne out with depressing regularity by the record of musical criticism to date – that it can often go very badly wrong unless defined in counterfactual terms as that upon which all judges would be sure to converge at the limit of optimal response.

As I have said, this should not be taken as an argument for assimilating music to the kind of fully fledged Platonist approach that would treat it on a par with mathematics and the formal sciences. That analogy breaks down on the problem of explaining how musical perception, understanding and evaluation could be held accountable to standards – like those of mathematical or logical proof – whose validity-conditions are in no way involved with the register of human responsive or phenomeno-logical capacities. Hence, as I have said, the error of supposing that the kinds of extreme contrapuntal and structural complexity exhibited by works such as Bach's *Musical Offering* or *Art of Fugue* give reason to think that the greatest music somehow aspires to the condition of pure math-ematics. For if this were the case then analysis of those works – or indeed of any music that qualified for treatment on similar terms – could best take the form of a proof-theoretic demonstration that certain thematic, harmonic and tonal problems were posed and resolved through a process of thought whose validity had nothing whatever to do with the work's expressive or communicative power. A good deal of present-day music analysis does seem to work on this mistaken supposition: that is, the idea that mathematical techniques such as pitch-class set analysis are somehow guaranteed to reveal what is most significant about the music's struc-tural or even its phenomenological character as perceived by a listener duly instructed in these or kindred technicalities.[54] Moreover, that idea might be said to have exerted a strong and (arguably) a malign influence not only on certain ultra-formalist trends in academic musicology but also on the way that such thinking is mirrored in a line of creative-compositional development running from middle-late period (i.e., twelve-tone serial) Schoenberg, via Anton Webern, to the Darmstadt School and their few remaining followers. Here we have another striking case of how analysis can sometimes risk losing touch with the deeper-laid sources of musical expressivity. Undoubtedly these have much to do with the various structural (e.g., thematic, harmonic and rhythmic) traits revealed by a sharp-eared analytical approach. However, the latter needs to be enhanced – guided and informed – by a prior sense of their musical significance as realized through a full and appreciative listener-response. Otherwise analysis will tend to over-emphasize those elements or aspects of the work that lend themselves most readily to treatment on formalist, structuralist or (quasi-)mathematical terms whilst undervaluing – even ignoring – those other more elusive yet phenomenologically salient aspects that resist such treatment.

For much the same reason, if philosophy of music presses too far toward a full-scale objectivist Platonism of the sort that finds its most frequent (if strongly disputed) application in mathematics, logic and the formal sciences then this may have a similar distorting effect. That is, it may prevent philosophers from acknowledging the extent to which musical works exist in and though their ongoing reception-history and the responsive capacities of those – performers, listeners and analysts alike – who seek to realize their structural as well as expressive qualities.

Thus the trouble with an unqualified Platonist approach is, as one might expect, just the opposite of that which afflicts any view of music as a matter of purely subjective or (in the widest, i.e., non-rigorous and un-Husserlian sense of the term) phenomenological response. And again, it is the opposite of that which arises with response-dispositional theories wherein music would figure as a topic of discourse subject to truth-values or conditions of warranted assertibility that can always be cashed out through a circular appeal to 'whatever it takes' for work *x* to possess quality *y* just so long as the listener likewise possesses 'whatever it takes' to recognize *y* in *x* under normal (or optimal) conditions. For if pure-bred Platonism captures the idea that musical works must in some sense be thought of as transcending the various contingent aspects of their reception-history to date then it does so only at the cost of failing to explain how listeners, no matter how responsive, could ever gain access to the experience of music, as distinct from its abstract representation. (One is reminded here of Hermann Hesse's novel *The Glass-Bead Game*, where a mandarin cultural elite is concerned with nothing so vulgar as musical composition or performance but spends all its time in devising elaborate mathematical permutations on existing works.)[55] However, this gives no reason to swing right across to the opposite extreme of a downright anti-Platonist, subjectivist or response-dependent approach that would deny the very possibility of music's possessing a mode of existence beyond its various transient realizations or beyond how it strikes the community of those presently deemed fittest to judge.

These issues are posed with particular force in the case of music – more so, I have argued, than when raised with reference to Locke on secondary qualities – since music occupies a kind of contested zone where philosophy will have to find room for some prima-facie sharply conflicting but none the less jointly binding conditions on any adequate approach. This is why I have drawn attention to Derrida's treatment of the various deep-laid antinomies that emerge throughout Husserl's project of transcendental phenomenology.[56] Although he (Derrida) has nothing to say directly about music he does raise the question, more generally, of how 'a certain' structuralism nowadays inherits the Platonist commitment to values of recognition-transcendent truth or 'absolute ideal objectivity', and also how this commitment relates to the phenomenological concern with intuitive acts of understanding, judgement, and conceptual-investigative grasp. I have argued elsewhere that analytic philosophy over the past half-century and more has been driven into a series of dead-ends – of ultimately sterile rather than productive or thought-provoking aporias – through its steadfast refusal (with just a few, mostly shortlived exceptions) to engage with issues that have typically preoccupied thinkers in the 'continental' line of descent after Husserl.[57] Here also the case of music has a special pertinence and diagnostic force. For it is hard to escape the impression that much analytical philosophy of music – and Anglophone aesthetic philosophy more generally – has long been in thrall to a narrow agenda of agreed-upon topics for debate which have to do mainly with issues of linguistic, conceptual or logico-semantic analysis, and has thereby avoided any deeper engagement with the kinds of issue taken up amongst thinkers in the 'other', mainland-European tradition. Yet in shying away from those questions it has tended to veer between the opposite extremes of an objectivist indifference to phenomenological concerns – stigmatized since Frege as mere 'psychologism' – and a series of reactive retreats into various sharply opposed (e.g., emotivist, project-ivist or other such non-cognitivist) positions.

Hence the strenuous but, it seems to me, the unavailing efforts of thinkers such as McDowell to dismount from this violently oscillating seesaw or damp down its movements to the point of restoring a state of equilibrium no longer disturbed by such contrary pushes and pulls. What emerges from McDowell's claims to this effect, as likewise from the response-dependence literature, is the curious way that such attempts to occupy a sensible, middle-ground position between realism and anti-realism end up by producing yet more complex and roundabout versions of the same old subject/object or mind/world dualism. Thus, according to McDowell,

> what we find in Kant is precisely the picture I have been recommending: a picture in which reality is not located outside a boundary that encloses the conceptual sphere ... The fact that experience involves receptivity ensures the required constraint from outside thinking and judging. But since the deliverances of receptivity already draw on capacities that belong to spontaneity, we can coherently suppose that the constraint is rational; that is how the picture avoids the pitfall of the Given.[58]

The tortuous, Chinese-box-like phrasing of this passage – the notion of reality as somehow no less 'real' for *not* being 'located outside a boundary that encloses the conceptual sphere' – is evidence enough that McDowell is still wrestling with problems that Kant bequeathed most directly to his heirs in the German idealist line of descent, whether 'subjective idealists' such as Fichte or 'objective idealists' like Schelling.[59] But it is also the kind of quandary that has typified a great deal of debate in the mainstream analytic tradition, from logical positivism down. That is to say, it results from that same Kantian problem of how one could ever reconcile two such intrinsically disparate or non-communicating realms as those of sensuous (phenomenal) intuition and objective (noumenal or mind-independent) reality.

I should not wish to claim – far from it – that I have here succeeded in putting together what just about every development in post-Kantian epistemology has somehow managed to drive asunder, most often (as with McDowell) despite and against its professed intent. On the other hand I do hope to have shown that this problem has a complex genealogy, one that has received a more adequate, historically informed and – be it said – philosophically sophisticated treatment in post-Husserlian continental than in mainstream analytic debate. One reason is that continental thinkers – even those (like Habermas and Derrida) who have little to say expressly on the subject of music – are none the less heirs to a history of speculative thought concerning the relationship between truth, knowledge and experience where issues of aesthetics have been central, rather than marginal, and where music has often figured as the greatest challenge to philosophy's self-image and powers of conceptualization. Nowhere is this more apparent than in the writings of a thinker such as Adorno, for whom that challenge was a matter of music's stubbornly autonomous formal character – its holding out against the lures of commodified mass-culture – yet also, paradoxically, of its capacity to reflect (albeit in a highly oblique or mediated fashion) the various forces at work in its social contexts of production and reception.

I can scarcely cite Adorno as a straightforward source of philosophical support for the kind of phenomenologically qualified Platonist approach to the ontology of music that I have proposed in the course of this chapter. After all, some of his most powerful and sustained critiques were directed at Husserl's phenomenological project and also toward what he saw as the self-deluding and ideologically complicitous idea that one could somehow subsume the unique particulars of musical (or indeed everyday) experience under the rubric of an abstract, hence reified general ontology.[60] Yet it is clear that Adorno's negative-dialectical approach to the sociology of music cannot do without the enabling premise that works have a certain structural autonomy, that is to say, an ontological status beyond whatever meaning or value is imputed to them by this or that (however well-attuned) listener in this or that (however favourable) context of reception. It is equally clear, despite his animadversions on Husserl, that Adorno's relentless critique of conceptual abstraction and his defence of the particular against the encroachments of system and method cannot but have recourse, at crucial points, to a phenomenology of musical and other perceptually based modes of experience. For there could otherwise be no explaining how certain works – those that elicit Adorno's dialectically hard-won approval – are such as to challenge our acculturated, ideologically conditioned habits of response. This is where Adorno's thinking comes closest to Derrida's deconstructive analyses of the various tensions in Husserl's project or the 'principled, essential and structural impossibility', as he puts it, 'of closing a structural phenomenology'.[61] It is also where reflection on the nature of music, its ontological status and relation to the range of our perceptual-cognitive capacities has most to offer by way of suggestive analogy in the context of current epistemological debate. In Chapter 3 I shall have more to say about the benefits to be had from a deeper acquaintance with developments in recent continental thought, along with the additional problems posed when some of those developments – especially in the field of 'literary' deconstruction – are over-zealously applied by music theorists with an ideological axe to grind.

3

What's In a Work? Music, Ontology and the 'Deconstructive Turn'

I

It is a claim often voiced (albeit most often by those on the 'continental' side of the fence) that analytical aesthetics, in particular philosophy of music, has nothing to show that remotely compares with the rich heritage of mainland-European, mostly German work in the field. Be this as it may – and I shall have more to say on the topic as my argument proceeds – there is incontestably a sense in which these two traditions of thought have pursued separate paths and given rise to very different ideas regarding the relationship between music and philosophy. Briefly put, the analytic approach has concerned itself mainly with the business of conceptual clarification, that is, with examining music – and our ways of thinking or talking about music – in order to reveal the various ideas, presuppositions, value-commitments, and so forth, which it takes to be implicit in our otherwise largely intuitive modes of response.[1] Thus it mostly starts out from a shared repertoire of concepts such as form, structure, thematic development, tonal progression or the claims of 'absolute' versus 'programme' music, and then offers a detailed account of how they relate to one another or how they are most properly, consistently or usefully applied. These concepts may be 'essentially contested' in the sense that they are always open to competing definitions or rival accounts of their relative priority *vis-à-vis* some particular conception of musical value. Still the analytic approach can fairly be characterized as one that concentrates on the second-order (conceptual or linguistic) elucidation of first-order musical issues and which therefore tends to operate at a certain, distinctly 'philosophic' remove from any direct engagement with the business of music criticism.

Hence the notable disinclination among most analytic philosophers of music to practise anything like the kind of 'analysis' (i.e., the detailed examination of music in its various formal or structural aspects) that has become the veritable stock-in-trade of academic musicology. As with aesthetics more generally, the emphasis has been on a metalevel mode of conceptual exegesis and critique where the primary aim is to be clear about the 'logical grammar' of our talk about music rather than to offer substantive proposals for rethinking the relationship between music, philosophy and other (e.g., historical or sociological) areas of discourse. Of course this leaves room for some sharp disagreements between those who take the Wittgensteinian descriptivist view that philosophy 'leaves everything as it is' and those who adopt a more revisionist approach, or who deploy the methods of conceptual analysis by way of challenging received ideas. Such, for instance, is the case with Jerrold Levinson's recent and highly controversial book *Music in the Moment*, which rejects all of the above-mentioned concepts and categories – along with just about the entire apparatus of present-day music theory – on the grounds that they absurdly overestimate the normal listener's powers of long-range structural (i.e., retentive or anticipatory) grasp.[2] Understandably enough, his arguments have provoked some strong reactions and defences of the more orthodox position amongst philosophers of music, such as Peter Kivy, who regard the capacity for structural listening not only as a mark of sophisticated musical response but also as a source of more refined and durable pleasure.[3]

So it is not just a case – as some 'continentally' inclined commentators would have it – of analytic philosophy avoiding all the big issues and contenting itself with the kind of subservient or under-labourer role recommended by Locke in relation to the natural sciences. On the contrary: the kind of disagreement that emerges between Kivy and Levinson (and which I shall discuss at greater length in Chapter 5) raises questions as searching and provocative as anything to be found in the work of an *echt*-'continental' dialectician such as Theodor Adorno. However, it does so always at a certain conceptual distance, or by way of philosophical reflection on what makes sense within the extant discourse of musical aesthetics and criticism. Continental approaches, on the other hand, are typified more by their strong speculative bent, their aim to transform (or at any rate to challenge) our very experience of music, and their extreme self-awareness with regard to philosophy's mediating role as a mode of thought which seeks to articulate the otherwise strictly ineffable truth-content of music. No doubt that role is envisaged very differently by thinkers such as Schopenhauer, Nietzsche, Bloch and Adorno. Even so, the 'continental' line of descent has enough common features – and enough points of contrast with work in the current analytic mode – to give the term more purchase here than in most areas of present-day philosophical debate.

Of course continental philosophy of music cannot be viewed as a monolithic school or movement, embracing as it does a wide range of often sharply contrasted approaches. Thus some find their chief inspiration in Husserlian phenomenology, while others – like Adorno's intensely dialectical, Marxian–Hegelian but also psychoanalytically inflected studies in the sociocultural dynamics of music – are such as to defy any kind of summary classification.[4] Also there are marked differences of emphasis within the broadly phenomenological school, as between Roman Ingarden's highly systematic and elaborately theorized approach to the many-layered ontology of the musical artwork – one that draws heavily on Husserl – and the more nuanced or 'appreciative' studies in the phenomenology of musical expression essayed by the philosopher-critic Vladimir Jankélevitch.[5] Still, this diversity should not be allowed to obscure the features that they do have in common and which set them decidedly apart from philosophy of music in the analytic mainstream. One is a concern – overt or not – with the kinds of issue that Derrida raises in his deconstructive readings of Husserl, namely the aporetic relationship between structure and genesis, form and expression, or the claims of a Platonist ontology grounded in the notion of 'absolute ideal objectivity' and those of a phenomenological approach that would bring such questions back within the remit of human responsive capacities and powers. This is not to deny that analytic philosophy has often been preoccupied with similar issues, as can be seen from the various attempted solutions to the problem of knowledge – such as John McDowell's revisionist reading of Kant – that have been proposed in the wake of Quine's famous attack on the two last dogmas of old-style logical empiricism.[6] However, as I have argued at length elsewhere, those 'solutions' do not so much mend the drastic (ultimately Kantian) rift between sensory and conceptual modes of cognitive uptake as raise the same problem over and again in a range of different, terminologically varied but no less intractable forms.[7]

II

What I seek to do in the rest of this chapter is to suggest certain aspects of that 'other', continental tradition of thought that might have a useful – even a transformative – effect if absorbed and brought to bear on debates within the mainstream analytic sphere. Philosophy of music is an area of discourse where these issues regularly come to the fore, not least in the dispute between Platonism and anti-Platonism: a dispute that has often assumed various surrogate (e.g., formalist versus expressivist or structuralist versus phenomenological) terms of engagement.[8] Indeed, it seems to me that the tension thereby produced is a strictly ineliminable aspect of any sensitive, intelligent, culturally informed and reflective response to music. That is to say, such listening itself has a dual character, on the one hand taking its orientation from the possibility of correct judgement – of understanding, interpreting or valuing the music at its true worth – whilst on the other allowing for the converse possibility that one may misperceive or misjudge what is heard through some lapse of attention, failure of structural grasp, tendency to over- or undervalue certain works for extraneous (cultural or private-associative) reasons, and so forth. Thus there are times and moods when I might derive far more enjoyment from listening to some of Grieg's *Lyric Pieces* than to a late Beethoven piano sonata, or from E. J. Moeran's G Minor Symphony than Schubert's Ninth, or from any number of favourite pieces that happen to exert some peculiar tonal, harmonic or rhythmic appeal than from even the finest performance of a work which leaves me largely unmoved yet whose superiority or claim to canonical status I would none the less readily acknowledge. And this – be it said – not merely out of deference to received or authorized opinion but through a sense of something 'there' in the work to which I am simply not responding in a musically adequate way. Sometimes, indeed, this dissociation can go so far as to create an almost schizophrenic state of mind whereby one can hear all sorts of thematically and structurally interesting things 'going on' in the music – things that a sufficiently sharp-eared analyst could no doubt discern – yet still fail to hear them as *musically* involving in the fullest sense of the term.

This has been my own experience with the music of several composers whose works have attracted some detailed, intensive and convincingly argued analysis which (sad to say) helps me scarcely at all in coming to a better, more appreciative grasp of what that music is all about. In some cases one may finally conclude that, after all, it is not so much one's own responses that are tested and found wanting but rather the music that fails to repay such devoted yet unavailing efforts. In other cases – the more problematic – one retains a nagging sense that the failure lies chiefly or solely on one's own side yet still cannot honestly claim to understand how the admirers (whose powers of judgement one perhaps rates higher than one's own) can possibly take that position. For the record: I can't shake off the former impression as regards Peter Maxwell Davies's music, or the latter with respect to some of Elliott Carter's works despite – or perhaps on account of – their (to me) highly elusive and tantalizing quality. Then again there are works, such as Wagner's *Ring* cycle, where I know that my negative responses are conditioned – or at any rate strongly influenced – by factors that may (as the Wagnerites would argue) have absolutely no bearing on the music's intrinsic quality, or else be thought of as deeply bound up with its ethos and palpable design on the listener, not to mention its chequered reception-history. (One is reminded here of Woody Allen's quip: 'Whenever I hear Wagner I feel like invading Poland.') However, such instances take us beyond the realm of discriminative musical response into areas of cultural politics, aesthetic ideology or the Wagner-cult as viewed from a socio-diagnostic viewpoint. My point is, rather, that so long as we remain within the sphere of musical experience and judgement – as distinct from these strictly extraneous although, on their own terms, perfectly legitimate lines of approach – it is always an open possibility that our responses will fall short of those required for an adequate understanding and appreciation.

Moreover, *contra* the 'New Musicologists' and others who reject any such idea, that possibility exists only on condition that the work be taken to possess certain well-defined, structurally salient and value-conferring attributes that cannot be reduced without remainder to its contexts of production or reception.[9] No doubt one can go a long way toward explaining (say) the drastic undervaluation of J. S. Bach's works during the century or so after his death in terms of changing musical tastes and the various wider, extra-musical factors – historical, political, sociocultural – that may plausibly be adduced in that connection. Conversely, there is a case to be made that the current overvaluation of music in the minimalist or neo-Romantic mode has to do with that mode of 'regressive listening' – of reduced attention-span, lack of structural grasp, fixation on endlessly repeated popular 'highlights' – which Adorno traced (albeit via some complex dialectical mediations) to their source in the infantilized and fetishized habits of response engendered by commodity capitalism and the present-day culture industry.[10] Yet in both cases – Bach and the minimalists – any argument along these cultural-diagnostic lines will necessarily imply some tacit (even if strongly disavowed) reference to standards of adequate response or valid musical judgement which provide the only possible rationale for undertaking such a project in the first place.

Not that those standards enjoy any kind of ultimate privilege or exemption from the prospect of challenge with the advent of later, more perceptive or intelligent modes of musical response. However, this is just the point (as well as the limit-point) of a qualified musical Platonism: that it makes due allowance *both* for the idea of our getting certain things right where previous listeners had got them wrong, *and* for the requisite degree of modesty in conceding that our judgements are none the less fallible and might always yield to a better, more adequate range of descriptive, analytic or evaluative criteria. Thus it has the great virtue – so I would claim – of leaving room for response-transcendent standards of musical value which might, at the limit, conceivably surpass the appreciative powers of any present or even any future community of listeners, no matter how expert or well qualified by the lights of (what else?) that same community. Quite simply, 'best judgement' can always go wrong, as with the appointment committee members who regretted that Bach and not Telemann (the first-choice candidate) had won the post of Cantor at Leipzig. The same applies to many others at the time who much preferred Telemann's music, or those most responsive to changing tastes – to the new style of emotionally charged and overtly dramatic expression – who considered C. P. E. Bach (the eldest son) by far the more gifted composer since fully *au fait* with these latest developments.

Of course it is always good to retain a healthy measure of scepticism with regard to received or canonical views in a field where there is always room for disagreement and where, as T. S. Eliot remarked in a well-known essay, our present understanding of past works is constantly – however subtly – altered by our foreknowledge of later developments to which those works gave rise.[11] Thus Eliot's point about Donne's poetry applies just as much to the music of Bach: that we now hear the latter in ways that Bach himself could never have heard it, since our cultural experience contains a great deal (including Bach's own works and their reception-history) beyond his utmost powers to imagine. However, this is no reason to concur with present-day philosophic doctrines – such as anti-realism or at least some versions of response-dependence theory – which, in this context, would amount to a rejection of the Platonist claim that validity in matters of musical judgement is accountable to standards above and beyond those of best opinion, consensual warrant or even optimized listener-response under maximally favourable conditions.[12] The issue is very much like that which divides realists from anti-realists with respect to scientific, historical and other varieties of truth-claim. Thus the latter are wont to argue that realism, in whichever area of discourse, can only give rise to dogmatic and coercive modes of argument that bank on their privileged access to truth and brook no debate unless it is conducted on their own, highly restrictive terms. It is the same argument that is often put forward by advocates of social constructivism or the 'strong' programme in sociology of knowledge, i.e., that theirs is not only the more liberal, tolerant and open-minded but also the more scientifically productive and knowledge-conducive approach since it resists the imposition of dogmatic truth-claims and encourages the widest possible range of historical as well as present-day perspectives.[13] At which point the realist will most likely respond with a pair of related counter-arguments. These are (1) that the relativist's position is philosophically incoherent since it cannot account for any gains in knowledge (or our knowledge of the growth of knowledge) without some overt or covert appeal to criteria of truth and falsehood, and (2) that realism is the best defence against dogmatism since it always entails a due recognition of the constant possibility that even our best-established, currently indubitable items of 'knowledge' might yet turn out – as so often in the past – to fall short of objective truth.[14]

Still the question remains as to just how far, if at all, these arguments can be transposed from their usual context in epistemology and philosophy of science to aesthetics and, more specifically, to the kinds of issue that I have raised here with regard to the ontology of musical works and the status of our judgements concerning them. Thus it might well be claimed that they don't carry across except, perhaps, in a vaguely suggestive and distinctly problematical way, since here there is no question of *truth* in the sense that realists defend and anti-realists reject, that is to say, truth conceived as objective, recognition-transcendent, or epistemically uncon-strained. After all, this is a domain (unlike those of mathematics, logic or the formal sciences) where we have to acknowledge the involvement of another, some would say 'subjective' but more properly *phenomenological* dimension which cannot be reduced, despite the best efforts of certain musical analysts, to any description in the purely structural or quasi-mathematical mode. However, the proponent of qualified Platonism can readily make this concession without thereby yielding crucial ground on the issue as to whether music is entirely response-dependent or whether, *non obstante* that 'other' dimension, it offers a basis for descriptive or evaluative statements that are subject to validity-conditions beyond the register of merely subjective or emotive response.[15] For she can still hold to her major thesis that musical judgements are capable of bearing truth-values and, moreover, that those values are decided not just as a matter of individual or collective 'taste' but with reference to standards that might always transcend the discriminative powers of this or that listener in this or that cultural context. As I have said, this is partly a question of musical ontology, of the work's having a mode of existence which intrinsically allows for the coming-apart of our actual judgements from those that the music properly requires or that would (counterfactually) constitute a full and adequate response. But it is also a matter of how we listen to music in the hope that repeated hearings will bring new perceptions, unexpected insights and a greater depth of appreciative grasp which more closely approximates – though never quite achieves – that wished-for condition.

Thus the chief virtue of what I have here called a 'qualified Platonist' approach is that it leaves room for a phenomenology of musical response – and hence for the absence of strictly objective criteria in such matters – whilst none the less acknowledging the various ways in which best judgement can still fall short of adequate musical warrant. This is where my suggested comparison with the realist/anti-realist debate in epistemology does have a useful if limited and area-specific bearing. Anti-realists about truth – together with cultural relativists and 'strong' sociologists – very often mount their case on the so-called 'sceptical meta-induction' or generalized 'argument from error'.[16] After all, they remark, it is an undeniable fact that by far the greater portion of hitherto accepted scientific 'knowledge' has turned out to be false, or else (like Newton's theories of space–time and gravitational attraction) valid only within certain specified and tightly restrictive limits. In which case it is sheer hubris to suppose that our current state of 'knowledge' is any less open to falsification or relegation to the status of a regional (domain-relative) science by future developments in this or that field. However, this invites the realist to respond by asking *on what possible grounds* – consistent with their own position – the anti-realist or the epistemological sceptic can appeal to the evidence of past error by way of asserting the unattain-ability (even the non-existence) of anything that could ever, now or in future, count as veridical knowledge. For it is clear that any version of the argument from error – or the sceptical meta-induction – must at some point appeal to the idea of truth as a yardstick against which to measure the various kinds or degrees of erroneous belief that have typified the history of science to date. In that case it is plainly a self-refuting argument since it can only go through on condition that we do – *ex hypothesi* – have certain standards or criteria by which to distinguish truth from falsehood or knowledge-conducive from knowledge-obstructive theories, hypotheses or truth-claims.[17] Such is the realist counter-thesis in its gener-alized or relatively abstract form, one that would in principle apply to any version of the (likewise generalized) anti-realist position. However, it can also be stated more directly in terms of the 'no miracles' (or 'cosmic coincidence') argument. Thus it would indeed be a miracle if science had managed to come up with such a range of successful (i.e., applied-technological ideas) unless most of its theories were true – or at any rate truth-tracking – and unless most of its operative concepts (among them its postulated referents across the whole scale from atoms to galaxies) were likewise on the right track.[18]

Anti-realists and social constructivists are wont to view this as a quick and dirty argument that blatantly begs the question with regard to the meaning (or the cultural–historical–ideological context) of terms such as 'successful' and 'truth-tracking'. Yet it is one that captures the standing intuitions of those with a decent working knowledge of the sciences who have not yet been got at by sceptical philosophers, or those who have been got at but none the less preserved a robust sense of evidential weightings and priorities. Michael Devitt speaks strongly for this point of view when he remarks that realism in epistemology and philosophy of science

> is an overarching empirical (scientific) theory or principle. It is initially plausible. It is supported by arguments that make no appeal to theories of language or understanding … What firmer place could there be to stand than Realism, as we theorize in such undeveloped areas as those of language and understanding? In contrast, the poor state of theories in those areas, whether verificationist or not, makes them a bad place from which to start theorizing, particularly in determining overarching principles about the nature of reality. To think otherwise is to put the cart before the horse.[19]

The same could be said of those recent approaches that invert the standard (on their account, deeply conservative) order of priorities between music conceived, in qualified Platonist terms, as a mode of experience best understood through its jointly expressive and structural aspects and music conceived as primarily an object of sociocultural, ideological or gender-based analysis.[20] What is wrong with such approaches is not just the fact of their focusing on topics – mostly with respect to the cultural contexts of production or reception – that tend to downplay (even ignore) those other, more traditional concerns. Nor is it solely the current idea amongst New Musicologists that any talk of structure, thematic transform-ation, tonal development, large-scale 'organic' form, etc., may well be a sign of the analyst's subscribing to a kind of 'aesthetic ideology' that has more to do with their deeply ingrained and professionally bred precon-ceptions than with anything demonstrably 'there' in the work.[21] Rather, as I have said, it is the systematic inversion of priorities which treats the very business of analysis – whether in its formalist/structuralist or its phenomenological (i.e., listener-oriented) mode – as an approach that itself needs explaining (or deconstructing) with the aid of those methods lately developed by critical theorists, sociologists of culture and others who have managed to resist the lure of such mystificatory notions. More than that, so it is argued: the failure to take their point can only give rise to a conception of music that extends the organicist metaphor from the privileged status of certain artworks to the privileged status of certain national cultures, and thereby comes to exert a dubious, even dangerous, influence on our thinking about matters of history and politics.

It is here that the New Musicologists' position invites something like Devitt's riposte to anti-realists or adepts of the 'linguistic turn' in epistemology and philosophy of science. That is to say, it is another instance of 'putting the cart before the horse', or the strictly preposterous idea that there is greater *musical* as well as cultural–political–historical insight to be had from non-music-centred disciplines or fields of study. The effect is not only to distract attention from the work in hand but to raise such distraction to a high point of principle by declaring that the very concept of 'the work' – bound up as it is with all manner of formalist, organicist and other deeply suspect notions – must likewise be counted just a product of aesthetic ideology, and hence as long overdue for deconstructive treatment.[22] I have argued elsewhere that musicology – or music theory – doesn't always stand to gain from this wholesale and often rather indiscriminate borrowing of methods and theories from outside its own disciplinary domain.[23] In particular it runs the risk of ignoring not only certain basic aspects of our musical experience but also certain ways in which music criticism and analysis can make a genuine – sometimes decisive – contribution to our better understanding and deeper, more appreciative grasp of that same experience.

Over the past few years there have been various voices raised against this (supposedly) self-interested claim that analysis of the kind carried on by experts or specialists in the business of academic musicology can actually enhance the enjoyment of music at a straightforward intuitive level.[24] On the contrary, they argue: it is merely a device for preserving the canon of acknowledged 'great works' and also for securing the experts' position as those with the know-how – the accredited competence – to judge in such specialized matters. Such opposition comes mainly from critics on the cultural left for whom the whole idea of 'structural listening' should be seen as just another technique of self-promotion on the part of a mandarin cultural elite. Thus the values and priorities attached to that idea are expressed not only by conservative upholders of the canon but also by those, like Adorno, who strive to locate the last sources of resistance in a complex dialectic of musical form and highly 'mediated' sociocultural content which itself needs some expert decoding if that resistance is to register with anything like the requisite force.[25] From this standpoint, the left/right divide in academic-cultural politics is really just so much window-dressing that conceals the existence of a shared ideology, a commitment to values which can only be defined in contradistinction to those of a stereotyped mass-culture. And of course the chief hallmark of this latter, debased kind of musical consumption – whether for Adorno or his sworn foes amongst the upholders of orthodox bourgeois 'taste' – is precisely its lack of the sustained, attentive, cultivated habit of mind that distinguishes 'structural listening'. Hence the widespread, often fiercely combative, rejection of Adorno's approach by cultural critics with a primary interest in popular music who deplore his contemptuous blanket dismissal of the 'culture-industry' and all its works, along with what they see as his own high-bourgeois disdain for anything (or anyone) failing to meet those narrowly exclusive standards.[26]

Moreover, there are others of a far-from-'radical' or left-leaning persuasion – among them, as we have seen, the analytic philosopher Jerrold Levinson – who have likewise argued against the idea of 'structural listening' as a basically a fiction invented by music analysts in order to keep themselves in business.[27] Thus, according to Levinson, it is beyond the powers of any listener who is actually hearing and enjoying the music to make the kinds of long-range thematic, harmonic and tonal connection that they would have to make if their experience was anything like that described by Schenkerian or other such ultra-formalist analytical techniques.[28] Rather, when we listen we most likely have a fairly vivid though rapidly fading recollection of what happened a few seconds ago and perhaps, if we know the work well, a likewise fairly vivid sense of how it is going to unfold in the next few seconds. Beyond that we have only the vaguest idea – and at a level of abstraction far removed from our immediate experience – of how present episodes link back, thematically or tonally, to earlier episodes or forward to those that we know (again in a highly abstract sense of 'knowledge') are yet to come. Any further, more ambitious or longer-range claims for our capacity of structural listening are therefore to be treated as a product of wishful thinking or, more pointedly, of professional self-interest on the part of music analysts. As I said, Levinson's book has been greeted with a large measure of scepticism or downright hostility amongst most in its target readership, while from one self-confessed 'structural listener' – Peter Kivy – it has drawn a more temperate but deeply puzzled and deeply personal response.[29] However, what is chiefly at stake is also what underlies the antagonism between Adorno and his left-populist detractors. That is to say, it is the question whether music can be thought of as always potentially transcending the limits of any given (individual or communal) mode of response, and whether – if so – that potential is best explained by its possessing certain jointly formal and phenomenological attributes that would warrant the qualified Platonist approach recommended here.

III

This is why I have drawn a parallel with issues in recent philosophy of science and mathematics where debate between realists and anti-realists likewise turns on the existence/non-existence of recognition-transcendent truths.[30] Of course there are large problems in the way of any too direct or, as Adorno would say, insufficiently 'mediated' passage from the way such debate has typically gone in those core areas of analytic philosophy to their possible bearing on issues of aesthetic understanding. Thus it would take a very bold (or downright reckless) philosopher to argue that musical judgements, like those in mathematics, were capable of objective truth or falsehood quite apart from the register of human perceptual, cognitive and phenomenological modes of response, or again, that the validity-conditions for such judgements might be specified in terms entirely independent of the various historical and cultural contexts in which they were arrived at. Any plausible version of the Platonist case as applied to music will need to acknowledge the degree to which musical responses – whether actual or optimal – play a role in deciding what counts as a true (i.e., both structurally and phenomenologically valid) judgement. However, this is *not* to claim, with the advocates of a 'strong' response-dependent approach, that those responses constitute the sole criterion or ultimate court of appeal for any judgement with regard to music and its various formal or value-conferring attributes. For there is, as I have said, a standing possibility built into the very nature of musical experience that it may fall short of doing justice not only to those work-specific attributes but also to the scope and capacities of human appreciative grasp. Where my 'qualified Platonist' approach has a difficult path to tread is in balancing the twin – on the face of it irreconcilable – demands of acknowledging the response-transcendent character or status of musical works whilst at the same time conceding the strictly undeniable fact that *in a certain sense* music cannot exist in the absence of sufficiently perceptive, responsive or musically competent listeners.

This might seem reminiscent of the old Berkeleian-idealist chestnut about whether a tree that falls in the forest when there is nobody (or no sentient creature) around to hear it can truly or plausibly be said to create the sound of a tree falling. However, the issue is in fact very different, since here – in the case of music – we have to do with a phenomenologically and structurally informed order of perception rather than a basic (phenomenal) register of sensory responses that may involve some highly complex auditory processing but not of the same qualitative kind or with anything like the same scope for meaningful divergences of judgement. It is the phenomenalist approach that has prevailed within the mainly

Anglophone line of descent from Locke, Berkeley and Hume to the logical positivists and thence, via sundry (e.g., Dummettian) updates on the verificationist theme, to the idea of response-dependence as a means of escape from all our epistemological woes.[31] However, it can now be seen to have produced a long series of technically varied but in the end unproductive quasi-solutions to the empiricist problem of knowledge. For it will always resurface as soon as one raises the Kantian *quid juris* question as to how – by what legitimate (self-validating) means – those sensuous or phenomenal intuitions can be 'brought under' adequate or perfectly corresponding concepts.[32] And if Kant's attempted resolution left the problem firmly in place – if his a priori arguments from the conditions of possibility for knowledge and experience in general failed to reconcile his twin doctrines of transcendental idealism and empirical realism – then the same must be said of subsequent efforts, like McDowell's, to come up with a 'naturalized' or de-transcendentalized version of Kant that would somehow achieve the wished-for deliverance.[33] That is to say, such ventures will always run aground on the impossibility of closing the gap opened up by this tenacious dualism of scheme and content or concept and intuition, whether in its native empiricist or its lately re-imported and scaled-down Kantian guise.

It is here that these debates stand to gain through a closer engagement with the 'continental' (i.e., post-Kantian, mainland-European) tradition of thought wherein epistemology has mostly taken a phenomenological rather than a downright phenomenalist (hence anti-realist and scepticism-inducing) line of approach. What is needed, in short, is a different perspective that allows us to see beyond the false dilemma exploited by those who would have it that the choice falls between objectivist truth and humanly attainable knowledge, or again, the impasse which often results when proposals for a middle-ground solution – like response-dependence theory – turn out to view truth as epistemically constrained, and hence as subject to the standard anti-realist caveats and qualifications. Any genuine or workable solution, I suggest, will need to take stock of developments outside the mainstream analytic tradition, in particular those that have emerged in the wake of Husserlian phenomenology. Just lately there have been signs of a movement in this general (i.e., 'continental') direction by certain analytic (maybe 'post-analytic') philosophers – McDowell and Robert Brandom among them – in response to the perceived bankruptcy of logical empiricism and its various successor movements.[34] However, these have so far tended to focus on Kant and Hegel as tutelary figures or sources of the looked-for liberation, and not to more recent developments. Also there is a strong sense, in McDowell's case at least, of their still being hooked on the same old dualisms that have hobbled epistemology ever since Kant's ultimate failure to reconcile the realms of sensuous intuition and conceptual understanding. Hence McDowell's constant swinging back and forth between, on the one hand, a notion of 'receptivity' which claims to avoid the empiricist myth of the given by incorporating just enough 'spontaneity' to give the mind an active role in the process of knowledge-acquisition and, on the other, a notion of 'spontaneity' that strives to incorporate just enough empirical constraint from the outside world to avoid the opposite (idealist) nemesis.[35]

I have argued elsewhere that this pattern of expressly disowning such bad dichotomies while in fact reproducing them in various oblique, displaced or surrogate forms is one that can be found across a wide swathe of present-day 'post-empiricist' or 'post-analytic' thought.[36] One reason is the failure to engage with those modern continental developments – from Husserl to Derrida – that have raised these issues in a more sustained, self-critical and reflective way. This is perhaps what Derrida has in mind when he remarks that the chief lesson to be learned from Husserl's thinking about issues in the philosophy of language, logic and mathematics is 'the absolute, principled, and structural impossibility of closing a structural phenomenology'.[37] Or again, '[w]hat I can never understand, in a structure, is that by means of which it is not closed'.[38] It is clear enough that the terms 'structure' and 'structuralism' here have to do not only with a twentieth-century movement of thought based on the linguistic theories of Saussure but also – more importantly – with the sense in which, as Derrida says, 'a certain structuralism has always been philosophy's most spontaneous gesture'.[39] That is, they denote the form most recently taken by that Platonist commitment to modes of reasoning, so to speak, 'in the absolute' which has always – inevitably – come into conflict with approaches that place their chief emphasis on matters of genesis, historical development or the expressive/creative (as opposed to the formal or rule-governed) aspect of language and thought. Which is *not* to say – far from it – that we had best follow those who despair of achieving any viable solution to this quandary and who therefore recommend one or other of the various anti-realist, pragmatist, constructivist, cultural-relativist, framework-internalist or downright sceptical escape-routes currently on offer.[40] For if philosophy (or the history of philosophy) has one constantly repeated lesson to teach it is the fact that problems which have turned out to lack any straightforward solution may none the less be worth continued attention and give rise to insights unattainable elsewhere.

It seems to me that Derrida is right in claiming that the stand-off between structuralism and phenomenology – in the extended, non-parochial sense of those terms – is among the most intractable but also the deepest and most philosophically productive problems inherited by present-day thinkers. Moreover, it is one that arises with particular pertinence and force with regard to philosophy of music since here – as I have argued – there is a need to accommodate two sharply conflicting intuitions, both of which have a strong claim to truth in the experience of most philosophically minded and musically responsive listeners. One is the Platonist (and, in Derrida's parlance, 'structuralist') thesis: that in the case of certain musical works our understanding and evaluation of them is itself subject to assessment by standards that are *not* just those of individual taste, cultural fashion, received 'expert' opinion, etc. On the contrary, such standards have to do with intrinsic structures, attributes and qualities which may be more or less adequately realized in any given performance/audition of the work yet which cannot be reduced to the sum-total of performances/auditions to date, nor even to some optimal subset defined by reference to the best opinion of those deemed fittest to judge. The other intuition, with which this first seems irreconcilably at odds, is that music is nothing – that it lacks any qualities, attributes, meaning, value or plausible ontology – except in so far as it is heard, understood, appreciated and valued by a listener (or community of listeners) whose responses are the very conditions of possibility for its existing *qua* musical work, rather than in some abstract limbo of the Platonist imaginary.

Such is the claim mounted by those who look to response-dependence theory in search of an adequate (i.e., a duly normalized, or optimized) account of what it takes in terms of perceptual powers or ambient conditions for this or that report of sensory response to possess veridical warrant.[41] Arguments of this kind can be shown to fall short – or so I have maintained elsewhere – when it comes to explaining how even the best-placed observer/listener/respondent can sometimes be in error even with regard to those basic perceptual modalities – such as the classic Lockean instances of colour, sound, taste and smell – where communal or intersubjective agreement goes a long way toward settling the issue.[42] Still less can they be thought to hold good in matters of musical judgement where there is far greater room not only for subjective variations in response but also for the sorts of conflict that can often arise between listeners who reach sharply differing estimates despite their each possessing a high degree of aural perceptiveness, structural grasp, analytic acuity and informed (musically literate) understanding. That is to say, the Platonist argument has somehow to be squared with a phenomenological approach that avoids the vacuously circular upshot of pure-bred response-dependence theories ('best judgement *just is* what counts as such by our best communal lights') by providing a more substantive account of what it takes for musical responses to be (1) more or less up to the mark in the above-mentioned respects and (2) *responsive to* salient features or aspects of the work which justify certain descriptive or evaluative claims. It is in this sense, I suggest, that we should understand Derrida's reiterated point about the absolute need to pursue the twin projects of structuralism and phenomenology as far as possible even though – or perhaps just because – their joint pursuit gives rise to such deep conceptual and methodological problems. It is also for this reason that I have here used the phrase 'qualified Platonism' with respect to philosophy of music in order to denote a double and, seemingly at least, downright contradictory imperative. That is to say, it is a phrase which usefully betokens *on the one hand* the need for a musical ontology that allows the truth-value (i.e., the truth or falsehood) of our various musical descriptions and judgements sometimes to exceed our best powers of appreciative grasp and *on the other* the need for any such ontology to reckon with those aspects of musical experience – its perceptually and cognitively mediated character – which set it apart from logic, mathematics and the formal sciences.

Thus, when Derrida speaks of 'structuralism' by way of contrast to phenomenologically oriented modes of thought, it is with an eye both to the generalized sense of that term which covers a range of Platonist, objectivist or formalist approaches and the modern, more restricted sense whereby it denotes certain regional developments in the human sciences with their proximate source in Saussurean linguistics. Amongst them – and most obviously relevant in this context – is the structuralist approach to musical analysis that seemed to be making great strides in the 1970s and early 80s but has since then, it is fair to say, not fulfilled that initial high promise.[43] Among various likely reasons is the fact that it often amounts to just a different technical gloss on other, more familiar kinds of music-analytical discourse, that is to say, one that imports a whole battery of Saussure-derived binary distinctions – *langue/parole*, signifier/signified, synchronic/diachronic, paradigm/syntagm – whose effect is merely to lend an appearance of increased methodological rigour.[44] But there is another reason that goes rather deeper, and which Derrida brings out most tellingly in his reflections on the aporetic nature of the encounter between structuralism and phenomenology. Thus 'the structuralist quest', he remarks, is always in its ultimate intention the quest for 'a form or function organised according to an internal legality in which elements have meaning only in the solidarity of their correlation or their opposition'.[45] Nor (presumably) would any self-professed structuralist wish to reject that characterization, invoking as it does the central tenet of Saussurean semiology along with those later movements of thought that claim Saussurean warrant: namely, the idea of language and its various analogues as systems of meaning made up entirely of differential relationships 'without positive terms'.[46] However, it is just Derrida's point – one that emerges most clearly in his readings of Husserl – that while 'a certain structuralism' may well be intrinsic not only to philosophical discourse but to any attempt at revealing linguistic or other (e.g., geometrical) modes of intelligibility, nevertheless that approach will always, of necessity, leave something out of account.[47]

Hence, to repeat, his interlinked claims that '[w]hat I can never understand, in a structure, is that by means of which it is not closed' and that the chief insight to be gained from a deconstructive reading of Husserl's texts is 'the principled, essential, and structural impossibility of closing a structural phenomenology'.[48] What eludes the structuralist project – what marks the furthest limit of intelligibility when conceived in such terms – is that element of jointly genetic, expressive and intentional signification which structuralism *necessarily* ignores by reason of its basic theoretical and methodological commitments. Commentators mostly fail to perceive this relationship of mutual interrogative exchange – rather than reciprocal mistrust or downright antagonism – between structuralism and phenomenology. Thus, according to the widely accepted (often post-structuralist) account, structuralism displaced or superseded phenomenology through its critique of the latter's 'naïvely' subject-centred or expressivist approach to language and signifying systems in general, only to be superseded in turn by the rapidly emergent post-structuralist critique of its residual 'logocentric' assumptions.[49] No doubt it is the case that some of Derrida's most influential early writings – especially his essay 'Structure, Sign and Play in the Discourse of the Human Sciences' – were instrumental in bringing about the eclipse of classic 'high' structuralism, at least amongst the arbiters of avant-garde intellectual fashion.[50] Yet, as should be clear by now, this was a drastically simplified approach: one that ignored not only his insistence that 'a certain' structuralism (or drive for conceptual clarity and precision) was intrinsic to any philosophical enterprise meriting the name, but also – yet more strikingly at odds with prevailing cultural trends – his claim that a passage through Husserlian phenomenology in its various stages of development was likewise prerequisite to any understanding of structuralism's scope and limits.

Nothing could be further from the textbook account of how post-structuralism – to which Derrida's work is very often (and wrongly) assimilated – took its place as the outcome and radical upshot of a movement of thought whereby those previous episodes were left decisively behind. For if one thing should be plain to any properly attentive reader it is his rejection – his 'absolute and principled' rejection – of such grossly simplistic ideas. Rather, what is called for and exemplified in Derrida's readings of Husserl is just the kind of patient, meticulous, detailed and (in the non-parochial sense) closely *analytic* thinking-through of the encounter between structuralism and phenomenology which he considers indispensable to any adequate treatment of these issues.

IV

Derrida has little to say about music apart from his lengthy disquisition, in *Of Grammatology*, concerning Rousseau's self-contradictory attempts to establish the 'natural' basis of authentic musical expression in a language of the passions – a kind of primitive speech-song – as yet untouched by the corrupting influence of harmony, counterpoint, stylistic convention, structural complexity, and so forth.[51] Given time it would be possible to show how this discussion relates to our topic here, that is to say, how the aporetic character of Rousseau's discourse results from its commitment to a range of strictly unsustainable or self-subverting value-priorities. Chief among them is Rousseau's express belief – though one that is undermined by the logic of his own argument – in the absolute primacy of melody over harmony, nature over culture, and straightforward, uncomplicated passional utterance (whether in music or speech) over other, more articulate or 'civilized' forms of expression.

Hence what Derrida terms the 'logic of supplementarity' that is everywhere to be found as a covert yet disruptive subtext in Rousseau's multifarious writings on music, language, cultural history, political institutions, civil society and the question of authentic (primitive and communal) versus inauthentic (complex and stratified) forms of social existence. In each case the supposedly derivative, decadent, corrupting, or 'supplementary' negative term can be shown – through a logico-semantic analysis of Rousseau's text – to constitute the very condition of possibility for any discourse on its positive (supposedly original, proper and self-sufficient) counterpart. And so it transpires, in Derrida words (paraphrasing Rousseau), that

> [t]he growth of music, the desolating separation of song and speech, has the form of writing as 'dangerous supplement': calculation and grammaticality, loss of energy and substitution. The history of music is

parallel to the history of language, its evil is in essence graphic. When he undertakes to explain how music has degenerated, Rousseau recalls the unhappy history of the language and its disastrous 'perfecting': 'To the degree that the language improved, melody, being governed by new rules, imperceptibly lost its previous energy, and the calculus of intervals was substituted for nicety of inflection.'[52]

However, Rousseau's attempt to hold these distinctions and priorities firmly in place is everywhere thwarted by that other, 'supplementary' logic whose effect is not simply to invert them – thus leaving their basic structure intact – but rather to produce ever more complex internal (i.e., intraconceptual) oppositions and splittings which work to destabilize that structure from within. Thus:

> Just as there is a good musical form (melody) and a bad musical form (harmony), there is a good and a bad melodic form. By a dichotomous operation that one must ever begin anew and carry further, Rousseau exhausts himself in trying to separate, as two exterior and heterogeneous forces, a positive and a negative principle. Of course, the malign element in melody communicates with the malign element in music in general, that is to say with harmony. This second dissociation between good and bad melodic form puts the first exteriority into question: there is harmony already within melody.[53]

Whilst scarcely doing justice to the subtlety, perceptiveness and (not least) the logical rigour of Derrida's exegesis, I trust that this brief discussion will have brought out its relevance to the topic in hand. It shows how his thinking engages issues that are *not* – as sundry detractors would have it – just products of a certain perverse ingenuity in seeking out textual problems where no such problems truly exist. What renders this charge so manifestly off the point is its failure to grasp that Derrida is here broaching issues that have just as much to do with music – with the phenomenology of musical experience, its perceptual modalities, structural aspects and various tonal-harmonic resources – as with the textual complications that Rousseau confronts in striving to make his case.

Thus if the 'supplementary' logic of his discourse constrains Rousseau to acknowledge that there *simply cannot be* – can *never have been* – a pure melody devoid of harmonic implications, aspects or overtones, then this is something more than a matter of locating those symptomatic passages in which there emerges, as Derrida puts it, 'a certain relationship, unperceived by the writer, between what he commands and what he does not command of the patterns of the language that he uses'.[54] For it is also a truth borne out by reflection on the character of musical response that even a plain, unaccompanied melodic line – say a folksong or piece of plainchant – will none the less be heard as possessing an implied harmonic dimension. In part this has to do with the science of acoustics, that is, with the fact that there is no such thing in nature as a 'pure', harmonically unalloyed tone, since every sound (even if produced by a sine-wave generator) always carries along with it a series of decreasingly perceptible overtones up and down through the circle of fifths. Moreover, there is phenomenological evidence to similar effect (i.e., that melody depends upon harmony) in so far as, for any receptive listener, it is the patterns of harmonic implication – of mounting or diminishing tension, of discordant or concordant tonality, of resolved or unresolved chordal progressions, conclusive or interrupted cadences, etc. – which define our sense of melodic contour and character. So it just won't do for purveyors of the 'textualist' charge to claim that Derrida is merely concerned with rhetorical complexities (or pseudo-complexities) which result from his desire to make trouble for our normal understanding of language or for orthodox readings of thinkers such as Plato, Rousseau and Husserl. What this ignores is firstly the logical acuity of Derrida's analyses, drawing as they do – albeit by way of textual exegesis and critique – on a range of modal, epistemic, deontic and temporal considerations that should not be beyond the grasp of those with a knowledge of developments in recent, non-classical philosophy of logic.[55] Secondly, it takes no account of the way these analyses bear on matters of extra-textual knowledge and experience, whether (as I have said) in the particular case of music or as regards Rousseau's kindred thoughts about language, culture, history, politics, ethics and civil society.

Here likewise it can readily be shown that his overt priorities self-deconstruct not only through the presence of certain indicative textual complications but also, more concretely, on the evidence of what we can know or find out through other (e.g., phenomenological, empirical or socio-historical) methods of enquiry. Just as harmony turns out to be the necessary basis or condition of possibility for melody, so language turns out – *contra* Rousseau's express belief – to be reliant necessarily and of its very nature on those various 'supplementary' features (everything pertaining to its structural, grammatical, semantic or social-communicative aspect) in the absence of which we cannot conceive how language could ever have developed. And again, it is a lesson to be learned not only from a deconstructive reading of Rousseau on the idealized 'state of nature' but also through conceptual analysis or anthropological reflection that in truth there can *never have been* such a state, since even the earliest, most 'primitive' forms of human society were already – by very definition – subject to various cultural distinctions of kinship, caste, rank, age, gender, authority, occupational role, and so forth. In each case there emerges a deviant, non-classical yet none the less cogent logic whereby what *ought to be* thought of (on Rousseau's account) as merely a later, inessential and most often corrupting addition to the pure self-sufficiency of nature turns out *necessarily* to be there at the source and hence not a 'supplement' in anything like that belittling or pejorative sense of the term. Rather it is a 'supplement' in the other, essentially palliative sense: 'that which makes good some existing lack', or 'that which must be added in order to complete some otherwise partial, defective or non-self-sufficient state of things'. Thus etymologically the word itself can be seen to contain just the striking ambiguity – or proneness to generate chains of conflicting logico-semantic implication – that Derrida traces through Rousseau's writings on language, music, cultural history and many other topics besides. It is therefore a question, he writes, 'of Rousseau's situation within the language and the logic that assures to this word or this concept sufficiently *surprising* resources so that the presumed subject of the sentence might always say, through using the "supplement", more, less, or something other than he would mean [*voudrait dire*]'.[56] And again: it is a matter of locating and accounting for those moments of conceptual strain in the text where an attentive reader becomes most aware of what Derrida calls '[the] difference between implication, nominal presence, and thematic application'.[57]

Now it may not be altogether clear, even to such a reader, how these points about Derrida's critical exegesis of passages in Rousseau link up with my previous discussion of issues in philosophy of music, especially the issue concerning musical Platonism. What provides that link, I suggest, is the fact that Derrida is at pains to insist on the necessity – the 'absolute and principled' necessity – (1) that texts, whether those of Rousseau or Husserl, should be read in such a way as to reveal this supplementary logic at work; (2) that it will (and must) stand revealed as the outcome of any sufficiently attentive and rigorous deconstructive reading; and (3) that what is thereby brought to our notice is not just some super-subtle point of 'textualist' contriving but a truth about language, logic, mathematics, music, or those other topic-areas upon which his writings are focused. Hence his carefully specified claim with regard to the operative scope and limits of any appeal to authorial intention: namely, that 'Rousseau's discourse lets itself be constrained by a complexity which always has the form of a supplement of or from the origin ... [h]is declared intention is not annulled by this but rather *inscribed* within a system which it no longer dominates.'[58] My point is that this idea of 'constraint' has multiple dimensions in Derrida's thought, including as it does both the various constraints imposed upon Rousseau's discourse by recalcitrant features of the topic in hand, and also those constraints upon the reader that require the abandonment of certain received or orthodox interpretative notions when confronted with likewise recalcitrant details of Rousseau's text.

Here we are close to the central theme of Derrida's writings on Husserl, that is to say, the strictly undecidable issue between structuralism and phenomenology. More generally, it is the conflict of priorities between an approach that perforce disregards the expressive 'surplus' of meaning and intention in its quest for preconstituted structures of intelligibility and an approach that renounces that quest for the sake of conveying, evoking, or at any rate not ignoring, the expressive dimension of language.[59] This is also – I would suggest – well within reach of the issue between Platonist and anti-Platonist ways of thinking about music in relation to the formal sciences (i.e., logic and mathematics) on the one hand and, on the other, to those various creative, expressive or non-formalizable dimensions of human thought that lie beyond reach of any objectivist account. Hence my proposal for a 'qualified Platonist' approach that would maintain the conception of musical works as always potentially transcending the limits of their cultural context, reception-history, valuation by this or that community of listeners, etc., yet at the same time acknowledge their response-dependent character in a certain, distinctly phenomenological sense of that otherwise misleading phrase. What is most attractive about this proposal is the fact that it can draw on a wide range of tributary sources, whether those – such as the work of Merleau-Ponty – that have emerged in the wake of Husserl or those that have developed through the fruitful conjunction of music theory and analysis with an awareness of wider philosophical issues.[60] Thus the chief virtue of this approach – one that takes stock of 'continental' developments from phenomenology, through structuralism, to deconstruction – is its capacity to focus on the various conditions for a full and adequate musical response: that is, those having to do with both the formal attributes of the work in question and the modes of perceptual-cognitive uptake or appreciative grasp to which they give rise. Where response-dependence theories inherit their agenda from old-style logical empiricism – along with its inertly phenomenalist epistemology and philosophy of mind – this alternative approach finds room for a far more complex, substantive and philosophically developed though also (as we have seen) more acutely problematical conception of the issues involved.[61]

V

My mention of Merleau-Ponty is worth developing further since his works give a fascinating view from the other side, so to speak, of that crucial encounter between phenomenology and structuralism that Derrida broaches in his early writings on Husserl. Thus for Merleau-Ponty, as for Derrida in an essay such as 'Force and Signification', it is a matter of striving to convey how the expressive dimension of language can always potentially surpass or exceed what is graspable in terms of 'preconstituted' signification: that is, whatever lends itself readily to analysis by structuralist, formalist or other such methodologically powerful but overly restrictive means.[62] As Merleau-Ponty describes it, this aspect of language should impel us to reflect on 'that paradoxical operation through which, by using words of a given sense, and already available meanings, we try to follow up an *intention* which necessarily outstrips, modifies and in the last analysis stabilizes the meanings of the words that translate it'.[63]

If the kinship between his and Derrida's thinking in this regard has not been widely recognized it is perhaps because Derrida also – more famously – argues to contrary effect. That is, he puts the case that this expressive/intentional dimension of language (Saussurean *parole*) necessarily entails and presupposes a grasp of those various preconstituted structural features (Saussure's *la langue*) which alone make it possible for language to exist and develop as an effective means of communication. Still it is clear, in his early essays on Husserl, that Derrida is so far from denying or demoting the expressive 'surplus' of signification that he insists on the absolute impossibility of 'closing' a structuralist analysis. Moreover, this applies especially to literary texts which very often involve a maximal divergence or sense of creative dislocation between what is given as a matter of established linguistic convention and what is conveyed through certain distinctive traits of metaphor, idiom or style. Indeed, Derrida makes the point through a striking simile of his own, comparing the result of certain structuralist analyses – here one thinks of Roman Jakobson's virtuoso exercises in this vein – with a city that has been stricken by some natural or humanly visited catastrophe, all its buildings and physical landmarks intact but utterly devoid of life.[64] Such, he suggests, is or would be the case if that approach were carried through to the point where it actually succeeded in its ultimate methodological aim: that of reducing the expressive to the structural (or purely indicative) functions of language. That it cannot in practice be carried right through – that the expressive-intentional aspect of language must always count crucially even for hardline structuralists when they seek to explain why their findings should be thought valid or relevant – doesn't prevent such methods from exerting an effect reminiscent of Derrida's striking simile.

Merleau-Ponty's later essays on painting often manage to catch what I have here been trying to define, that is to say, a thinking on the cusp between various opposed priorities, among them the claims of structure and genesis, form and meaning, or – in Derrida's early terminology – 'signification' and 'force'.[65] They are also balanced with extraordinary tact between the rival claims of a phenomenology that was just then encountering the challenge of emergent structuralism and a structuralism prone to overstate its claims and thereby leave itself bereft of certain still-valid phenomenological insights. One topic was a documentary film about Matisse which showed the artist in the process of putting the final touch – the decisive stroke – to a painting. What so fascinates Merleau-Ponty is the interplay of freedom and necessity, or of choice and formal constraint, at just the moment when an artwork (though the same would apply to a written or spoken utterance) takes on a kind of quasi-inevitability despite its having seemed right up until that moment that various other possibilities were still in play. As he puts it: 'the chosen line was chosen in such a way as to observe, scattered out over the painting, twenty conditions which were unformulated and even informulable for anyone but Matisse, since they were only defined and imposed by the intention of executing *this painting which did not yet exist*'.[66] Here again, there is a striking convergence between Merleau-Ponty's phenomenological way of broaching certain nascent structuralist themes – such as those elusive 'conditions' of formal intelligibility that must somehow have pre-existed yet could only have been defined through the finishing stroke – and Derrida's deconstructive meditations on the impossibility of 'closing' a structural phenomenology. If deconstruction owes more than is commonly acknowledged to these post-Husserlian phenomenological developments then it is equally the case that Merleau-Ponty's later essays on language, literature and the visual arts already show signs of a willingness to measure the force of structuralist arguments and to modify some aspects of his thinking in response.

There are valuable insights to be had from this conjuncture of two, closely related yet in many ways antagonistic modes of thought whereby each draws out the other's implications and provides, in effect, an immanent critique of its operative scope and limits. What is also significant here – in the context of our primary concern with music and its ontological status – is the fact that this encounter between structuralism and phenomenology cannot but take place against the background of certain shared philosophical assumptions. Among them, I suggest, is the qualified Platonist belief that statements about musical structure or form are genuinely truth-apt (i.e., possess specifiable validity-conditions) yet can best be treated in relation to the various modalities of human sensory, cognitive and structural-phenomenological grasp. For although music seldom figures as an overt topic in Merleau-Ponty's writings, and in Derrida's only at a second remove via his reading of Rousseau, it is none the less clear that philosophy of music has much to learn from these thinkers' sustained and intensive engagement with the various antinomies of structure and meaning, form and force, or language in its twofold (expressive and indicative) aspects. Thus, for instance, what Merleau-Ponty has to say about Matisse – about the complex dialectic of freedom and necessity or creative choice and formal constraint – could just as well apply to our conflicting intuitions as regards the most valued, i.e., most challenging and (at least to the responsive listener) inexhaustibly rewarding musical works.

This is why 'deconstructive' musicologists go wrong when they take a lead from Paul de Man's sombre meditations and routinely denounce any talk of 'organic form', thematic integration, tonal development, and the like, as at best just a product of the analyst's foregone descriptive-evaluative bias, and at worst a projection of that deep-seated 'national aestheticist' ideology which (so it is claimed) goes along with some dubious, not to say dangerous, cultural-political beliefs.[67] Quite apart from the highly questionable nature of any such sweeping claim, there is also the basic fallacy of supposing that the kinds of criteria typically invoked by literary critics or music analysts when they seek to demonstrate the presence of such unifying features in this or that work are such as to imply an order of necessity – of formal compulsion – with its closest analogue (indeed its ultimate political realization) in the totalitarian state.[68] What is so tendentious, indeed grossly misleading about such comparisons is their failure to grasp the crucial point that Merleau-Ponty makes so strikingly in his essay on Matisse, and which is also articulated with great precision in Derrida's writings on the interface between phenomenology and structuralism. That is, they involve something very like the kind of dogmatic prescription which these theorists are wont to denounce, namely the hardline determinist idea that values such as structural coherence, developing variation or (worst of all) 'organic form' must be thought to exclude all possibility of creative or even (if one takes the analogy at full force) of social and political freedom.

Here it is worth recalling what de Man has to say about Heinrich von Kleist's curious parable 'On the Puppet-Theatre', which he reads alongside

Schiller's *Letters on Aesthetic Education* in order to point up the affinity – as de Man would have it, the sinister affinity – between these two, otherwise very different texts.[69] It concerns the way that certain kinds of extreme formal precision in the arts – such as those achieved through a perfectly coordinated dance or gymnastic display – may be felt to give access to a state of aesthetic grace beyond all the vexing antinomies of form and content, mind and nature, or free-will and necessity, while none the less exhibiting (like the puppet-theatre) a purely mechanistic, hence totally programmed and coercive exercise of power over body and mind alike. For Schiller, it is a post-Kantian article of faith that aesthetic experience can and should serve as the highest, most humanly fulfilling means of reconciliation between our otherwise sharply dissociated modes of sensuous cognition on the one hand and intellectual, moral and spiritual knowledge (or self-knowledge) on the other. Thus what the image of a perfectly choreographed dance evokes in Schiller's idealist rendering is the means whereby 'everything fits so skilfully, yet so spontaneously, that everyone seems to be following his own lead, without ever getting in anyone's way'.[70] According to de Man, this translates philosophically as 'a wisdom that lies somehow beyond cognition and self-knowledge, yet can only be reached by ways of the process it is said to overcome'.[71] In other words, 'aesthetic education' on Schiller's account is the sole means of transcending those dichotomies – between concept and intuition, understanding and reason, pure and practical reason, determinate and indeterminate (reflective) judgement – that Kant had striven (and ultimately failed) to reconcile through his doctrine of the faculties and the various orders of reciprocal dependence or interinvolvement amongst them.

However, de Man sees this as just the first in a long series of misreadings, distortions or uncritical appropriations of Kant the chief effect of which has been to promote that strain of aesthetic ideology which took hold with the rise of a Romanticism premised on notions such as organic form and the transcendent, reconciling power of poetic language, and which still dominates most varieties of present-day critical discourse. Thus '[t]he "state" that is here being advocated [by Schiller] is not just a state of mind or of soul, but a principle of political value and authority that has its own claims on the shape and the limits of our freedom'.[72] And again, with more particular reference to the bearing of Kleist's allegorical narrative on this high-Romantic creed: '[t]he point is not that the dance fails and that Schiller's idyllic description of a graceful but confined freedom is aberrant'.[73] Rather, as de Man and his followers would have it, such ideas continue to exercise a strong and well-nigh compulsive fascination over

critics, theorists, music analysts and (not least) those mistaken readers
– or non-readers – of Kant who ignore the resistance that his texts put up
to any such naïve or ideologically complicitous account. Thus '[a]esthetic
education by no means fails; it succeeds all too well, to the point of hiding
the violence that makes it possible'.[74]

Nevertheless it is worth asking whether this diagnosis really holds
good, especially since it has tended to exert just the kind of powerful,
seductive, almost spellbinding, influence on some of his more orthodox
disciples that de Man attributes to the workings of that same aesthetic
ideology. In particular it is worth raising this question in the context
of present-day 'deconstructive' musicology where such ideas have come
to occupy the high-ground of advanced, theoretically informed debate.
My point is that avant-garde theorists are just as apt to be seduced by
these strong but reductive and doctrinally driven modes of argument
as are those mainstream critics or analysts who place their faith in
received ideas of organic form, structural coherence, long-range tonal-
thematic integration, and the like. What drops out of sight when either
approach is pushed to a dogmatic extreme – but especially when deconstructive musicologists attack those ideas as *nothing more* than a delusive
reflection/projection of prevailing (deeply conservative) cultural norms
– is that whole complex interplay of freedom and necessity, choice and
constraint, or expressive 'force' and structural 'form' that emerges from
Merleau-Ponty's or Derrida's reflections on language and art. Moreover,
this is not solely a question of their deeper philosophical or abstract
conceptual grasp but has to do with the way that their thinking captures
certain salient aspects of musical experience which cannot be described
or accounted for on a hardline deconstructive account. Thus if one really
went along – not just 'in theory' but as a matter of conviction and auditory
practice – with the programmatic veto on 'structural listening', or with
the notion that any such 'experience' is sure to be the product of a self-
deluding aesthetic ideology, then there is a great deal of music that simply
wouldn't register as anything other than a loose concatenation of more-
or-less pleasant sounds. And likewise, if one follows some recent theorists
in rejecting the very idea of the musical 'work', along with that of 'the
canon' in however flexible, open-ended or always-revisable a form, then
one simply won't be able to hear that music in the way it properly asks to
be heard.

That is to say, what provides the best criterion of musical value as
well as the best measure of adequate or optimal listener-response is
our perception of the constant interplay between various background
generic, stylistic or period-specific norms and those foreground depart-

ures from established convention that make for the sense of a creative and distinctive musical intelligence at work. But it is hard to see how such standards could apply – or such perceptions claim anything like veridical warrant – were it not for the capacity of some music (that which offers the greatest, most lasting rewards) to achieve what the deconstructionists reject as a product of naïve organicist thinking. For they would see just another symptom of aesthetic ideology – or another retreat to the elitist citadel of long-range 'structural listening' – in such mandarin talk of the value-conferring tension between background norms of musically literate expectation and foreground elements of norm-breaking creativity. Yet this is surely one of the chief factors in our understanding and appreciation of the qualities that mark out great from excellent, excellent from accomplished and accomplished from merely routine, conventional, or run-of-the-mill compositions. It is what makes the difference between (say) Haydn's early (pre-Op. 20) and his later, more mature and individual string quartets, or Mozart's symphonies after his early, *divertimento*-like exercises in the genre, or again – amongst many other examples – Sibelius's First and Second Symphonies, with their expansive, Russian-influenced, immensely stirring but as yet not fully characteristic style, and Nos Three to Seven with their increasingly distinctive and (as we now hear it) uniquely 'Sibelian' idiom.

VI

To deconstructive musicologists this sort of claim would bear out all their worst suspicions with regard to the pernicious hold exerted by organicist ideas of formal and thematic development. That is to say, it would stand as a cautionary instance of the analyst's habit of extrapolating straight from (supposed) 'intrinsic' features or structural traits of the individual work to (supposed) markers of a kindred 'organic' pattern of development taken to characterize the composer's œuvre as a whole. And from here, so it is argued, there is a slippery slope to Schenkerian 'national-aestheticist' notions of a single, historically pre-eminent (i.e., Austro-German) line of musical descent which alone lays claim to the requisite spiritual and cultural resources.[75] Nor can it easily be denied that such chauvinist assumptions are deeply entrenched in Schenker's analyses and, to a lesser extent, in some of the present-day analytic work which adopts no such overtly partisan nationalist creed yet still takes for granted those same dominant values and priorities. However, it is wrong to suppose that any work – or sequence of works – that exhibits (or is claimed to exhibit) a progressive, coherent, formally intelligible pattern of development must *for that very reason* be complicit with the workings of aesthetic ideology.

Nor again can this blanket charge justifiably be laid against any analysis or critical approach that puts up an adequate (sufficiently detailed and sharp-eared) case for hearing this or that work as an instance of extended sonata form, developing variation, progressive tonality, or whatever. For it is a lesson to be learned from Adorno's far subtler, more intelligent and musically (as well as philosophically) informed writings that any real, as opposed to merely notional, resistance to aesthetic ideology must come from a close analytical engagement not only on the part of critics and theorists but also by performers who will otherwise fail to grasp how the music itself resists assimilation to orthodox or preconceived notions of formal unity.[76] Thus there is no point approaching these issues with a set of fixed ideas about (e.g.) the collusive relation between organicist models or metaphors and the discourse of 'national aestheticism' if this is taken to discredit the very enterprise of music analysis and hence to debar the theorist from attempting to analyse just what it is about certain works – certain stubbornly resistant particularities of style, structure or form – that holds out against such blandly assimilative treatment.

Nobody has shown better than Adorno how analysis can always go along with an acute sense of music's historical or sociological bearings (both in its original context of production and its present-day context of reception) and a likewise acutely dialectical sense of the need to reject any too reductive or 'unmediated' line of approach. Above all, what his writings emphasize is the crucial role of analysis – or of 'structural listening' in the sense decried by some New Musicologists – as a means of locating those recalcitrant details or anomalous features whose effect is precisely to challenge and subvert our habituated modes of response. What they also bring out is the need for a qualified Platonist conception of musical form and meaning in relation to the listener's more or less developed capacity for perceptive, intelligent and structurally aware understanding. This is a version of Platonism that still merits the name in so far as it finds room for truth-apt statements about music whose truth-value might always exceed our present-best powers and capacities of musical response. At the same time it is a 'qualified' version in so far as it rejects the implausible idea that music inhabits a realm of suprasensible forms to which initiates can gain access – like the sequestered mandarins in Hermann Hesse's novel *The Glass-Bead Game* – only by renouncing the mundane pleasures of performance or auditory contact and instead directing their attention solely to its formal, abstract or (quasi-)mathematical structures.[77] It is here, I would suggest, that reflection on music has most to gain from the encounter between structuralism and phenomenology, or from a critical engagement with the two much broader and longer-lived movements of thought that can roughly be categorized under those headings. For if one thing is clear about the nature of music and modalities of human musical response it is the close, indeed inextricable tie between their formal and perceptual dimensions.

Between Phenomenology and Structuralism: Alternative Resources for Music Theory

I

In this chapter I shall look at some possible connections or grounds for comparison between issues in philosophy of music and issues that have lately come to the fore in epistemological debate. This latter I take, conventionally enough, to be concerned with questions like: What is knowledge? What is the relationship between knowledge and truth? Can knowledge be unproblematically defined as 'justified true belief'? What other kinds of justificatory warrant (such as a causal link between knowledge and the objects of knowledge) might be needed in order to strengthen that classical account? and again – perhaps most relevant in this context – Can it make sense to affirm the existence of recognition-transcendent truths?[1] Central here is the issue of realism or objectivism about truth as opposed to various forms of anti-realism or scaled-down conceptions of 'truth' as epistemically constrained, response-dependent, or subject to assessment in terms of best opinion amongst those best qualified to judge.[2] With regard to music, a realist approach might be developed along Platonist lines: that is, by treating musical works as abstract objects concerning which we can make certain statements that are true or false, even though – like the objects of mathematics and the formal sciences – they cannot be accessed through any mode of sensory-perceptual grasp.[3] Otherwise realism might take the form of a more down-to-earth or empirically grounded epistemology that holds such knowledge to be chiefly a matter of the extent to which, as responsive listeners, we register those salient (sensory-perceptual as well as formal) properties of the work that should engage our attention. On either construal, the opposed, anti-realist position would be one that denied the existence of anything objectively 'there' in the music, or anything – whether formal structures or sensuous particulars – that would render our descriptions true or false quite apart from best judgement or expert opinion.

Thus, strictly speaking, the issue about realism as raised in this present-day form has more to do with metaphysics, ontology and philosophy of language than with epistemology (or the problem of knowledge) in its more traditional guise. That is to say, it concerns the objectivity of truth or, conversely, the anti-realist claim that it makes no sense to conceive of statements as possessing an objective (recognition-transcendent) truth-value irrespective of whether we can – or in principle could – establish that value by the best means at our epistemic disposal. This issue is very far from resolved even in fields such as philosophy of mathematics, logic and the formal sciences where Platonism mounts its strongest, or at any rate its most intuitively plausible case.[4] So one cannot expect much agreement with regard to such inherently contested zones as philosophy of music where that case needs somehow to make sufficient room for music's constitutive involvement with – though not (I shall argue) its total dependence on – certain normative modes of human perceptual and phenomenological response. To this extent it might seem just the kind of issue that Kant placed beyond any hope of settlement on rational-conceptual terms since aesthetic questions required the appeal to an order of reflective or indeterminate judgements.[5] That is, they had to do with normative claims of an open-ended, 'essentially contested' character which, unlike matters of merely sensuous (e.g., gustatory) taste, were aimed toward securing the widest measure of intersubjective agreement. On the other hand, such judgements could not be treated – like those of theoretical understanding – as conducive to knowledge through the bringing of phenomenal intuitions under adequate (determinate) concepts.[6] However, this analogy is somewhat misplaced, not least in view of Kant's low regard for music, his deeming it intrinsically less valuable than the other (visual and literary) arts due to its lack – so far as he could tell – of any significant formal dimension. Hence, Kant believed, its deplorable tendency to gratify those sensuous tastes and inclinations that should be thought of as 'pathological' in so far as they belong to our appetitive natures and are therefore inimical to the interests of human rational and moral autonomy. More to the point is the fact that this negative appraisal resulted from the Kantian conjunction of a high formalist doctrine strongly averse to the notion of art as a source of sensory pleasure with a failure to perceive just those elements in music – those jointly formal and sensuous elements – which lifted it above that condition. In other words it was the absence of a properly *phenomenological* dimension to Kant's understanding of music that left him at a loss to assign it any role save that of a strictly inferior, since formally deficient and purely self-gratifying, mode of aesthetic experience.

What also seems to have aroused his suspicion was the idea of music as a kind of 'intensive manifold' which could somehow register directly with our sensuous intuitions and hence bypass the cardinal rule that art should be accountable, if not to any rules of determinate concept-formation, than at least to a *sensus communis* grounded in the values of shared appreciation or acknowledged good taste.[7] Thus music figured, to Kant's way of thinking, as an anomalous and even threatening reminder that the 'aesthetic' might always revert to something more like its original (etymological) and pre-Kantian sense, that is, as having to do with a modality of sensuous experience whose nature was precisely to pre-empt and subvert the claims of aesthetic judgement, properly so called.[8] Various commentators – Derrida among them – have traced the extraordinary shifts of analogical and metaphoric thought to which Kant is forced by his resolute will to maintain this strict demarcation between sensuous pleasure and those higher, more acceptable modes of aesthetic judgement.[9] What distinguishes the latter is not their lack of sensuous content – since he fully acknowledges that this must be involved in any kind of aesthetic experience – but rather the fact that they partake of a strong counterbalancing drive toward formal intelligibility as a mark of our striving for that which transcends the limits of sensuous cognition. Yet, as Derrida shows, this effort of prescriptive boundary-setting leads Kant to some odd, not to say absurd conclusions. Chief among them is his high formalist idea that the work 'itself' must be taken to exclude such strictly adventitious ('parergonal') features as the clothing or drapery on statues, the various kinds of outwork – such as flying buttresses – that perform a merely functional role in architecture, or colour and texture in painting as opposed to its formal attributes. At least there would seem to be large problems for any theory based on the notional dichotomy of abstract form versus sensuous content.

Moreover, these problems arise once again with Kant's insistence on the strict demarcation between cognitive judgements (whereby, to repeat, sensuous intuitions are 'brought under' adequate concepts) and judge-ments of taste whose character is 'indeterminate' or constantly open to revision whenever we encounter some new mode of aesthetic experience. The former can be treated as rule-governed and subject to certain speci-fiable validity-conditions (i.e., standards of empirical warrant or a priori truth), while the latter always admit some leeway for differences of view that can only be resolved through the harmonious free-play of faculties within and between suitably responsive individuals. In which case, clearly, the discourse of aesthetic philosophy cannot itself give rise to aesthetic experience in so far as it belongs to the conceptual realm – the realm of analysis and rational argumentation – and not to the domain of indeter-minate judgements which constitutes its field of application. And again, or so it would appear on this Kantian account, aesthetic experience cannot be affected by exposure to works such as Kant's third *Critique*, or by our reading a piece of musical analysis, art criticism or literary theory which makes use of various conceptual resources and distinctions yet none the less purports to bring about some change in our received or habituated modes of response. Kant is in something of a cleft stick here – an aporia, as Derrida would term it – in so far as his distinction between determinate and indeterminate orders of judgement must require that the third *Critique* and its operative concepts (of aesthetic disinterest, formal autonomy, the beautiful, the sublime, and so forth) can have no bearing on whatever transpires in our experience of art or of nature under its aesthetic, contemplative aspect. Thus it leaves him hard-pressed to explain how that distinction could possibly apply, since our responses to music, literature or the visual arts may in fact be decisively affected – for better or worse – through our acquaintance with just those kinds of 'parergonal' (e.g., philosophic or critical) discourse that Kant would regard as strictly extraneous to the aesthetic domain.

Besides, there is strong evidence from other present-day disciplines (notably cognitive science) that, in the case of music, perceptual responses can indeed be informed by various sorts of conceptual knowledge. Such knowledge may derive from reading a sensitive, intelligent work of analysis or from keeping up with the best scholarship and hence listening with an ear more sharply attuned to period conventions of language, style or genre. What this shows – according to some theorists – is that the human capacity for musical response is not (in the jargon) strongly 'modular', 'encapsulated' or 'cognitively impervious'; that it allows for a variety of inputs from extra-perceptual sources the effect of which is to deepen or extend our range of structural-appreciative grasp.[10] Here they are at one with erstwhile proponents of 'strong' modularity, like Jerry Fodor, who have lately seen fit to moderate their claims or restrict them to just those cognitive functions – such as sensory processing or straightforward grammatical parsing – where speed and efficiency are more at a premium than fine discriminations or subtlety and depth of response.[11] Thus Fodor now takes the view that his modularity-thesis comes up against its limit in certain kinds of reasoning (such as abduction or inference to the best, most plausible explanation) which cannot be reduced to any purely formal or functionalist account since clearly they involve a great range of background beliefs, tacit assumptions and context-relative hypotheses.[12] The mind may very well be strongly modular with respect to those functions that work best or can be shown to give greatest adaptive/selective benefit when screened off from other, potentially distracting inputs or sources. However, that thesis doesn't hold water – in fact becomes hugely implausible – when extended by its more zealous advocates to the kinds of higher-level mental processing which require so much in the way of intermodular, contextual or global explanation as effectively to rule it out of court.

What this entails in the case of language is that while the syntactic component may indeed be strongly modular – at least when divorced from the semantic and pragmatic dimensions of language-use – it cannot be so treated if one seeks to make sense of communicative utterance in other than specialist terms. What it entails in the case of music is that a modular approach might perhaps hope to explain certain rudimentary aspects of melodic, harmonic, tonal, rhythmic or even (at a stretch) thematic-developmental form but would quickly run out of conceptual resources when it came to the more complex, subtle or long-range structural aspects. For these involve just the sorts of phenomenologically salient response and just the kinds of structurally salient detail that require a mode of listening much wider and deeper than could ever be captured by a strictly modular account. This is why there is a need for philosophy of music to move beyond those various drastic dichotomies that have regularly surfaced in its history to date, from Plato to Kant and thereafter through a range of developments whose latest chapter is Derrida's acutely perceptive probing of the issue between structuralism and phenomenology.[13] That issue can itself best be seen as a further product of the same deep-seated dualist habit of thought that has been such a hallmark of Western philosophical thinking right down from its ancient Greek origins. It is the problem that Derrida brings to light in his reading of Husserl's exemplary attempt to reconcile the claims of 'structure' and 'genesis', or mathematical truths on the one hand conceived in terms of 'absolute ideal objectivity' and on the other treated as the outcome of various successive, historically emergent discoveries.[14] Where the former lay claim to an order of strictly atemporal and mind-independent validity, the latter must be taken to have had their source in some inaugural insight on the part of some individual geometer and then to have required a constant effort of repeated 'reactivation' in the minds of those subsequent thinkers who would seek or purport to comprehend them.

II

I have suggested that philosophy of music comes up against a version of this same problem, albeit one that may appear less urgent than in the case of mathematics, logic and the formal sciences. After all, its challenge can scarcely undermine our accustomed modes of musical perception, experience or enjoyment and is thus more a provocation to speculative thought than a threat to the very foundations of musical criticism or theory. Still it is an issue that should not be pushed aside in the interests of analytic tidiness or with a view to avoiding just the kinds of conceptual difficulty that followers of Wittgenstein typically put down to our 'bewitchment' by bother-headed styles of philosophical talk.[15] For there is a genuine and not a merely notional or hypercultivated problem about squaring these two conceptions, each with a strong intuitive claim on our musical (as well as philosophical) understanding, yet hard to reconcile one with another unless through some form of anodyne linguistic therapy that in truth does nothing to clarify, let alone resolve, the issue. Thus any *echt*-Platonist or doctrinaire formalist approach will fail to make adequate allowance for the subjective (and in some sense work-constitutive) component of musical response, whilst any purely response-dependent or subjectivist account will fail to reckon with those formal or structural aspects of the work which distinguish it as *just that* particular work throughout and despite all the shifting tides of reception-history, cultural change, performing convention, audience taste, and so forth. However, to pose the issue in these terms is again to fall back into that chronically dualist and oscillating pattern of thought that has characterized so much of this debate not only in music theory and aesthetics but also in epistemology, philosophy of mind and philosophical semantics. That is to say, it can easily be posed as a stark dilemma between the idea of valid judgement as answering to standards of objective, recognition-transcendent truth which are thus, *ipso facto*, beyond reach of human perceptual or epistemic powers and the idea of valid judgement as always necessarily a matter of shared opinion amongst those deemed fittest or best qualified to judge.[16]

I would argue that this is a false dilemma, although one that presents itself with well-nigh inescapable force when we reflect on the kinds of problem thrown up by the ontology of abstract objects. These latter include numbers, concepts, logical relations, types as distinct from tokens, and – in a relevant though crucially different way – musical works as distinct from their reception-history or whatever pertains to the listener's share in their realization and continued availability.[17] The difference is a matter of our having to recognize that music has a mode of existence which can never be entirely detached from its sensuous embodiment in structures of organized sound or from the sorts of response that those structures typically do or ideally should evoke in musically responsive subjects. No doubt this invites the charge of patent circularity in so far as it is taken to equate with the claim: 'work *x* has the distinctive set of attributes *y* just in case that judgement is borne out by the assenting disposition of competent listeners sufficiently acquainted with the relevant generic, stylistic, or cultural norms and exposed to the work under specified (normal or optimal) auditory conditions'. Such is the trivial upshot of response-dependence theory in the analytic mode, or at least that version of it which reduces to a flat tautology since it fails to specify in adequate detail what is meant by musical 'competence' and what precisely the relationship is between the kinds of judgement thus evoked and the kinds of analytically salient feature that would offer adequate grounds for the claim in question.[18] The only means to fill that justificatory gap, I would suggest, is by adopting a qualified Platonist (or jointly Platonist and phenomenological) approach that grants due weight to considerations on both sides of the issue. In other words, it is an approach that doesn't seek refuge in any attempt to make the problem disappear through some all-purpose salvific technique of conceptual analysis or some therapeutic strategy for treating it as merely as product of our chronic 'bewitchment by language'.

This is not to conclude – far from it – that philosophy of music should find no place for the sorts of analysis (whether musical or conceptual) which may do much to clarify our grasp of what is involved in the otherwise mysterious process whereby our sensuous responses are raised to a level at which aesthetic predicates or value-judgements properly come into play. On the contrary: without such clarificatory efforts it would scarcely have progressed beyond downright subjectivism or, at the opposite extreme, a thoroughgoing formalist-objectivist conception that reduced music to a kind of sonorous mathematics or – as in Hermann Hesse's prescient novel *The Glass-Bead Game* – an ingenious play of purely abstract possibilities. Yet analytic approaches often tend toward this latter condition in so far as they focus on the 'logical grammar' of our musical concepts and categories: that is to say, on getting clear about the various entailments and presuppositions of our talk about music, rather than on the phenomenology of musical response.[19] It is the same point that Derrida makes about structuralism in the wider, non-parochial sense of that term according to which 'a certain structuralism' has recurrently emerged, from Plato via Kant to one aspect of Husserl's thinking, as 'philosophy's most spontaneous gesture'.[20] What he has in mind here is the quest for intelligible forms, structures or conceptual ensembles that would somehow float free of their genesis in acts of expressive or purposive-intentional signification and thereby achieve an objective mode of existence outside and above the history of human creative-exploratory thought.

Thus the structuralist quest, as Derrida conceives it, is always for 'a form or function organised according to an internal legality in which elements have meaning only in the solidarity of their correlation or their opposition'.[21] And again: whatever its heuristic value as a method of analysis in various contexts structuralism operates always at a certain abstract, conceptual, or metalinguistic remove and is hence unable to pass beyond 'a reflection of the accomplished, the constituted, the *constructed*'.[22] At the same time, there is no question of simply abandoning a Platonist ontology of abstract realia that would conserve the truth-value – the 'absolute ideal objectivity' – of those various statements, theorems, hypotheses, proof-procedures, and so forth, which constitute the history of the formal sciences. To this extent at least Derrida agrees with a fully fledged Platonist like Frege: that they cannot be reduced to just so many episodes of historically emergent, culturally located or psychologically explicable 'genesis' without thereby relinquishing any claim to conceptual validity and hence falling into one or another philosophically disabling variety of relativism. Where Derrida differs with Frege and most representatives of the mainstream analytic tradition is in rejecting the idea that questions of genesis can or should play no role whatsoever in our better understanding of the processes of thought through which truths are arrived at or discoveries made. More precisely: that role need not be confined (as those thinkers would somewhat grudgingly concede) to matters concerning the strictly second-order cultural, historical or psychobiographical 'context of discovery' but may also have a bearing on issues that pertain to the scientific 'context of justification'.[23]

Such is indeed a main point of divergence between the analytic and continental lines of descent: not that the latter tends toward a cultural-relativist or social-constructivist outlook which lacks the former's eminent virtues of logical rigour and conceptual precision, but rather that mainland-European philosophers have typically taken more adequate account of the ways in which knowledge accrues through a complex interplay of genesis and structure.[24] This is evident not only in the phenomenological tradition deriving from Husserl but also in the work of a thinker like Gaston Bachelard, that is to say, an 'applied rationalist' approach that retains the Cartesian emphasis on clear and distinct ideas but sets out to show how those ideas emerge through a process of conceptual 'rectification and critique' brought to bear on the proto-scientific repertoire of image, metaphor and anthropomorphic projection.[25] What sets both traditions apart from the predominant strains of analytic philosophy is not any habit of simply collapsing the 'two contexts' principle – which would render that process totally opaque or treat it as merely an upshot of selective Whiggish hindsight – but their willingness to view it as a constant dialectic between factors that impede and factors that promote the advancement of scientific knowledge. Moreover, Bachelard is one of those thinkers who can be seen to have exerted a strong influence on Derrida's early work, above all with regard to this need for philosophy to retain the highest standards of logical, conceptual and analytic rigour, while none the less acknowledging the pertinence of just such (as some would have it) philosophically extraneous concerns.[26]

A broadly analogous case can be made with regard to the 'two traditions' in philosophy of music, taking these to divide along much the same lines as in epistemology and philosophy of science from the 1930s on. What distinguishes the kinds of approach that fall under the 'continental' rubric is an openness to issues – such as those raised by Derrida in the passages cited above – which go well beyond the business of conceptual analysis, narrowly defined, to engage the central question of how one might reconcile a viable conception of musical form with one that makes adequate allowance for music's sensuous, perceptual and phenomenological aspects.[27] Such an outlook of 'qualified Platonism', as I have called it, would accept that works have a mode of existence that cannot be reduced to their reception-history or the various modalities of listener-response that have made up that history to date. Nor can their identity-conditions be defined, as in Nelson Goodman's ultra-nominalist approach, through a strict deployment of the type/token distinction which insists that the work *just is* what is given by the score, and that no performance can or should count as a performance of *that* specific work unless it complies with the score's every last detail and marking.[28] This strikes me as a *reductio ad absurdum* of the nominalist position and hence as good reason to weigh the benefits of a Platonist alternative that doesn't entail any such extreme or drastically counter-intuitive consequences. On the other hand, Platonism invites a similar charge if taken to involve the full-strength ontological claim that works can exist in an abstract realm – like Fregean 'thoughts' – quite apart from their various instantiations in scores, performances, cultural traditions or kinds of listener-response.[29] For it is precisely their dual mode of existence – as allowed for on the qualified Platonist account – that enables us to talk about differing renditions of this or that work, rather than (as Goodman's theory would require) an endless variety of altogether different since not-strictly-true-to-the-letter-of-the-score works. Any approach that doesn't find room for both of these apparently conflicting intuitions will fail to meet music's philosophical challenge as well as its demands upon the competent but not overly self-confident listener who is willing to concede that his or her responses may not come up to what the music implicitly requires.

This is why Platonism stands in need of certain significant qualifications if it is to offer an adequate or plausible answer to issues in the philosophy of music. Thus it has to allow that some works – often those that rank highest in terms of intrinsic value – are more readily thought of (in Platonist terms) as possessing a quasi-objective mode of existence above and beyond our experience of them or even the sum-total of experiences evoked in the best, most responsive and appreciative listeners throughout their performing history to date. And conversely, there may be music that we cherish for all sorts of reasons yet to which we would not assign so high a value as to other works that, alas, we can admire only in a somewhat detached and impersonal way. I think that this experience of a tug between music that we simply, unself-critically enjoy and music that we don't so much enjoy but recognize as potentially offering rewards beyond our present-best capacities of musical response is one that is quite common among seasoned listeners and bears out the case for a qualified Platonist approach. That is, it suggests how we might reconcile the phenomenological conception of music as existing only in and through its appeal to our perceptual and responsive capacities with the case that music is potentially response-transcendent in so far as it can always surpass – and somehow be felt or known to surpass – our powers of understanding, appreciative grasp or evaluative judgement. This also captures the crucial distinction between areas of discourse (such as mathematics, logic and the formal sciences) where the Platonist case, if valid, must be taken to apply at full ontological strength (i.e., as entailing the 'absolute ideal objectivity' of truth) and areas – such as musical aesthetics – where any plausible version of Platonism will need to go by way of a rapprochement with the phenomenological approach.

I have suggested that the place where this issue has received its most searching philosophical treatment is at the point of intersection between structuralism and phenomenology. More specifically, it is raised to a high-point of critical awareness in those texts of Derrida where 'a certain' structuralism with distinctly Platonist leanings comes up against its limits in the need to account for the genetic and expressive (as opposed to the purely structural-synchronic) aspects of language, literature and art.[30] For it is here that philosophy engages most directly with those vexing antinomies – of form and content, structure and genesis, or the claims of analytic versus those of 'appreciative' criticism – that have long preoccupied the discourse of musical aesthetics. It seems to me, for all the reasons offered above, that an outlook of qualified Platonism coupled with the insights of a likewise qualified phenomemological approach goes furthest toward making sense of these otherwise sharply conflicting claims. The kind of phenomenology in question is one that has been subject to a structuralist critique but also deployed in order to test the limits of a pure-bred (Platonist) structuralism. That is to say, in more general terms, it is an approach that finds adequate room for the claim that musical works may always elude our best powers of perceptual or appreciative grasp yet still retain their constitutive appeal to just those modalities of human response that define the very nature of musical experience and judgement. What saves this claim from self-contradiction or wilful paradox-mongering is the fact that music occupies that border-zone between, on the one hand, the abstract objects of mathematics, logic and the formal sciences and, on the other, an aesthetic realm – 'aesthetic' in the original (sensory-perceptual) meaning of the term – with which it brings us more directly into contact than any other art-form.[31] This is why philosophers of diverse persuasion have discovered in music a peculiarly intimate and challenging topic of reflection. Such has been the case whether (like Kant) they responded reactively by erecting conceptual defences against it, or whether – like Schopenhauer, Nietzsche and Adorno – they sought different ways of meeting that challenge through a transformation of philosophy's role in response to the demands placed on it by music's power of teasing thought beyond the limits of conceptual representation. That is to say, they have been coming at the same central issue that Mendelssohn famously posed when he rejected the hitherto dominant idea that any 'meaning' music might possess was too vague or indefinite to be stated in verbal form and declared, on the contrary, that its meaning was far too precise and specific ever to be captured in words.

III

Recent scholarship has convincingly shown how that idea took hold in the mid to late eighteenth century through a combination of various historical and sociocultural factors, among them – most importantly – the emancipation of music from its erstwhile subservience to religious or secular texts.[32] From here can be traced the emergence of an 'absolute' conception wherein the other arts (principally literature and painting) were eventually conceived – by poet-philosophers in the German post-Kantian line of descent, and later by the French symbolists – as striving to shed their residual attachment to notions of mimesis or pictorial representation and hence as aspiring to the condition of music.[33] Thus the classical injunction '*ut pictura poesis*' (that poetry should emulate the visual arts) gave way to a more autonomist conception of literature and, beyond that, to the idea that poetry should so far as possible aim to break free of its everyday-prosaic referential constraints. This in turn went along with a heightened interest in the sublime as a mode of apprehension that was likewise taken to transcend the utmost limits of conceptual thought or determinate content.[34]

The relevant scholarship has mostly come from critical theorists of a deconstructive or cultural-materialist bent, which disposes them to treat these developments as nothing more than the product of a newly dominant bourgeois ideology for which they served in an oblique but none the less useful legitimizing role.[35] Its other manifestations included the emergence of a sizeable concert-going public with a taste for just such reassuring displays of their own purely disinterested judgement and their capacity to rise clean above any narrowly partisan, socially invested or class-related mode of enjoyment. Thus – according to this line of argument – the classical symphony, string quartet and other such paradigm genres of 'absolute' music can be seen to have achieved their rapid development and elevation to canonical status through a range of sociocultural factors that rendered them ideologically fit for the purpose. That role was accomplished all the more effectively through the advent of extended sonata-form movements – along with a receptive audience primed by nascent organicist models and metaphors – which likewise worked to reinforce the idea of music as a mode of expression uniquely able to transcend or reconcile otherwise conflicting interests. In short, the chief tendency of much criticism in this vein is to undermine those conjoint values (of structural autonomy, aesthetic disinterest and Platonism in however qualified a form) which it views as just a smokescreen put up to disguise the workings of a once-vigorous (since freshly emergent) but now threadbare (since merely residual or outworn) ideology.

However, there is a logical fallacy involved in the notion that *just because* certain precepts and value-commitments can be shown to have promoted certain ideological interests amongst certain individuals or class-representatives at a certain time, *therefore* those precepts and commitments must be devoid of *anything but* such delusive ideological content. After all, as Leo Treitler pointedly remarks:

[i]f the idea of the autonomy of symphonic music served German nationalist self-interest and mythology, that does not render the idea false, or taint the music, or render the study of the music in the aspect of its autonomy invalid. The idea of aesthetic autonomy is not *inherently* tied to political thought of a particular kind – nineteenth-century

German thought about an 'aesthetic state', even though it was appropriate for a programme of political action in the musical arena.[36]

It is a similar fallacy which holds that, since critical talk about 'sonata form' didn't catch on until a good while after composers (notably Haydn) are supposed to have invented or developed that form, therefore such talk is misapplied to those composers and should be seen as just a backward projection of that same ideological bias. For here also there is a questionable leap from the fact that critics were late to recognize and codify the structures involved, to the idea that those structures cannot have existed – cannot have emerged in the course of Haydn's (and Mozart's) early-to-middle period quartets and symphonies – except through a misconceived effort of wishful thinking on the part of their devoted analysts. Compare, if you will, the argument advanced by some literary theorists: that since the term 'literature' once (until around 1750) referred to all sorts of writing rather than just that particular sort reckoned to possess 'literary' worth, therefore we are wrong to apply it in the modern (evaluative) sense to texts that were written before that date.[37]

What's more, as in the musical case, this argument is often extended to works that were written or composed long after the pertinent shift of meaning yet whose claim to fall under any such description – i.e., that they merit assessment on 'literary' terms or should be heard as a more-or-less inventive deployment of sonata-form principles – is now treated as merely a product of 'aesthetic ideology'.[38] Yet the fallacy here should again be obvious enough to any musically responsive listener with a basic grasp of those principles and an ear sufficiently attuned to shifts of period style, generic expectation and the complex interplay between foreground (distinctive) and background (routine or conventional) elements that marked the emergence of the 'classical style'.[39] Thus it is neither anachronistic nor evidence of ideological complicity to assert that sonata-form can be heard emerging from its various baroque antecedents in the development of Haydn's string quartets, from his earliest, divertimento-like essays in the genre, through the Op. 20 set to those of Op. 33 which achieve what can justifiably be claimed as a fully fledged, maximally versatile handling of its hitherto latent resources.[40] Nor can such charges be brought against the claim that a kind of reverse process occurs in the stylistic transition from Beethoven's 'middle' to 'late' period quartets. For in this case one can hear how sonata principles – albeit in a loosened, expanded or greatly modified form – are combined with something like a return to the baroque manner of contrasted, often suite-like, elusively interconnected movements whose effect is to put up increasing resistance to analysis along standard 'classical' lines.

My point is that such analytic talk is not, or not necessarily, in hock to some naïve or ideologically motivated dogma of organic form. Rather it can be as flexible and subtly responsive to deviations from the classical norm as are the works wherein that norm is both established and constantly subject to modes of creative extension and revision. Indeed, the late Beethoven quartets might serve as a useful corrective to the extreme anti-organicist viewpoint adopted by some 'deconstructive' musicologists. I am thinking here of a well-known exchange between Jonathan Dunsby and Alan Street when the former claimed to find unifying elements, tonal and thematic, in Brahms's sequence of piano *Fantasies,* Op. 116, while the latter roundly denounced this claim as just another showing of the same old aesthetic ideology or the collusive desire, among music analysts, to boost both the music's and their own reputation by proving this to be the case.[41] What the comparison with late Beethoven helps to bring out, conversely, is the fact that neither music nor musical analysis can do without certain enabling presuppositions – like the idea of structural unity – that may sometimes be honoured more in the breach than the observance but which still constitute the normative basis of all musically informed perception and judgement. Thus Dunsby's thesis with regard to those Brahms *Fantasies* – that they form a distinctive kind of 'multi-piece' with a strong sense of thematic continuity – is one that might perhaps be challenged on account of their being linked mainly by felt affinities or contrasts of mood, and hence prima facie lacking such a high degree of formal coherence. Certainly, that unity is far less evident – whether through analysis or as it strikes the attentive listener – than in the case of Beethoven's late quartets, even at their most formally elusive. All the same, Dunsby's analysis does manage to pinpoint certain thematic relationships whose presence *in the music* and not just in his own professionally or ideologically driven zeal to 'discover' them is something that listeners can readily check against their own responses.

The same goes for those other cases – like the Haydn quartets – where theorists are prone to argue from the fact that 'sonata-form' hadn't yet (in Haydn's time) entered the lexicon of music criticism that the label is anachronistic and hence just a product of selective cultural hindsight. For once again, any musically competent listener will perceive that Haydn was composing sonata-form movements, not to mention making use of progressive tonality and other advanced techniques, even though he might not have recognized these descriptions. It seems to me that one result of such mistaken reasoning has been to promote critical approaches that drastically inflate the role of theory – or of 'theory' in its current deconstructive or cultural-materialist guise – while just as drastically deflating the ontology of music to the point where it becomes a mere figment or plaything of various competing ideologies. Besides, there is a glaring problem with much of this work in so far as it sternly rejects the appeal to musical 'experience' as just another symptom of that same aestheticist error (i.e., the confusion, as de Man describes it, between formal structures and phenomenal or sensory-perceptual data) and yet falls back upon just that idea when interpreting the social, cultural, political or gendered-inflected content of various musical works.[42] Thus, as Treitler very reasonably asks,

> [i]f postmodern theory would put aside the aestheticisation of music that was a project of the early nineteenth century, then how can postmodern historical interpretation be based on musical analysis that claims to reveal musical *experience* which, no matter how broadly drawn, arises from those aesthetic conceptions? This contradiction is not evaded by musical analysis that is superficial and unengaged, that lacks the conviction of hammer-and-tongs analysis, as though to avoid entrapment in the aesthetic.[43]

And again, with more specific reference to Susan McClary's class-based and gender-oriented deciphering of Mozart's G major Piano Concerto, K.453:

> '[t]he scenario that is sketched is presented, really, as a programme. It gives concrete content to the music's aesthetic content, and it seems to avoid the appearance of preoccupation with the aesthetic by offering only analysis sketches ... [Thus] the question of the real status of the interpretation as historical is left hanging.[44]

(See Chapter 5 for a more detailed discussion of McClary's approach and related lines of argument in the New Musicology.)

Where these theorists go wrong is by pushing too far in a contextualist direction which leads them to denounce any notion of 'the work' as an object of analysis, knowledge or musical experience, and which thus leaves them hard put to explain just what they are talking *about* when they describe – for instance – the conflicts of class identity encoded in the Mozart concerto or the complex and ambivalent gender politics of Schumann's *Carnaval*.[45] For if indeed it is the case – as they assert, following de Man – that any talk of such experience betrays the effects of a delusive (and potentially coercive) 'aesthetic ideology' resulting from that same phenomenalist error, then clearly there is a problem about how to interpret these claims. Hence my proposal: that we adopt a duly qualified Platonist approach to the ontological issue combined with a phenomenological appeal to those normative (since intersubjectively agreed-upon) modes of listener-response that can plausibly be claimed to transcend the vagaries of personal or idiosyncratic taste. What the latter holds out is an answer to those who reject any version of musical Platonism on account of its supposedly placing the work in a *topos ouranos* – a realm of suprasensuous forms or paradigms – to which we could have no access save through some kind of abstract, quasi-mathematical power of understanding. What the former provides is an adequate sense of the musical work as a unique, enduring and (in certain respects) autonomous entity which cannot be dissolved – as the cultural constructivists would have it – into the various ideologically invested codes, conventions and value-systems that have made up its reception-history to date. For the work can then be thought of as possessing distinctive identity-conditions which explain how it is that we are able to do such otherwise impossible things as refer to it from one context to another, recognize multiple (perhaps widely discrepant) performances as renderings of the same work, and advance certain claims with regard to its formal structure, thematic development, tonal progression, and so forth. Or again, in more distinctly Platonist terms, it accounts for what I take to be the widespread conviction amongst seasoned and reflective listeners that works may possess a great many value-conferring attributes or qualities that elude our best yet always limited powers of musical perception or judgement.

Of course this whole set of claims would be rejected outright by cultural theorists and deconstructive musicologists for whom any talk of 'the work' – let alone its defining characteristics or ontological properties – is in hock to that same aesthetic ideology or doctrine of organic form whose dubious credentials they are constantly at pains to expose. However, I would hope to have established the case that such arguments are self-stultifying in so far as, if taken seriously, they leave the theorist with nothing to theorize about except other, more traditional (organicist) theories and the range of delusory pseudo-objects – 'works', 'structures', 'sonata form', 'development sections', or whatever – whose ontological standing is much on a par with centaurs, mermaids or Homer's gods. After all, there is not much point in deconstructing the discourse of mainstream musical analysis unless it can be shown *with reference to the music and to certain anomalous or analytically unaccounted-for features of it* that the discourse in question works to occlude those features and thereby avoid any challenge to its own self-assured methods, values and priorities. Otherwise the theorists' most radical claim – to reveal the extent of that ideological bias and its distorting effect on our perceptions of the music – will sound very much like bombinating in the void, or changing bolts on the stable-door after turning the horses loose. There is a similar problem about other forms of strong-descriptivist, social-constructivist, or cultural-relativist thinking in various disciplines that have taken the present-day linguistic 'turn'. Thus the result of pushing through with this line of argument is effectively to treat one's objects of study – be they social facts, historical events, atoms, DNA molecules, astrophysical bodies, mathematical theorems, or whatever – as so many textual or discursive constructs which cannot be thought to fix the truth-value of our statements concerning them since that value is itself just another such construct.

As I have said, the case of music is somewhat different since it scarcely makes sense to posit the existence (or reality) of musical works in a realm quite apart from the phenomenology of musical response or the capacity of well-equipped listeners to perceive and comprehend what the work in question has to offer. Hence the idea that we are faced with a choice between, on the one hand, an objectivist approach that fails to reckon with the listener's strictly indispensable role in this process and, on the other, a subjectivist approach whereby 'the work' exists only as a product of the listener's acculturated habits of response. Thus it might well seem that philosophy of music finds itself in much the same cleft stick as philosophy of mathematics according to those of a pyrrhic disposition who claim that, quite simply, 'nothing works' in this discipline since one can *either* have objective (verification-transcendent) truth *or* mathematical knowledge within the bounds of attainable proof, but surely not both since they are mutually exclusive on any logically consistent account. In which case, it is argued, the only solution is a scaled-down (e.g., anti-realist or response-dependent) version of 'truth' which holds it within epistemic constraints or redefines it in accordance with the scope and limits of human cognitive command.[46]

Yet it is just my point – one ignored by most analytic philosophers since the 'two traditions' went their largely separate ways – that this will only seem a genuine dilemma or instance of *tertium non datur* if one ignores the available alternatives. Chief among them, to repeat, is the phenomenological approach and its thinking-through of the various problems that were temporarily pushed out of sight by the proponents of logical positivism/empiricism, but which have now returned to haunt the discourse of present-day analytic philosophy. These emerge very clearly in the kinds of debate that currently go on between realists, anti-realists and response-dependence theorists in areas such as epistemology, ethics and philosophy of language where the issue typically comes down to a question of whether – and precisely how – one can save some workable notion of 'truth' from the standard range of anti-realist objections. Philosophy of music has a special pertinence in this regard since it raises a number of crucial questions concerning the relationship between truth and knowledge (or ontology and epistemology), and does so – uniquely – in a way that casts light on kindred problems as they affect both the formal sciences, mathematics especially, and the procedures of empirical (everyday or natural-scientific) enquiry. For if philosophy of music has its work cut out – more so than ever at present in response to a range of cultural-relativist, postmodernist and other such sceptical-debunking movements of thought – it is in the task of reconciling two, apparently incompatible yet equally vital (since domain-specific and discipline-constitutive) claims. That is, it has to show how musical works and their distinctive (e.g., formal, structural, thematic or tonal) attributes can be thought of as possessing sufficient specificity to fix the truth-value of statements concerning them and yet – consistently with that – as dependent for their adequate realization on certain duly normalized or optimized modes of performance or listener-response.

IV

I have argued that this outcome cannot be achieved by response-dependence theory in its present-day (analytic) form since that approach, if applied to music, would in effect come down to a formally elaborate but substantively underspecified thesis regarding the criteria of right judgement. (Thus: 'work x possesses properties y and z just in case it is judged to possess them when heard by musically competent listeners in a decent performance under favourable ambient conditions'.)[47] Otherwise it reduces to sheer triviality through being cashed out in more strictly a priori terms, that is, as a claim that any descriptive or evaluative statement concerning x – say, that x is an instance (or a fine instance) of sonata-form, of progressive tonality, or of the fully developed classical style – is true if and only if made in good faith by a well-equipped, musically literate and highly responsive listener when exposed to a consummately gifted and accomplished performance under ideal ambient conditions.

This again harks back to the issue in Plato's *Euthyphro* – taken up by theorists of response-dependence – as to whether pious acts have that character in virtue of the gods' approval (i.e., their sovereign value-conferring estimation) or whether, conversely, the gods are constrained to approve them since the acts are themselves intrinsically (objectively) good and the gods by definition have a fail-safe power of tracking or detecting their goodness.[48] It seems to me that this analogy is distinctly revealing with regard to the debate around response-dependence, although not in quite the way that its proponents intend. What it shows – and what the instance of music brings out with particular force – is the need for analytic philosophy to broaden its horizons and absorb certain insights from the 'other', mainland-European tradition so as to avoid the kinds of dead-end predicament that have marked its history since the heyday of logical empiricism.[49] This possibility was brusquely closed off when Gilbert Ryle renounced his early interest in Husserl, having decided that the latter's whole project was just another form of ill-disguised psychologism.[50] It was subsequently glimpsed, only to be closed off again, when J. L Austin toyed with the phrase 'linguistic phenomenology' as a description of what he was doing, but clearly had doubts and therefore chose to stick with the safer, less continental-sounding 'ordinary language' appellation.[51]

I have put the case that nothing more strikingly exemplifies the limits of pure-bred conceptual or linguistic analysis than the sorts of problem it runs up against in trying to account for our experience of music. Among them – crucially – is the problem of explaining how it comes about that our musical responses can be felt to fall short of what the work properly requires, or to create that sense of a gap between actual and potential depth of insight or level of appreciative grasp which lends weight to the Platonist case. At the same time, and by way of necessary qualification, it is clear that full-strength Platonism just won't work in the musical context as it does (arguably) in the case of mathematics, logic and the formal sciences.[52] After all, we could scarcely register that 'sense of a gap' – as I have rather awkwardly phrased it – unless we had responded to *something* in the work that left an impression, no matter how fugitive, elusive or inchoate that impression might have been. Otherwise the claim would be deeply problematic (even logically self-refuting), like T. S. Eliot's curious idea that *Hamlet* is an unsatisfactory play because it fails to find an 'objective correlative' or an adequate (i.e., poetico-dramatically realized) form for the painful complex of emotions with which it attempts to deal.[53] For then one has to ask: on what possible grounds can Eliot have seen fit to advance this claim if not by reason of his having experienced that same complex of emotions when reading or watching *Hamlet*, in which case *a fortiori* the play cannot be deficient in the way he describes?

Of course there is a crucial difference as regards the issue with musical Platonism since here it is not so much a case of (supposedly) inchoate emotions struggling to find some 'objective' form as of a musical experience which may involve a high degree of formal, structural or analytic grasp but which none the less leaves the listener aware of some dimension beyond their present-best powers of response. In other words, what is in question here is a sense of 'transcendence' that is Platonic in so far as it involves formal attributes which may always in principle surpass the capacities of actual listener-response yet which cannot be conceived apart from their potential realization through the phenomenology of musical experience raised to a higher power. So perhaps where this differs from the otherwise strikingly analogous case of Eliot on *Hamlet* is through the fact that Eliot – trained up as he was philosophically in the school of Bradleian idealism – fails to specify just how that 'objective correlative' might be lacking with respect to some particular (e.g., his own) experience of the play and yet be thought of as potentially accessible to a more responsive, perhaps less inhibited or psychologically resistant, approach.[54]

It is here that Husserl's project has valuable lessons to impart since his chief purpose was precisely to explain how the concept of transcendence (in the formal sciences and elsewhere) could be reconciled with a phenomenological approach that retained its grounding in the various modalities of human perceptual, cognitive or epistemic grasp.[55] This is also the area where musical analysis does its most useful work: that is, through the kind of consciousness-raising which makes us more alert to structural details that might otherwise escape notice, or be 'noticed' only as a matter of vague or subliminal response. Hence, I would suggest, the way in which a good (i.e., sensitive, perceptive and intelligent) piece of analysis will often carry conviction not so much by revealing some (to us) entirely new detail or aspect of a work but rather by describing with particular clarity and a keen sense of its larger structural relevance what we had already been aware of but not in so consciously accessible a way. This might seem reminiscent of Plato's set-piece demonstration, in the *Meno*, of how knowledge comes about through a kind of 'unforgetting' (*anamnesis*), a process whereby the learner – in this case a slave-boy undergoing instruction in the elements of geometry – is prompted to enunciate certain truths that in some sense he 'knew' all along but the memory of which had been overlaid or clouded by his fallible powers of recollection.[56] For Plato, the episode is intended to prove that such truths belong to a realm of supra-sensuous essences or forms which the mind (or soul) is enabled to grasp through a mode of transcendence that lifts it above the mere flux of transient phenomena. Once shorn of its mystical tonings this notion has a fair claim to capture what is most distinctive – though also most deeply problematic – about the truths of geometry and the other formal sciences. That is, it offers an evocative (if fanciful) account of the way that such truths may thought to possess a character of absolute ideal objectivity which sets them categorically apart from any knowledge acquired by empirical, hence unreliable since non-apodictic, methods.

Needless to say, this assurance has been drastically shaken not only by what now seems its fatal reliance on a highly implausible metaphysics but also – since Kant – by the growing recognition that a priori truth-claims of whatever kind are always at risk of being undermined by scientific developments such as non-Euclidean geometry and relativistic space–time physics.[57] All the same, as I have said, this should not be construed as a knockdown argument against Platonism in any form, or adduced in support of the nominalist case for rejecting all talk of abstract entities such as numbers, sets, classes or indeed musical works. For such talk is indispensable not only as a matter of convenience but in order to provide both a workable account of truth and knowledge in the formal sciences and also – with certain qualifications – an account of musical experience that allows for our conception of the work as always quite possibly transcending the limits of even the subtlest, most perceptive or highly attuned listener-response. Where these instances differ, as I have said, is in the fact that (at least on a realist-objectivist view) the truth-value of mathematical statements, theorems or conjectures cannot but be conceived as possessing an abstract or 'absolute ideal' character and hence a mode of recognition-transcendence that a priori excludes all reference to issues of empirical or experiential warrant. In the case of music, conversely, any truth-value that attaches to our claims about works or their thematic, tonal and structural features must involve some more than token appeal to how they do – or ideally should – strike a listener whose sensory-perceptual responses as well as her powers of conceptual-analytic grasp are fully and effectively engaged. And it is here, in the region where (as Derrida puts it) 'a certain' structuralism encounters the claims of 'a certain' phenomenology, that music exerts its greatest challenge to our powers of conceptual understanding.[58]

Nor is this merely the kind of issue that offers a notional point of purchase for high-flown philosophical debates with little or no relation to our actual experience of music. On the contrary, I would say, it is precisely this experience of a variable, sometimes diminishing yet ever-present gap between our actual responses and our sense of what the music implicitly demands or potentially has to offer that provides the chief spur to more attentive, perceptive and intelligent listening. Some works are widely felt to exemplify this quality at its most striking, although different listeners would no doubt vary just as widely as they moved down their separate shortlists. Thus I would be fairly confident in venturing the claim that most musically literate respondents with a knowledge of the mainstream Western-European tradition would include (say) such canonical works as Bach's B Minor Mass, Haydn's *Creation*, Mozart's *Jupiter* Symphony, Beethoven's late string quartets, Schubert's B Flat Major Piano Sonata D. 960, Brahms's *German Requiem*, Bruckner's Eighth and Sibelius's Fourth Symphony. They might not share my fervent conviction that the same kind of inexhaustibly rewarding experience is to be had from Martinu's Fourth Symphony, Vaughan Williams' Fourth and Fifth, Walton's First and his Cello Concerto, Nielsen's Third and Fourth, Shostakovich's Piano Quintet, Joonas Kokkonen's opera *The Last Temptations*, or – to go even further out on this self-indulgent limb – Fredric Rzewski's extraordinary hour-long set of piano variations on 'The People United Will Never be Defeated'.

However, my point is not so much to press these particular evaluative claims as to bring out the extent to which any such judgement, if advanced on adequate (musically responsive and analytically cogent) grounds, will involve just the kind of qualified Platonist outlook that I have here sought to defend. That is, it will move between the twin poles of an awareness that music may always transcend the scope and limits of any given, no matter how perceptive or appreciative hearing, and a conjoint awareness – paradoxical though this might seem – that the transcendence in question can only take rise from within the actual experience of music or the phenomenology of musical response. Not that the paradox is merely apparent, or easily resolved through what I have here proposed as a qualified (i.e., phenomenologically tempered) Platonist approach. For there is still the large conceptual problem, as with mathematics (albeit in a somewhat less sharp and vexatious form), of how one can possibly reconcile the claims of recognition-transcendent truth on the one hand and epistemically accessible knowledge or experience on the other. What makes music such an interesting case – and such a standing provocation to philosophers from Plato to the present – is the fact that it poses this issue in a striking and, on account of its sensuous appeal, a peculiarly intimate or subjectively involving way.

V

As so often, it is Adorno whose intensely dialectical, relentlessly demanding yet (at times) highly evocative prose comes closest to describing that moment of transcendence whereby music offers a constant challenge to the analyst or sharp-eared listener whilst yet giving access to the deepest, most significant and in some sense most humanly familiar regions of subjective response. Such is indeed the 'problem of analysis' as Adorno defines it in a late essay: the fact that analytical approaches will always tend to fall back upon known methods and techniques, even (or especially) when confronted with works that threaten to disrupt or subvert habituated modes of understanding. Thus:

> [w]hether we like it or not analysis is inevitably to some extent, of its very nature, the reduction of the unknown, the 'new' ... to the already known, inasmuch as it is the 'old'. However, in that every modern composition contains an essential, inbuilt moment that combats this mechanism of the familiar and the known, in so far can it be said that the analysis of modern works is also always a betrayal of the work – although at the same time it is actually demanded by the work itself. From this there also arises the question as to how analysis puts right the wrong that it inflicts on the work; and the way to an answer lies, I believe, precisely in the fact that analysis serves to pinpoint that which I call the 'problem' of a particular composition – the paradox, so to speak, or the 'impossible' that every piece of music wants to make possible.[59]

This is also how Adorno seeks to explain what he calls the 'language-character' of music, that is, the likewise paradoxical way in which music intrinsically eludes any adequate verbal description yet also intrinsically demands such treatment by reason of its lacking determinate (conceptual) content, and hence its inability to state or articulate whatever lies encrypted in its formal structures. Thus 'analysis is itself a form in its own right, like translation, criticism, and commentary, as one of those media through which the very work unfolds ... Works need analysis for their "truth-content" to be revealed.' And again: '[i]f, without analysis, such works [he has here been discussing Beethoven and Webern] cannot be presented in even the simplest sense as being meaningful, then this is as much as to say that analysis ... is an essential element of art itself'.[60]

What precisely Adorno means by the 'truth-content' of musical works has been the topic of much, often highly specialized, debate and cannot be pursued in detail here.[61] Sufficient to say that it credits the work with a power to resist any kind of reductive treatment, whether in the form of a vulgar-sociological approach that ignores its salient structural features or a formalist approach that focuses exclusively on just those features and thereby neglects the sociocultural or ideological dimension wherein they assume a larger significance. Of course it would wrong – at any rate tendentious – to claim Adorno for the Platonist (even the qualified Platonist) camp, given this latter aspect of his thought and its relentless dialectical critique of the idea that musical works should ever be conceived as purely autonomous, self-enclosed monads apart from their cultural contexts of production and/or reception. Yet Adorno is just as fierce in denouncing any 'positivist' sociology of music – such as he encountered (and was briefly forced to undertake) during his period of US exile – that thinks itself capable of simply reading off the sociocultural 'content' of music through a documentary method very largely devoid of formal analysis.[62] Hence his claim that 'the ultimate "surplus" over and beyond the factual level is the *truth content*, and naturally it is only critique that can discover [this] content'. Moreover, '[n]o analysis is of any value if it does not terminate in the truth content of the work, and this, for its part, is mediated through the work's technical structure'.[63] It seems to me – on the evidence not only of these, rather sketchy and programmatic statements but also of Adorno's texts on Beethoven, Mahler, Schoenberg, Berg, Stravinsky and others – that the 'surplus' here equated with musical 'truth content' is such as can be rendered intelligible only in qualified Platonist terms.[64] That is, one has to think it of it as involving a moment of transcendence that exceeds the limits of our normal, habitual, even analytically informed habits of musical response but also – despite that – an ultimate appeal to those capacities of structural-phenomenological grasp that constitute the basis of a truly attentive and perceptive understanding of music.

A useful analogy is with Derrida's reading of Rousseau where he traces the emergence of a deviant, non-standard or paraconsistent logic that marks Rousseau's usage of the word 'supplement' in a great many diverse contexts, among them those of music history and theory.[65] What is most striking about this 'supplementary' logic is the way that it requires each occurrence of the word to bear both of its opposed or (as classical logic would dictate) contradictory and mutually exclusive senses: 'supplement' = 'mere addition, optional extra, inessential appendage' and 'supplement' = 'that which must be added so as to complete or make whole what would otherwise be lacking in some crucial respect'. I shall not comment at length on Derrida's immensely detailed, perceptive and cogent analysis save to remark that on one particular topic – Rousseau's thesis concerning the priority of melody over harmony – it relates directly to the line of argument pursued here. That is, it brings out the curious though constant and – once the reader is alerted to it – the strictly unignorable twist of implication through which Rousseau's explicit claims in this regard are subverted not only by the logic of his own argument but also by reflection on the nature of music, its sonorous properties (e.g., the overtone-series) and its perceptual or phenomenological mode of apprehension.

In short, 'no melody without harmony' since this harmonic dimension is a 'supplement' in just the opposite of Rousseau's intended sense, one that turns out to be the necessary adjunct – indeed the very condition of possibility – for whatever is capable of striking the ear as possessed of a melodic contour or character. Thus, in Derrida's words:

> [t]his fissure [i.e., the harmonic interval] is not one among others. It is *the* fissure: the necessity of interval, the harsh law of spacing. It could not endanger song except by being inscribed in it from its birth and in its essence. Spacing is not the accident of song. Or rather, as accident and accessory, fall and supplement, it is that also without which, strictly speaking, the song would not have come into being ... [T]he interval is part of the definition of song. It is therefore, so to speak, an originary accessory and an essential accident.[66]

I must refer the reader to Derrida's text if s/he wishes to gain a more adequate sense of the extreme logical acuity and conceptual precision with which he argues for these (seemingly) counter-intuitive conclusions. Elsewhere I have put the case that his critical exegesis of Rousseau on the topics of language, music, civil society, nature versus culture, speech versus writing, and the origins of morality might best be viewed as a highly original contribution to recent debates in philosophy of logic, especially those having to do with issues of modality.[67] However, my point here is that it offers support for the qualified Platonist claim that there exist certain ways of responding to or thinking about music which can be subject to assessment on grounds more objective (or logically accountable) than anything envisaged by the advocates of a response-dependent, listener-relative, or downright subjectivist approach. That it also connects with Derrida's sustained and intensive thinking-through of the relationship between structuralism and phenomenology is further reason, as I have said, to look in this direction for some useful pointers beyond the current stage of music-theoretical debate, whether in the mainstream analytic tradition or the more advanced (by their own estimate) quarters of the New Musicology.

What emerges from a critical survey of the field is a strong vindication of Adorno's claim that philosophy of music can have little of value to say without some appeal to the truth-content of musical works. This involves a 'surplus' of formal complexity over anything describable in terms of expressive content, yet also a 'surplus' of expressive yield over anything that falls within the scope of a purely formal or structural analysis. That is to say – risking the charge of blatant self-contradiction on any but Derrida's deconstructive or Adorno's negative-dialectical view – certain works possess a truth-content that eludes or transcends our present powers of perceptual-cognitive response, while none the less involving an ultimate appeal to the phenomenology of musical perception, understanding and judgement. It seems to me that thinkers in the 'continental' (i.e., post-Kantian mainland-European) line of descent have a stronger claim to have engaged this paradox and drawn out its most challenging implications than Anglophone philosophers who have mostly deployed the techniques of linguistic or conceptual analysis by way of expounding the logical grammar of our talk about music.[68] This is partly, no doubt, the difference between a dialectical and a non-dialectical approach, or one (like Adorno's) that strenuously holds out against the lures of conceptual reification or premature method and one that attaches greatest importance to the analytic virtues of clarity, precision and secure conceptual grasp. However, it is also – and perhaps more crucially – the difference between a philosophy of music that has taken the phenomenological path, even if (as with Derrida and Adorno) in a manner that contests or complicates certain of its grounding assumptions, and on the other hand a philosophy of music that has developed very largely in isolation from phenomenological interests and concerns. I have argued that both ways of thinking must entail at least a qualified commitment to Platonism if they are to offer a plausible ontology of music. For that commitment is endorsed – whether overtly or not – by any adequate account of the identity-conditions for musical works, their capacity to meet those conditions across widely varying styles of performance or modes of listener-response, and the extent to which these latter can be judged and assessed in terms of their capturing (or failing to capture) what is most distinctive or valuable about the work in question.

Needless to say, this whole set of claims will be rejected out of hand by theorists who regard the very concept of 'the work' as a thoroughly ideological and now discredited notion, along with its associated values of *werktreu* (faithful) performance and a proper sensitivity to period-style or idiom on the listener's part.[69] One likely reason is the growing revolt against various excesses of the 'authentic' performance movement, along with the suspicion – voiced most trenchantly by Adorno – that this insistence on restoring or retrieving the music as heard by its first audiences can amount to no more than a nostalgic mystique dressed up in dubious scholarly colours. However, an outlook of qualified Platonism, as I have described it here, is by no means committed to any such notion of the work as a kind of noumenal *Ding-an-Sich* that somehow (impossibly) permits us to commune with its creator's original expressive intent quite apart from all the changing conditions of its material and sociocultural reception history. On the contrary, it is able to take due account of those conditions while also making adequate allowance for the phenomenology of musical response, whether as concerns the more durable aspects of tonal, harmonic and rhythmic perception or the various ways in which they may be affected by just such contingent factors. From both points of view – the phenomenological and the sociocultural – it is clear that any adequate defence of Platonism in the musical context will need to accommodate certain apparently conflicting intuitions, among them the fact that music is inescapably tied to our modes of perceptual-cognitive response and, moreover, that these are in some degree subject to alteration over time. But it is also clear, as I hope to have shown, that neither approach can sustain its claim to make sense of our basic working assumptions about the nature of musical experience, understanding and judgement except in so far as it rests that claim on the basis of a qualified Platonist ontology.

In Chapter 5 I shall look more closely at the kinds of challenge posed to my argument by the New Musicologists and others of a similar mind who seek to 'deconstruct' (more aptly: to debunk or discredit) any such conception of the musical work as transcending the various contexts or vicissitudes of its reception-history to date. This will also mean taking careful stock – more careful (one is tempted to say) than is often taken by those who routinely invoke their authority – of certain texts by Derrida and Paul de Man which may prove less than ideally suited to these theorists' interests and purposes.

Music, Pleasure and the Claims of Analysis

I

It is a long time now – getting on for a century – since literary critics first became involved in earnest (often heated) debate about the relative merits of 'appreciative' and 'analytic' criticism. In fact one can date the most significant outbreak to the period just following the 1930 publication of William Empson's *Seven Types of Ambiguity,* a text that is nowadays perhaps more talked about than actually read but which remains (in my judgement) altogether unsurpassed for sheer brilliance, acuity, analytic insight and – be it said – occasional flights of soaring free-associative fancy.[1] No work since then has come anywhere close to *Seven Types* for the extent of its influence (especially on the US New Criticism) and the way that it opened up new possibilities of detailed textual exegesis combined with the strongly speculative bent of a first-rate analytical intelligence. Indeed, it is fair to say that this transformative impact was as much upon the poems or passages that Empson singled out for scrutiny as upon those receptive – and to that extent 'appreciative' – readers for whom poetry would never be quite the same again. Nevertheless the book attracted, and continues to attract, a good deal of hostile commentary from two main quarters. On the one hand are scholar-critics, such as Rosamond Tuve, who have attacked Empson for his flagrant 'misreadings', most often brought about – they claim – through his blithely anachronistic approach or cavalier disregard for the standards of interpretative truth imposed by a due respect for the constraints of philological research, authorial intent and period-based generic convention.[2] On the other – more relevant in the present context – is the charge brought against him by those who maintain that our experience of poetry is first and foremost a matter of 'appreciation', that is to say, an intuitive mode of response that cannot – or should not – be subject to any such pleasure-destroying excesses of analytic rigour.

This objection was voiced by John Sparrow in an article, published in the journal *Oxford Outlook,* to which Empson replied with a vigorous defence of his own, typically 'Cambridge' outlook of sturdy scientific rationalism versus

Sparrow's typically 'Oxford' offence at the idea of having his fine-tuned aesthetic responses so rudely laid open to inspection.[3] In other words, there was no real danger that (in Empson's phrase) by 'pruning down too far towards the emotional roots' the critic might thereby destroy the delicate flower. Any good poem (i.e., one that merited such close analytical attention) would surely stand to gain through this process of helping the reader to appreciate at a more conscious or reflective level what had hitherto been largely a matter of inchoate, ill-defined emotive response. And again, if the poem – or the reader's enjoyment – was spoiled by the analyst's approach then most likely that enjoyment was misplaced, whether because the poem didn't deserve it or because the reader was responding in some wrong or inappropriate (e.g., emotionally self-indulgent) way. Thus, for Empson, the chief virtue of analytic criticism was in drawing conscious attention to a range of otherwise unnoticed (or subliminal) nuances and depths of meaning, and thereby offering the reader a firmer, more confident basis for arriving at judgements of value. At the same time it could happily avoid the kind of vague, unsupported or downright dogmatic evaluative talk that all too often resulted when critics such as Sparrow fell back on the appeal to unaided intuition as the sole arbiter of aesthetic or literary worth. That is to say, any judgement could be taken as implicit in the fact that the poem or passage concerned had not only been singled out for close attention but shown itself responsive to an analytic treatment whose success – in so far as it achieved its aims – was sufficient guarantee of such worth. At this stage opponents are likely to object that the whole process has become purely circular, since 'good' poetry is now defined as just the sort that lends itself best to the analyst's foregone methods and predilections, while these are in turn borne out by (what else?) their working so well with the poetry in question. To which Empson's response, quite simply, is that the mind takes pleasure in achieving a better, more conscious grasp of its own operations and hence that any doctrine – like that of his opponents – which prevents it from so doing is one with harmful consequences not only for our appreciation of poetry but also, by extension, for the conduct of our intellectual, moral and everyday social lives.[4]

So much for the back-and-forth of this debate as it emerged in response to Empson's *Seven Types* and has continued to rumble on since then, as for instance in the later round of 'theory-wars' provoked by deconstruction, post-structuralism, and other such dubious continental imports as viewed by the (mainly Anglophone) upholders of intuitive or common-sense wisdom. However, it would over-simplify the issue to state it in quite these terms since, as anyone will know who has followed developments in French critical thought over the past three decades, things have moved on apace since the heyday of structuralism in its 'classic' (i.e., intensely theoretical and, at least by its then-current lights, methodologically rigorous) phase. The challenge to that erstwhile confident self-image came from various quarters, among them Derrida's deconstructive reading of Saussurean structural linguistics and Lévi-Strauss's structural anthropology.[5] It also took a lead from Roland Barthes' reflections – in *The Pleasure of the Text* and elsewhere – on that whole missing dimension of affective and erotic experience (*plaisir* and *jouissance*) which could not but elude the grim paternal law of a full-fledged structuralist approach, as adopted in some of his own earlier writings.[6] Still it is hard to avoid the impression that Barthes' turn 'against theory' is one that not only draws intellectual sustenance from all those past encounters (with Saussure, Lacan and Althusser, among others) but also leaves room for a great deal of very subtle between-the-lines theoretical and speculative thought.[7]

In most respects no two critics could be more different than Empson and Barthes, the one a commonsensical, distinctly 'British' kind of rationalist with strong empiricist leanings who tended to excoriate literary theory (especially in its French manifestations) as so much intellectual hot air, the other (so to speak) a theorist *malgré lui*, even in his moments of intimate reflection on the erotics of reader-response.[8] All the same they have at least this much in common: that they conceive the relationship between theory, analysis and pleasure (or appreciation) as one that goes wrong – gives rise to much sterile debate – as soon as those activities are thought of as in any way separable one from another. Moreover, they have both – Empson especially – influenced the thinking of Charles Rosen, a scholar-critic, concert pianist, cultural historian and music analyst whose writings are among the most acutely perceptive contributions to the recent literature.[9] Indeed, Rosen's book *The Classical Style* shows to striking effect how certain literary-critical terms and ideas – such as Empson's 'ambiguity' and his idiosyncratic deployment of the 'pastoral' concept – can be absorbed into the discourse of music criticism with great benefits in the way of interpretative insight and without any sense of the music's becoming just a platform for displays of hermeneutic, deconstructive or wire-drawn 'textualist' ingenuity.[10] His work may therefore stand as an instructive counter-example to some of those other, more theory-driven and (in my view) less musically rewarding interdisciplinary ventures that will be my chief topic in this chapter.

II

Another reason (or excuse) for this prefatory detour via Empson is the current emergence of debates strongly redolent of that between Empson and Sparrow, but now with regard to the merits of musical analysis as a means of enhancing or – as some would have it – of obstructing our straightforward, intuitive grasp of what music has to offer by way of pleasurable experience.[11] This analogy is itself rather less than straightforward for various historical, cultural and discipline-specific reasons. One is the fact that music analysis was pretty well established as a *modus operandi* from the mid nineteenth century on, albeit in forms that would scarcely pass muster by present-day academic standards. For it was then that the idea emerged, most forcefully in Hanslick's writings, that any genuine appreciation of music – or adequate account of musical meaning and value – would need to respect its 'absolute' status and would hence do well to resist or discount any notion of programmatic content.[12] Such was the basic philosophical premise of what thereafter became a veritable item of faith for critics who professed to be concerned with the musical work 'itself', rather than with various (no doubt interesting but strictly extrinsic) aspects of its cultural background, psychological genesis, reception-history, and so forth.

Thus the trend toward ever more refined and sophisticated methods of formal-structural analysis is one that took hold very largely through the growth of academic musicology and its attendant division of intellectual labour between, on the one hand, positivistically inclined music historians or sociologists and, on the other, theorist-critics with a strong autonomist bias.[13] Its benchmark expression – for proponents and antagonists alike – was Schenker's ultra-formalist insistence on tracing every detail of a work's surface structure to some underlying generative theme or motif which then served as justification for the claim of structural coherence or 'organic' form.[14] Indeed, this approach went so far as to assert that the ultimate aim of analysis was to derive the entire composition from the tonic triad (or root chord) in relation to which it could then be seen as a massive yet always homebound excursion through various thematic transformations, tonal departures, or long-drawn cadential and other such suspensive devices. To be sure this invites a number of objections, among them the familiar circularity-charge (to put it crudely: that analyst and work are engaged in a process of mutual reputation-boosting) and the claim that such methods, Schenker's in particular, are reductionist to the point where all music is treated – absurdly – as a mere detour *en route* to restoring that primordial 'chord of nature'.[15] Furthermore, suspicions have lately been raised that the origins of this approach were deeply bound up with a form of 'aesthetic ideology' which deployed metaphors of organic growth and development in the service of a cultural-nationalist creed with distinctly hegemonic, highly conservative and (some would say) protofascist inclinations.[16] After all, Schenker took it as self-evident – a truth infallibly borne out by analysis – that the greatest works were those belonging to the mainstream Austro-German line of descent from Bach, through Haydn, Mozart and Beethoven, to Schubert and Brahms. This status had to do not only with their superior degree of thematic complexity and formal integration but also with their standing in just that kind of privileged lineal relationship: one that effectively transferred those values from the individual work – organically conceived – to a version of musical history likewise premised on organicist (i.e., strongly teleological) notions of predestined development and growth.

Whence, so the charge-sheet continues, Schenker's attitude of undisguised contempt for any music – including, notoriously, that of Debussy – whose sensuous appeal, thematic elusiveness or lack of 'structure' in the operative (Schenker-approved) sense rendered them resistant or opaque to analysis and thus placed them firmly beyond the canonical pale. Moreover, in hindsight, that attitude takes on a whole range of disturbing, even sinister, overtones to the extent that it foreshadows those kinds of 'national aestheticism' – exemplified above all in the Wagner-cult and associated forms of Nazi cultural propaganda – which likewise entailed a demotion or suppression of other, so-called 'decadent' or 'degenerate' art.[17] In short, there is a dangerous pseudo-logic that can easily lead from claims concerning the structural integrity or 'organic' character of certain works, via claims with regard to their intrinsic value thus defined and analytically revealed, to claims that such value is the sole prerogative of just those cultures – or just that singular, rightfully predominant culture – which brought them to birth. That Schenker is well known to have espoused political views very much in keeping with such musico-aesthetic values and predilections is yet further grist to the deconstructive mill of those present-day theorists – exponents of the 'New Musicology' – who have taken to denouncing the whole enterprise of 'analysis' as merely an expression of deep-laid ideological bias concealed behind a fake appearance of objectivity and rigour.[18] Along with this, very often, goes a protest in the name of musical pleasure, enjoyment or appreciation as against the kind of 'structural listening' enjoined by critics who assume – in typically 'analytic' style – that any hearing of a work which fails to perceive its long-term patterns of thematic transformation, motivic development, tonal progression, and so forth, is a hearing that manifestly fails to grasp its true significance and value.[19]

Such claims are by no means confined to analysts of a broadly orthodox, that is to say, for the most part academically based and – by their own account – politically neutral persuasion. Indeed, the case for 'structural listening' is one that is put with great emphasis by Adorno since he considers it the only means by which music can effectively challenge – or be heard and understood to challenge – the kinds of uncritical, facile or stereotyped response that otherwise typify every aspect of our social and cultural lives under the conditions of late commodity capitalism.[20] Thus, for him, it stands opposed to those forms of mass-media entertainment (such as music that lends itself readily to large-scale popular consumption) whose relentless promotion by the 'culture industry' is among the most effective agencies of social control, working as it does to repress or destroy any last remnant of the critical-emancipatory impulse.[21] Hence Adorno's stark diagnosis of the trend toward 'regressive listening' which fails (or refuses) to engage with the long-term structural elements of musical form and contents itself solely with the kinds of enjoyment to be had from the standard fare of 'popular classics', or from favourite chunks of those works wrenched out of context so as to demand least effort of musical comprehension.

For many readers this just goes to show that Adorno, whatever his supposedly 'radical' (i.e., Marxist-influenced) ideas, was in fact an upholder of the cultural status quo and a defender of elitist values which were none the less so for his presenting them in the guise of a critical theory that proclaimed its opposition to every form of ideological conditioning.[22] As evidence of this they cite (among other things) his constant appeal to the canonical masterworks of Western musical tradition, his indiscriminate lumping-together of 'authentic' jazz with its tin-pan-alley derivatives, and (above all) his contempt for any music that didn't measure up to those classically derived standards of formal integrity and good taste. The latter is a phrase that would scarcely have entered Adorno's critical lexicon, but one – so his adversaries argue – that none the less captures the ethos and the tone of his writing once shorn of its pseudo-radical posturing. Thus, in their view, there is something distinctly strained – even self-defeatingly perverse – about Adorno's attempt to reconcile a high-formalist stress on the need for detailed and rigorous musical analysis with a self-professed commitment to radical or emancipatory values in the wider ethical, cultural and sociopolitical sphere. Moreover, his approach when striving hardest to define the negative-dialectical relation between music and its material conditions of production or reception tends always toward the former priority, that is, toward a notion of structural listening which effectively disqualifies any response that falls short of its own exacting (for which read 'elitist') criteria. What this amounts to – so the charge-sheet continues – is a further propping-up of 'the canon' and its hegemonic status, along with those increasingly refined analytical methods (albeit here bearing a Marxist inflection) that have served to maintain that status through various well-practised techniques of ideological co-option.

Such is at any rate the kind of criticism often levelled against Adorno by a range of hostile commentators, from defenders of 'popular' music in its various forms, genres or styles to those who reject what they see as his residual Kantian (or covertly formalist) bias against any kind of aesthetic 'appreciation' that errs on the side of sensuous pleasure or downright hedonist indulgence. Amongst the New Musicologists, one who has argued very forcefully to this effect is Rose Rosengard Subotnik in her book *Deconstructive Variations*.[23] Here she puts the case that any such emphasis on the virtues of 'structural listening' – whether by mainstream music analysts or by those, like Adorno, who claim to deploy it in the service of sociocultural critique – should be seen as just another standard device for shoring up those ideological values invested in the canon of received 'great' works. Subotnik finds nothing but highbrow cultural prejudice linked to professional self-interest in the notion that those works are intrinsically such as to demand an effort of sustained analytical attention, and that this provides not only a measure of their true greatness but a touchstone of musical perceptiveness and intelligence on the listener's part. Hence Adorno's attitude of sovereign contempt for those other, less elevated modes of response – ruthlessly exploited by the 'culture-industry' – which, so far from requiring a capacity for long-term structural grasp, encourage the listener to attend spasmodically, to pick out favourite passages for repeated hearing, and completely to ignore any aspects of musical form beyond the most basic, easily assimilated melodies and harmonic progressions. To his way of thinking, this marked the prevalence of a regressive, even infantile, fixation on the kinds of purely sensuous pleasure – or desire for immediate gratification – that went along with other signs of a widespread malaise in the body politic, such as the demise of autonomous critical reflection among those who took their beliefs and values ready-made from mass media sources. Thus the stultification of collective intelligence went on apace, aided in no small part by the endless recycling of clichéd, stereotyped modes of listener-response whose effect – as with jazz, on Adorno's notoriously negative view of it – was to create an illusion of spontaneity which in fact worked to conceal its thoroughly banal and commodified character.[24]

In an earlier book, *Developing Variations*, Subotnik had drawn quite extensively on Adorno's musical and sociological analyses, not least in making her case for a feminist and class-based critique of the dominant paradigms in academic musicology.[25] In the sequel, as I have said, she pretty much disowns this allegiance and comes out very strongly against his idea that 'structural listening' to works that invite or reward such attention is the *sine qua non* for any critical practice that would keep faith with music's now much diminished and yet – as Adorno strives to maintain – still latent emancipatory potential or occluded truth-content.[26] On the contrary, she argues: this Adornian perspective is just another chapter in the long history of high-toned formalist and philosophic put-downs suffered by popular culture at the hands of those who would denigrate its pleasures as nothing more than frivolous distractions or ways of remaining blissfully well deceived. Thus Subotnik sees nothing wrong – nothing at all 'unmusical' – in the kinds of unfocused, intermittent, easily side-tracked, half-conscious, or free-associative listening that Adorno finds grimly symptomatic of our twilight cultural state. Still less does she go along with his distinctly Kantian mistrust of any pleasure in modes of aesthetic experience – such as the enjoyment of music at a sensuous level – that cannot be subject to formal analysis, or to treatment in conceptual (philosophic) terms.

To be sure, a central theme and motivating impulse in much of Adorno's work is the need to resist that totalizing (potentially totalitarian) drive toward absolute conceptual mastery that tends always to repress or ignore the stubborn particularities of lived experience.[27] Yet it is often hard to escape the impression that Adorno's own dialectical drive – albeit in the name of a 'negative dialectics' that strives to resist such closure – is itself so strong and conceptually hard-driven as to place that aim in some doubt. Thus his critics have a point when they remark on this tension in Adorno's thought between an overt dedication to saving the particular from the ravages of abstract generality and an approach that risks doing precisely the opposite through its relentless pursuit of dialectical arguments whose result – very often – is to force a procrustean either/or logic onto musical works and musico-historical developments. Such is, for instance, the doctrinaire juxtaposition of Schoenberg versus Stravinsky in *Philosophy of Modern Music* and the constant presumption in Adorno's writing that any musical 'appreciation' meriting the name must go by way of so intensive an analytical engagement as to place it quite beyond reach of any but the most refined and highly trained musical intellects. So to this extent at least there is a certain justice in the charge often levelled against Adorno of his having drastically devalued the role of pleasure (or sensuous fulfilment) in our experience of music and, by the same token, overrated the importance of analytic grasp – or 'structural listening' – as a measure of what such experience properly involves.

All the same this argument may be thought to have gone too far if it concludes that analysis has no place in our musical responses, or that pleasurable listening has nothing whatever to do with the kinds of longer-term structural awareness that analysts are expert in finding out. Thus Adorno was right to insist – as against Subotnik and others who attack his 'elitist' approach – that there is something intrinsically valuable about the kinds of listening (and the kinds of work) that find room for a perception of long-range tonal, thematic and developmental structure as well as for the more immediate pleasures of short-term sensuous response. To adopt such a view is not merely, as some sociologists of culture would have it, an expression of class-prejudice or gender-bias encoded in a highly technical language (i.e., the discourse of present-day, post-Schenkerian music analysis) whose seeming objectivity and effort to avoid any taint of programmatic or affective content is precisely the mark of its ideological character.[28] That is to say, borrowing a useful distinction from philosophy of science, interests of this sort may well play a role in the 'context of discovery' where music critics – and listeners bent upon increasing their stock of 'cultural capital' – are no doubt subject to all manner of social, professional, academic, psychobiographical and other such extraneous motivating factors. However, they have no bearing on issues raised in the 'context of justification' where it is a matter of making good one's claims with respect to (say) structures of tonal development or motivic and thematic transformation.[29] For those claims are typically advanced with respect to certain agreed-upon standards – of evidence, precision, demonstrative warrant, sensitivity to context, and so forth – in consequence of which they can properly be held to stand on their merits and transcend any reductive sociological account.

Of course it will be said by opponents that these are just the sorts of self-confirming, purely circular and hence empirically vacuous criteria that typify the analytic enterprise, determined as it is to keep itself in business by producing ever more elaborate analyses which merely take for granted the superiority of music that suits its own preconceived values. Thus the two main prongs of this adversary case are, first, that such values apply only to a narrow, canonically privileged subset of musical works and practices, and second, that they are not so much 'there' to be discovered through objective analysis as projected onto those works through a strong disposition in favour of ideas such as thematic development, organic form, structural complexity, etc. Hence Subotnik's later, more 'radical' position according to which there is something intrinsically suspect – ideologically compromised – about the whole business of music analysis, even where this takes the form (as in Adorno) of a project with overtly critical, progressive and social-emancipatory aims.

III

These developments in recent, broadly 'deconstructive' music theory can be traced back to an influential 1983 essay by the critic Joseph Kerman, whose work up to then had combined an analytic with a cultural–historical approach and done so without any overt sense of a looming crisis in either discipline, or the relationship between them.[30] The essay ('How We Got into Analysis, and How to Get Out') sought to put an end to this comfortable state of affairs by declaring the crisis already upon us and offering a diagnostic account of its symptoms and their cultural aetiology. Briefly stated, analysis as practised hitherto by mainstream musicologists was a product of that same 'aesthetic ideology' which literary theorists had long since recognized as a potent source of illusory notions – such as that of 'organic form' – whose extension into the wider (sociocultural and political) domain was at best an unfortunate category-mistake and at worst a highly dangerous conflation of realms.[31] It was just this delusion which had given rise to that particular strain of 'aestheticized' politics whose expressions ranged from the more overtly nationalist versions of German idealism and romanticism to Wagner's ideal of the *Gesamtkunstwerk*, or from Schenker's conception of musical form as growing out of certain germinal motifs to his likewise deeply organicist view of those same values as bearing out his claim for the superior quality of works in the Austro-German line of descent. Thus Kerman put the case that musicologists had yet to catch up with certain crucial developments in literary theory – chiefly of a French provenance – which had gone far toward deconstructing the kinds of ideological baggage that went along with the analytic programme, albeit (no doubt) unbeknownst to most of its practitioners. What the discipline needed was a healthy injection of 'theory', this latter equated by Kerman with a willingness to examine its own deep-laid, even (it might be) discipline-constitutive values, assumptions and priorities. Only thus – by taking various leaves out of the deconstructionist book – might analysis shed that bad Schenkerian legacy of national-aestheticist thinking and learn to question those hegemonic notions (of form, unity, thematic integration, 'structural listening', and so forth) that presently exerted such a harmful grip on its working principles and practices.

What made the situation worse, according to Kerman, was the way that music analysis of this sort went along with an approach to musical history that was likewise in hock to certain outworn, nineteenth-century 'positivist' conceptions of scholarly method. Here also, musicologists proceeded as if their discipline could and should remain entirely untouched by those major developments in other fields – hermeneutics, critical historiography, narrative poetics, structuralism, post-structuralism, feminism, deconstruction – whose deployment elsewhere had exerted such a powerful transformative impact. Once they started taking stock of such developments, Kerman surmised, they would find themselves impelled not only to rethink the methodological foundations of their work but also to raise serious doubts with regard to its ideological complicities, not least as concerned that *entente cordiale* – rather nicely exemplified, one is tempted to remark, in Kerman's own previous work – between music history and music analysis as currently practised.[32] In particular they would have to ask whether the very fact of this peaceful coexistence might not indicate a symptomatic failure or refusal to examine that complex, essentially contested and ideologically charged relationship. Even a cursory acquaintance with the writings of a literary theorist such as Paul de Man would suffice to show that they had come nowhere near thinking it through with the requisite degree of self-critical awareness.[33] And it would then become apparent, so Kerman claimed, that musicology in both departments was in urgent need of opening its doors to the kinds of thinking that had brought such benefits – as he definitely took them to be – when applied in those other, more advanced and speculative regions of debate.

When Kerman's essay first appeared he could plausibly strike the heroic tone of one crying in the academic wilderness, or of Milton's archangel Abdiel, 'alone against the forces of night'. Now, twenty years on, his plea for musicologists to broaden their theoretical horizons and absorb the lessons of deconstruction and other such cutting-edge developments is apt to sound distinctly old-hat or more like a fairly conservative prognosis of developments already under way. For it can hardly escape the notice of anyone who browses through the current music journals, bibliographies or publishers' catalogues that musicology has taken the 'deconstructive turn' with a vengeance, and that 'theory' has triumphed (or at any rate made territorial gains) beyond Kerman's wildest dreams.[34] Indeed, it wouldn't surprise me if he was less than happy about the extent to which – in certain quarters at least – his proposals have been taken on board and the rapidity with which they have become something very like an orthodox creed. Thus there is now a minor industry of 'deconstructive' musicology devoted to dismantling both the discourse of mainstream analysis – especially any talk of 'organic form' – and, beyond that, the habits of structural listening or long-term musical-cognitive uptake which are thought to fall in with just such ideologically complicitous notions.

Of these debates perhaps the most revealing is that between Jonathan Dunsby and Alan Street on the topic of Brahms' late piano *Fantasies*, Op.

116. In this sequence of pieces – most often thought of as loosely related in terms of style, mood and general character – Dunsby purports to hear (and to demonstrate by detailed analysis) a whole range of thematic cross-connections and subtle inter-movement unifying features.[35] To which Street responds that Dunsby's desire to 'discover' such features in the music is a projection of his own analytic (and ideologically driven) belief that a great work *must*, by very definition, manifest them in some degree and that the greatness of these particular pieces can be brought out all the more convincingly by showing their unity to transcend the limits of their surface episodic or suite-like form.[36] In the process Street draws upon a good many theoretical sources, among them de Man's deconstructive readings of numerous texts – philosophical, literary, literary-critical – which he (de Man) takes to exhibit all the signs of their having been seduced by that form of aesthetic ideology which consists in 'confusing linguistic with natural reality'.[37] Such is, for instance, the widespread idea among literary critics of otherwise diverse persuasion that poetic language somehow has the power not merely to describe, evoke, or represent features of the natural world but (through devices like metaphor and symbol) to render them with all the sensuous vividness that belongs to our various modes of perceptual experience. This elementary confusion – as de Man thinks it – gives rise to the further, more dangerous since ideologically charged error of attributing characteristics to language which are then metaphorically extended beyond the aesthetic domain to concepts of art, culture and (ultimately) the nation-state as expressions of a likewise natural process of organic development and growth.[38]

Hence, to repeat, his constant emphasis on the need for close attention to those crucial passages in certain exemplary thinkers – pre-eminently Rousseau and Kant – which show how they managed to avoid such temptations by maintaining the highest degree of critical vigilance, but also how their texts were later subject to various kinds of 'aberrant', ideologically driven misreading. It is this deManian imperative that Street and other deconstructive musicologists have in mind when they counsel an attitude of principled suspicion toward any method, technique or practice of analysis that rests its claims on such illusory (and, in their view, politically retrograde) notions as those of organic form or long-range structural unity. To which end they typically set about showing – as in Street's altercation with Dunsby – that the analyst's text itself contains certain symptomatic blind-spots or unnoticed and questionable turns of metaphor that unwittingly reveal its deep involvement with just such ideological values. Only thus, so the argument runs, can music criticism at last catch up with those developments in literary theory that have long since disposed of an organicist aesthetic, like that of the 'old' New Criticism, whose talk was of seemingly disruptive or 'non-totalizing' figures such as ambiguity, irony or paradox but whose overriding aim was to present the poem as a 'verbal icon' wherein such tensions were finally resolved or reconciled.[39] Here again de Man is taken to provide an object-lesson in the deconstructive reading of texts that are thereby forced to reveal their ideological hand.[40]

To be sure, Street brings some strong theoretical arguments to bear on the discourse of mainstream music analysis: arguments which make a plausible case for viewing it as heavily mortgaged to just those values that de Man finds complicit with the workings of aesthetic ideology. His proposed remedy – again taking a lead from de Man – is to read that discourse against the grain by refusing to endorse the privilege it attaches to tropes such as metaphor and symbol, that is to say, 'totalizing' tropes which reliably facilitate the passage from particular details of the literary work to a conception of that work as exhibiting an overall, transcendent unity of theme and idea.[41] Such a reading would take as its principal aim the demonstration that metaphors self-deconstruct into chains of metonymic displacement, substitution or surreptitious part-for-whole transference, and moreover that the symbolist notion of organic form – as it figures (expressly or implicitly) in so many versions of aesthetic ideology – can likewise be shown to fall back upon textual mechanisms whose structure is that of allegory rather than symbol. This is hardly the place for a full-scale exposition of the various texts (in particular his readings of Rousseau, Nietzsche and Proust) where these claims are tested to the utmost degree of hard-pressed rhetorical analysis, not to mention – as some might add – the utmost limits of readerly endurance.[42] Suffice it to say that metonymy stands as the trope whose prosaic, down-to-earth, literal, non-'totalizing' character allows it most effectively to counter the claims of metaphor, that is, to remind us how the language of metaphor unravels or self-deconstructs into chains of contingently related metonymic detail that stubbornly resist assimilation to the realm of metaphorical quasi-transcendence. So likewise in the case of allegory versus symbol: where symbolist readings typically indulge in an over-willingness to take such claims at face value (i.e., as achieving a consummate union between subject and object, mind and nature, time-bound or mortal existence and a realm of transcendent eternal truths) allegorical readings typically insist on the temporal character of all under-standing and hence the sheer impossibility that language might attain that wished-for condition.

Thus allegory is not so much a well-defined literary genre – including such works as *The Faerie Queene, Pilgrim's Progress* or *Animal Farm* – but a certain mode of critically reflective and rhetorically alert close-reading which holds out against the seductive blandishments of symbolist thought. And again: metonymy is not (as often supposed) just a kind of poor relation to metaphor, that is to say, a trope whose mundane character – forming as it does the stock-in-trade of most non-'literary' (e.g., journalistic or workaday) prose – invites unfavourable comparison with the creative or world-disclosive potential of metaphoric language. Rather, on de Man's account, it is a trope that can be shown to inhabit that language and indeed to constitute the underlying structure of every (supposed) metaphor. Thus metonymy and allegory turn out to subvert the traditional order of priorities and the high claims vested in metaphor and symbol as somehow granting access to truths beyond the grasp of commonplace, prosaic understanding. So to read allegorically and with an eye to metonymic details that resist or obstruct the suasive power of other, more seductive metaphorical–symbolist readings is also to engage in a form of *Ideologiekritik* with large implications for our thinking about issues of ethics and politics. This is why, as de Man provocatively puts it, with an eye on his Marxist or cultural-materialist critics, '[t]hose who reproach literary theory for being oblivious to social and historical (that is to say ideological) reality are merely stating their fear at having their own ideological mystifications exposed by the tool they are trying to discredit. They are, in short, very poor readers of Marx's *German Ideology*'.[43]

However, there is a problem – I want to suggest – with attempts to transfer this approach from the realm of literary criticism to the domain of musical analysis where any claims advanced on behalf of this or that 'reading' must surely concede a certain priority to the perceptual or phenomenological experience of music. That is to say, the fact that many verbal analyses (like Dunsby on the Brahms *Fantasies*) can be shown to exhibit a strong attachment to organicist models or metaphors is no proof that they are distorting or misrepresenting the music to ideological ends, or indeed that those metaphors don't capture something intrinsic to the well-equipped listener's pleasure and appreciation. Where de Man's arguments get a hold is through the undisputed truth – undisputed by all save diehard adherents to a Cratylist doctrine of linguistic mimeticism – that language is a system of purely conventional ('arbitrary') relations between signifiers and signifieds, or again (in Saussurean structuralist parlance) of 'differences without positive terms'.[44] Thus apart from such oddities as onomatopoeia or cases, as with poetry, where the sound very often in some way 'echoes the sense' it is a clearly a fallacy – and one subjected to withering critical scrutiny by de Man – to suppose that verbal language can somehow partake of the 'natural' reality that makes up its field of reference. In de Man's somewhat tortuous phrasing: '[t]he phenomenality of the signifier, as sound, is unquestionably involved in the correspondence between the name and the thing named, but the link, the relationship between word and thing, is not phenomenal, but conventional'.[45] And again: '[l]iterature is fiction not because it somehow refuses to acknowledge "reality", but because it is not a priori certain that language functions according to principles which are those, or which are *like* those, of the phenomenal world'.[46] However, it is far from clear that this argument might plausibly be carried across from the textual–linguistic to the musical domain, or – what is chiefly at issue here – from deconstructive readings of the discourse of music analysis to claims concerning our perceptual or phenomenological experience of music. For these latter have to do with modalities of jointly sensuous and cognitive (i.e., conceptually informed) perception which cannot be treated as mere figments of 'aesthetic ideology', or as symptoms of the Cratylist delusion that naïvely conflates linguistic structures with the forms or processes pertaining to natural phenomena.

This is why, as I have said, theorists should not too hastily reject the idea of 'structural listening' – whether advanced by mainstream analysts or by a critical dialectician like Adorno – as just a product of those old elitist values that serve to shore up both the canon of established 'great works' and the business of academic musicology. For it is simply not the case – or, at least, not simply the case – that such listening (and the pleasure afforded by it) is confined to some few professional adepts and leisured cognoscenti who have access to the specialist books, journals or high-brow broadcast media whereby these values are diffused, along with the kinds of analytical approach that bolster their cultural standing. Rather, what is revealed by a good, sharp-eared, intelligent and (above all) intuitively valid essay in musical analysis is what the listener is able to hear for herself through close and sustained attention to the music although perhaps, without having read that essay, unable to articulate in verbal form with such point and precision. This is not to deny – far from it – that analysis can bring out aspects of a work, from subtleties of detail to aspects of long-range structure, that the listener might well have missed up to now or been 'aware' of only in so vague or unfocused a way as scarcely to count as conscious recognition. All the same, such analytic- ally arrived-at insights will themselves scarcely count as such unless they chime with something in the listener's intuitive musical response which then serves as a measure of just how far the analyst has managed to hit on the right (i.e., perceptually salient) aspects of detail and structure.

A rough but useful analogy here would be that of the grammarian whose theories of what constitutes a well-formed or ill-formed sentence, a normal or deviant active–passive transformation, and so forth, must always be checked against the verdicts of a competent native speaker if they are to claim any kind of descriptive validity. Indeed, one branch of recent, post-Schenkerian analysis that brings out this point very clearly is the transformational-generative model proposed by Lerdahl and Jackendorff, where listener-response must surely be a crucial test in evaluating some particular claim with regard to what's really going on in the process of depth-to-surface tonal and thematic transformation.[47] Nevertheless, here as with other kinds of analysis, one should also allow for the extent to which musical perceptions can be further, more deeply or even creatively informed by the kinds of consciousness-raising structural insight that such theories seek to provide. It is this possibility that seems to be barred – ruled out on ideological grounds – by those among the New Musicologists who see nothing but a rearguard defence of elitist cultural values in the premium attached to 'structural listening' as against the claims of straightforward, uncomplicated musical pleasure. That is say, these theorists may be indulging a form of inverted cultural snobbery whereby it is assumed that complex, long-range or sophisticated modes of musical appreciation are *ipso facto* beyond reach of a popular audience while other, more immediate forms of gratification – those pleasures to be had from 'music in the moment' – are the sort that do possess a widespread appeal and should therefore be defended against their detractors by anyone with a well-developed social and political conscience. However, this risks selling everyone short: the analysts (whose efforts are written off as mere products of aesthetic ideology), the 'structural listeners' (who are, after all, perfectly entitled to their own kinds of satisfaction), the creators and performers of 'popular' music (which itself covers a huge range in terms of musical complexity and value), and – not least – the mass-audience whom these theorists effectively rule off-bounds when it comes to other, more demanding (and perhaps more musically rewarding) modes of listener-involvement.

The phrase 'music in the moment', as used above, is actually the title of a book by Jerrold Levinson which raises some of these issues from a different but related philosophical angle.[48] Levinson agrees with the New Musicologists that analysis goes wrong by attaching such inordinate value to long-range structural aspects of music, as distinct from those far more vivid, direct and readily appreciated 'momentary' features – accessible to short-term memory – which constitute the listener's chief source of genuine (rather than abstract or hypercultivated) pleasure. However, his reasons for taking this view have less to do with any programme of sociocultural–political critique than with certain lessons which he thinks should be drawn from phenomenological or cognitive–psychological reflection on the scope and limits of perceptual responses to music. In brief, these are that our attention-span is more restricted than the analysts suppose, that our powers of retentive grasp are confined to just a short stretch of time, and moreover that even when we know a work well – and should thus (on the analytic view) have a long-term anticipatory awareness of developments yet to come – we are still listening very much 'in the moment' and largely oblivious of them unless at a level of abstraction far removed from the actual experience of music. Thus Levinson – like Subotnik but on different grounds – takes a pretty dim view of any analytic approach whose effect is to promote the virtues of structural listening and thereby devalue the pleasures that accrue (more precisely: that occur in rapid succession) if one lends an ear more attuned to those short-term modes of perceptual experience.

He is challenged on this by another philosopher, Peter Kivy, who not only disagrees strongly with Levinson concerning those tight limits on the human capacity for long-range musical perception but states his disagreement in unusually forceful and passionate terms.[49] For Kivy – and also, I should say, for myself as a matter of personal as well as theoretical conviction – it is a truth borne out on many occasions over the years that one's appreciation of music can be greatly enhanced by the reading of perceptive analyses which conduce to a heightened, more adequate grasp of large-scale structural attributes far beyond the sadly impoverished range of Levinson's amnesiac listener. Indeed, I would suggest that Levinson's low estimation of our normal capacities in this respect is such as to imply a likewise low estimation of the standards that music should meet – standards of inventiveness, thematic interest, sustained harmonic development, tonal progression, rhythmic subtlety, and so forth – if it is to offer the kinds of reward that come with repeated and properly attentive listening. Thus anyone whose powers of retentive or anticipatory awareness were really as limited as Levinson decrees would be very much at home with the compositions of Philip Glass, Michael Nyman, (the later) Arvo Pärt, John Tavener and other such exponents of a minimalist style which relies on the constant repetition of banal and easily recognized themes with just enough in the way of undemanding harmonic or rhythmic variation to jog the hearer into semi-consciousness once in a while. Or again, they would be equipped to appreciate a large amount of bottom-drawer baroque music which also involves an absolute minimum of 'structural listening' in so far as it rehearses a predictable range of well-worn stylistic and formal techniques with only minor departures from the expectations raised by an acquaintance with the relevant generic norms. However, their responses would fall drastically short when it came (say) to Bach, to Vivaldi's more inventive works, to those other baroque composers (or individual works) that rose above the stock-in-trade conventions of the time, or to all but the earliest of Haydn's quartets and symphonies. Still less could they achieve a properly informed appreciation – as distinct from a piecemeal enjoyment – of mature Mozart, late Beethoven, Schubert, Brahms or indeed any music where the interplay set up between expectations and the thwarting or subtle disrupting of those same expectations is a chief source of sensory-perceptual pleasure and intellectual stimulus alike.

IV

Hence, as I have said, the taint of inverted snobbery that hangs about the discourse of professional musicologists, theorists and philosophers who claim to be speaking on behalf of the common listener when they attack such 'elitist' values, but whose argument can just as plausibly be read as an attack on the overweening pretensions of any listener – 'common' or not – with a taste for more developed or sophisticated modes of musical response. This revolt against analysis (or structural listening) in the name of, ostensibly, more direct and non-exclusive musical pleasures is one that has other dubious results. They include the return – by various exponents of the 'New Musicology' – to an oddly reductive and literalist notion of programmatic content (often reminiscent of the old 'life-and-times' approach) motivated partly by their anti-formalist bias and partly by the concomitant desire to bring music and music criticism back down to earth through an account of their class-based, gender-inflected or ideologically 'constructed' character.

Here again Kivy has some sharp observations to make, especially concerning this current trend in its cruder, more doctrinaire manifestations. Thus there is, to say the least, something caricatural about hearing the pent-up dynamism in the first-movement development section of Beethoven's Fifth Symphony as an expression (or unwittingly blatant confession) of the aggressive and thwarted male drive for sexual mastery.[50] Nor does it conduce very much to our better musical understanding to be told that the contrast between 'masculine' first subject and 'feminine' second subject in the opening movement of Tchaikovsky's Fifth represents a desperate struggle in the composer's mind between socially enforced denial and deeply felt acceptance of his own homosexual desires.[51] Admittedly these are extreme cases and one could instance other readings of musical works with a view to their (often ambivalent) psychosexual or ideological subtext which involve nothing like so grossly reductive or – as followers of Adorno might say – so dialectically 'unmediated' an approach. Nevertheless, even at its most sensitive and well-informed, such thinking tends to push the anti-formalist reaction to a stage where it risks falling back into a naïve and critically disabling confusion of life and work. That is to say, it shows many signs of adopting a standpoint that has simply failed to catch up with Adorno's far subtler, more musically responsive, yet also – quite compatible with this – more historically and sociopolitically engaged mode of analytic discourse. Thus when theorists such as Subotnik claim to have thought their way through and beyond Adorno's influence – and to have done so, moreover, by an outright rejection of ideas such as that of 'structural listening' – one is entitled to question whether this constitutes any kind of intellectual advance or indeed (as advertised) a return to the values of genuine musical enjoyment as opposed to the abstract rigours of formal analysis.

Kivy makes the point rather neatly when he invites us to entertain a thought-experiment regarding the claims of programmatic or 'content'-based interpretation on the one hand and formalist or structurally oriented approaches on the other.[52] Consider, he suggests, the case of three accomplished but in varying degrees untypical appreciators of the arts – Peter, Paul and Mary – whose aesthetic responses each have a certain distinctive or peculiar feature. Peter is an enthusiast for German poetry who possesses an exceptionally acute ear for the phonetic qualities (rhyme-schemes, patterns of alliteration, or ways of playing off metrical structure against natural speech-rhythms) to be found in Goethe, Hölderlin and Rilke, but who doesn't understand a word of German and thus savours those qualities with not the least grasp of how the sound echoes or subtly qualifies the sense. Paul is a visual-art connoisseur who has developed an ultra-fine appreciation of various formal attributes – of balance, contrast, structural proportion, perspectival effects, the interplay of light and shade, etc. – but who suffers from a curious kind of aspect-blindness that prevents him from perceiving the representational content of figurative paintings. Then there is Mary, a music-lover, who doesn't merely 'know' (in the abstract) all that abstract stuff about sonata-form, first and second subjects, developing variation, progressive tonality, and so forth, but who truly understands, enjoys and appreciates what music has to offer on just those descriptive or analytical terms. That is to say, she is a 'formalist' or adept of 'structural listening' but one to whom this comes very much as second nature and for whom such descriptions genuinely chime with her first-hand, intuitive and passionately engaged experience of music. What puts her in the company of Peter and Paul, for the purposes of Kivy's thought-experiment, is that Mary just doesn't get it when people talk about the programmatic content of works such as the *Eroica* Symphony, or Haydn's *Creation*, or Richard Strauss's *Ein Heldenleben*, or Elgar's *Falstaff*, or indeed – perhaps more controversially – some of Bach's (to most ears) very striking mimetic devices in his settings of religious texts. (These are my examples, not Kivy's.) Thus Mary might be counted a fellow-sufferer in so far as she seems to be missing out on something that other, 'normally' equipped listeners can be expected to hear in the music and which presumably heightens their appreciative grasp of its content, meaning and value.

However, it is just Kivy's point that, despite appearances, these cases are in fact very different. Thus whereas Peter can scarcely be said to 'appreciate' German poetry at all, and whereas Paul must likewise be considered blind to something intrinsic to the nature of figurative art, Mary cannot rightly be said to lack anything essential to the proper understanding or appreciative grasp of music. Perhaps it may be said – by anti-formalists of various persuasion – that she does in fact miss out on certain kinds of pleasure enjoyed by other listeners (i.e., those receptive or responsive to such elements of programmatic content). However, so Kivy maintains, this is surely not a failure of *musical* intelligence, perception or involvement on her part, nor a deafness to anything intrinsically 'there' in the work, but rather a non-dependence on ways of listening that by very definition have at most an extraneous, secondary or strictly inessential role to play. More than that: in cases where the listener – or (possibly) the music – does rely heavily on attributions of programmatic content then this gives reason to suppose that one or other falls short of what the best, that is to say, most musically rewarding since least secondary-response-dependent works have to offer.

Now of course this will strike the opponent (whether old-style defender of content-based musical interpretation or new-style advocate of deconstructive, Foucauldian, feminist, neo-Marxist or kindred forms of *Ideologiekritik*) as just another, albeit neatly turned statement of the formalist case and hence as subject to the same charges of inherent circularity or empty self-confirmation. Indeed, it will no doubt stand accused of reinforcing that potent strain of 'aesthetic ideology' – transposed into the likewise highly suspect notion of 'structural listening' – which music theorists have been quick to take up from de Man's later writings. All the same, as I have said, such accusations run the risk of ignoring some pertinent (even ideologically crucial) distinctions, among them that between the kinds of deeply organicist, methodologically doctrinaire and often quite explicitly chauvinist formalism exemplified by Schenker and those other varieties of analysis – whatever their particular problems or shortcomings – that hardly conform to this stereotype. Thus Adorno's work provides one striking example of an expressly analytic approach (and a corresponding emphasis on the virtues of structural awareness) conjoined with a range of cultural, historical and – not least – philo-sophical reflections on the complex dialectical relationship between music and its social contexts of production and reception.[53] But there are, and for quite a while have been, plenty of other, less elaborately theorized instances of music criticism that manages to heal – or at any rate to bridge for its own specific purposes – the rift that Kerman so deplored between the discourse of music analysis and those wider contexts. Here I am thinking again of Charles Rosen's writings, where a singular depth and acuity of musical perception goes along with a detailed scholarly knowledge of the relevant sociocultural background and also a keenly intelligent sense of how debates in other areas (historiography, narrative theory, poetics, hermeneutics, and so forth) may help toward a better, more appreciative understanding.[54] I would also mention – among my own favourites – the wonderfully perceptive study of Ravel by Vladimir Jankélevitch, a critic whose other chief interests (in phenomenology, ethics, the philosophy of time and irony) can be seen to inform his responses to the music in numerous subtle and revealing ways.[55]

So I am inclined to disagree with Kerman as regards his 1982 diagnosis and to suggest that things were in fact nowhere near as bad with the then-current state of academic musicology as he made out. Moreover, as implied by the above comparisons, it strikes me that Rosen is justified in claiming that a good deal of work produced by its subsequent, theory-led and sociologically minded debunkers must be found to fall far short of the insights delivered by intelligent, context-sensitive analysis.[56] That is to say, there is something distinctly wrong-headed about the notion that these approaches cannot go together, that a penchant for analysis *must* entail an attitude of downright indifference to sociohistorical concerns and hence a complicity with dominant ideological values, or again – conversely – that a critical engagement with those same concerns and values will inevitably lead one to reject 'analysis' and all its works. On the contrary, I have argued: not only *can and do* they sometimes go very nicely together but it is also the case that neither approach can come close to an adequate understanding of music without those insights and conceptual resources provided by the other. This is one issue where literary theory might offer a useful lead, not so much in its more extreme (e.g., purist deconstructive or cultural-materialist) strains but more through its effort, over the past few decades, to achieve a synthesis or working balance between the formalist/structuralist imperative to analyse texts in strictly synchronic terms and the kinds of diachronic, historically based approach enjoined by Marxists, sociologists of literature and others of a seemingly opposite persuasion.[57] Thus, as Roland Barthes once wrote in a cryptic but typically pregnant passage, 'while a little formalism turns one away from history, a lot of formalism turns one back to it'.[58] At any rate there is more to be gained in this way, from the viewpoint of a critical musicology, than by following other doctrinally committed literary theorists to the point of an ultimate stand-off or breakdown of communication between the interests of analysis or 'structural listening' and the interests of historically informed commentary.

The same applies – so I have argued – to that other false antinomy between music as an object of analysis and music as a source of pleasure. What we need to do here is triangulate and see that there is pleasure to be taken not only in the process or activity of formal/structural understanding but also in the kinds of appreciative benefit brought by a knowledge of music in its cultural-historical context. This might seem at odds with my general endorsement of Kivy's case as regards the primacy of formal attributes – and our ability to perceive or apprehend them – over any such merely 'extraneous' concerns. However, one can take his argument on board (i.e., the primacy-thesis as a matter of aesthetic principle) without concluding that those latter sorts of knowledge or interest are therefore to be counted strictly irrelevant to musical experience, properly so called. There is support for this more accommodating version of the thesis from a range of disciplinary quarters, among them that of cognitive psychology where recent debate has often turned on the extent to which our various mental capacities should be thought of as 'encapsulated' or 'hard-wired'. That is to say, it is the issue as to just how far – if at all – they involve the operation of relatively discrete, self-contained or (in the jargon) 'cognitively impervious' modules which carry out their multiple specialized functions with little or no input from other, more global or widely distributed modes of cognitive processing.[59]

Jerry Fodor is the best-known defender of the 'strong'-modularity thesis according to which this applies to quite a range of otherwise diverse mental functions.[60] These would include our everyday syntactic competence as language-users (here taking a lead from Chomsky's work in transformational-generative grammar) and also types of behaviour – like the 'fight-or-flight' response – which may well have required a complex but rapid and unthinking (i.e., highly 'encapsulated') cognitive mechanism so as to facilitate species survival. However, Fodor has lately shown signs of softening that line, at least in so far as he now sees intractable problems with the strong thesis when it comes to offering some plausible account of how we manage to perform high-level, complex and inherently hard-to-formalize mental tasks – such as abduction, or inference to the best explanation – which must involve drawing on a wide range of background knowledge, much of it tacit or below the threshold of conscious awareness.[61] This also has a bearing on our thought about music, as Mark DeBellis has argued in a recent book on cognitive-psychological aspects of the dispute between formalism (or 'structural listening') and its various detractors.[62] In brief, he puts the case that our musical responses cannot be strongly modular since they are clearly affected – most often in positive or experience-enhancing ways – not only by our reading of perceptive musical analyses but also, if to less striking effect, by our knowledge of relevant historical and sociocultural background information. That such knowledge indeed belongs to the background, rather than the foreground where analysis has a more significant role to play, is a main plank in DeBellis's argument for the conceptually informed nature of musical understanding and hence – in cognitive-psychological terms – its 'permeability' by the kinds of knowledge conveyed by sharp-eared analysts or structural listeners. All the same, it is hard to see how a principled distinction could be drawn so as to hold the formalist line between one and the other sorts of musical consciousness-raising: i.e., that which results from acquaintance with 'genuine' analytic insights and that which contingently accrues through exposure to some more-or-less 'relevant' piece of musico-historical information.

Thus DeBellis, like Kivy, makes a strong case for the merits of analysis as an active, integral, even transformative component of our musical experience rather than – as the current debunkers would have it – a discourse whose deeply ideological character is signalled by its sheer remoteness from such experience as well as its commitment to suspect values like those of thematic development, structural coherence or (worst of all!) organic form. On the other hand their arguments also leave room for the intuitive conviction of many listeners, not all of them by any means naïve or musically illiterate, that knowledge of a work's historical context and even of certain psychobiographical factors can often have a more-than-anecdotal bearing on the listener's musical experience. Thus it may well be true – as DeBellis maintains – that such experience, though grounded to some extent in a 'modular' capacity of musical response, nevertheless draws widely on other cognitive resources including that of analytically informed structural listening. But then there seems no compelling reason (formalist prejudice apart) to reject the idea that information of other sorts might play a broadly comparable role, albeit subject to the twin conditions of (1) its demonstrable relevance to the work or passage in hand, and (2) the possibility of bringing out that relevance through an adequately detailed musical analysis in some shape or form. The chief problem with recent debate is that it has managed to create this artificially induced dilemma between a typecast 'formalism' wholly bereft of substantive historical or sociocultural content and a likewise typecast 'reductionist' approach in the latter vein. Moreover, both have tended – through a kind of Newtonian equal-and-opposite-reaction principle – to adopt increasingly doctrinaire stances on the main points at issue and thereby confirm their opponents' worst suspicions.

V

If deconstructive musicologists want to break out of this dead-end predicament then they might take a second (or maybe a first) look at Derrida's essay 'Parergon', where he reflects with extraordinary tact, subtlety and insight on the problems raised by Kant's formalist aesthetic.[63] What emerges from Derrida's reading of the third *Critique* is a series of deep-laid aporias – conflicts, dilemmas, moments of strictly unresolvable impasse – having to do with the Kantian insistence on formal autonomy as an absolute requirement of art and aesthetic disinterest as the absolute condition for appreciating art (or natural beauty) as a matter of purely contemplative (i.e., non-instrumental) pleasure.[64] Thus Kant is constantly obliged, by the logic of his own argument, to posit a range of *de jure* distinctions – as between form and content, 'free' and 'adherent' beauty, intrinsic and extrinsic attributes, 'determinate' and 'indeterminate' modes of judgement – which can be shown to self-deconstruct through the impossibility of holding them firmly in place. That is to say, the entire conceptual structure of this work – along with its crucial justificatory role *vis-à-vis* certain epistemological and ethical issues that were left unresolved in the previous two *Critiques* – turns out to depend upon the use of arguments, examples, metaphors and analogies that are strictly indispensable to Kant's case yet which complicate the logic of that case beyond its power fully to determine or control.

Such is what Derrida describes as the 'parergonal' character of Kant's reasoning (from the Greek '*parergon*' = 'frame', 'border' or 'that which surrounds, encloses, or sets off a work whilst not an integral part of it'). 'Parergonality' thus takes its place as another in the sequence of deviant, non-classical, or paraconsistent logics that Derrida first broached in his readings of 'supplementarity' in Rousseau, the *pharmakon* in Plato, *différance* in Husserl, and 'iterability' in the discourse of Austinian speech-act theory.[65] With Kant it emerges in some obvious ways, as for instance in his strange, surely untenable case for excluding from aesthetic consideration (i.e., from the domain of artistic form, properly so called) such 'parergonal' features as the drapery on statues, the colonnades of palaces, the flying buttresses or other 'merely' functional outworks that support Gothic cathedrals, and so forth. However, it also causes problems for his cardinal distinction between the realms of determinate and indeterminate judgement, or of knowledge (where sensuous intuitions are somehow 'brought under' adequate concepts) and aesthetic experience (where such concepts cannot apply since there would then be no room for that free and harmonious interplay of the faculties which signifies our appreciation of the beautiful). What these difficulties all come down to is the fact that any such Kantian attempt to 'frame' or delimit the proper sphere of aesthetic judgement will always run up against problems, aporias or counter-instances that make it strictly impossible to decide whether some feature should be counted 'intrinsic' or 'extrinsic' to the artwork or our experience of it.

Thus – to take the most obvious and literal case – the frame around a painting would seem parergonal by very definition, yet can scarcely be held to have no effect on our appreciation of the work, since the right choice of frame sets it off to best advantage while the wrong choice may detract from its aesthetic appeal. And things become more complicated still if one considers how far – or by what kind of a priori aesthetic jurisdiction – the frame can serve as an impermeable border between that which properly belongs inside it (i.e., the painting) and that which exists altogether outside its aesthetically privileged space, such as the wall on which it is hung, the other paintings that surround it, or any number of supposedly irrelevant 'background' factors. For here again it is only in deference to certain Kantian formalist distinctions – like those between intrinsic and extrinsic attributes, or 'free' and 'adherent' beauty – that we might feel impelled to maintain what is otherwise (as Derrida's reading brings out) a deeply problematical doctrine. Moreover, this difficulty goes yet deeper since it affects Kant's argument concerning the uniquely contemplative, disinterested, non-instrumental (and hence non-conceptual) character of aesthetic experience. For if this were indeed the case – if concepts (e.g., philosophical concepts) were wholly extrinsic to our appreciation of art – then that experience could in no way be influenced, for better or worse, by our acquaintance with Kant's third *Critique* or any other work of criticism, theory, analysis or aesthetic philosophy.

One has only to state the issue in these terms in order to see how implausible is that position and how pointedly Derrida's reading engages with the aporias not only of Kantian aesthetics but of Kant's entire critical project.

Still it would be wrong – a gross misreading of Derrida's essay – to conclude that this puts him firmly on the side of those (at present a large company of sociologists, cultural theorists, postmodernists and adepts of the New Musicology) who totally reject such formalist ideas as aesthetic autonomy or intrinsic value. Nor does he endorse the 'strong'-sociological claim – advanced most influentially by Pierre Bourdieu – that once disabused of these spurious notions we can view the entire discourse of Kantian and post-Kantian aesthetics as merely the expression of a bourgeois ideology passing itself off as the pure, disinterested judgement of taste.[66] For this is to ignore his repeated point: that such values are deeply intertwined with the wider (i.e., the ethical and sociopolitical) project of enlightened thought, and hence cannot (or should not) be renounced whatever the abuses to which they have been subject and the various ideological admixtures or impurities that have always gone along with them.[67] Thus Derrida expressly repudiates the kinds of wholesale anti-enlightenment thinking associated chiefly with postmodernist thinkers such as Lyotard, and also – on related grounds – the sorts of dismissive or downright contemptuous attitude toward any talk of disinterest, aesthetic value, the *sensus communis* of shared critical judgement, and so forth, adopted by the current debunking school of thought.[68] To be sure, he devotes much of his argument in 'Parergon' and other middle-period writings to a detailed analysis of the way that those cardinal Kantian distinctions – all of which turn on some variant of the pure/impure dichotomy – can be shown to break down, under deconstructive pressure, into further such value-laden binaries (like 'free' versus 'adherent' beauty) that prove just as hard to fix or maintain when subject to critical reading. All the same, as I have said, Derrida is very firm in upholding the 'absolute and principled' necessity that those aims, values and priorities should be kept constantly in view as the only means by which thinking can orient itself toward a better understanding of the various factors and forces that work against their attainment as a matter of ethical or sociopolitical justice.

This is why philosophy takes its place on the 'left bench' of the Kantian parliament of the faculties, that is to say, as a discipline utterly remote from the centres of executive or legislative power. Yet it is a faculty which, for that very reason, should be granted the freedom to question and criticize any uses or abuses of such power, or indeed any item of received belief

– political, moral or theological – that might be enjoined upon those right-bench occupants whose executive status allows them no equivalent freedom.[69] This is also why the discourse of aesthetic judgement, concerned as it is (on the Kantian account) with matters at the furthest possible remove from the interests of government and state, should none the less be seen – and again, for just that reason – as embodying certain, albeit as yet unrealized and perhaps unrealizable values which offer a constant implicit critique of the executive branch. So it can hardly be denied that Derrida's reading goes various elaborate ways around in order to question or to deconstruct the concepts, categories and presuppositions of Kantian formalist aesthetics. However – and it is here that the New Musicologists have most to learn – it does so always in such a way as to conserve their critical valence and thereby maintain the crucial tension between this way of thinking (or the kinds of experience envisaged by its advocates) and the conditions under which it must presently remain a discourse marked by various kinds of contaminating ideological influence. Given time, one could trace this nexus of themes right back to some of Derrida's earliest essays where they are engaged by way of the conflict of interpretations between, on the one hand, a structuralist approach that treats the literary text as an autonomous, self-referential, ahistorical entity and, on the other, a phenomenological approach that treats it as expressing – inevitably so – a wide range of sociocultural as well as individual or subjective meanings.[70] Here again he adopts not a blandly accommodating line that would simply defuse the issue but, in the strictest sense, a deconstructive mode of engagement that locates the precise points of tension, aporias or methodological blindspots on both sides so as to achieve a more adequate grasp of the interests and commitments at stake.

My point in all this is that the New Musicologists – or some of them – have been too quick to claim Derridean warrant for certain of their claims with regard to the bankrupt, ideologically complicitous character of music analysis in general and (more specifically) formalist notions of structural listening or long-range thematic and tonal integration. What is being played out in these somewhat predictable debates – like that between Dunsby and Street – is yet another version of the well-worn 'analytic' versus 'continental' spat in recent (mainly Anglophone) philosophy. Thus analytical types charge the continentals with indulging deplorably lax standards of conceptual clarity and grasp while the latter see nothing in that rival discourse but a narrow-minded professionalism which treats all philosophy as aspiring to the strictly self-evident (hence tautological or vacuous) status of the analytic proposition.[71] If there is one area of study where such pseudo-dilemmas should have no place it is that of music criticism, taken (one would hope uncontroversially) to embrace whatever kinds of approach can be shown to enhance our understanding of and pleasure in the experience of music. No doubt there are some theorists who will indeed controvert the naïve or hopefully ecumenical assumption underlying that last sentence. That is, they will take issue with the joint claim that better, more refined or structurally informed understanding is itself a great source of musical pleasure, and again, that such pleasure is by no means just an unwitting product of 'aesthetic ideology' or a mere distraction from the sorts of hard-headed *Ideologiekritik* that would expose its less-than-edifying cultural and sociopolitical origins. Amongst them, as I have said, are certain deconstructive musicologists who cast a cold eye on the very idea – the 'eudaimonic' delusion, in de Man's parlance – that pleasure might have any significant role to play in an undeceived, rigorous, critically alert response to those works (or to the discourse about them) that solicit our enjoyment on terms unacceptable by any such exacting standard.[72]

All the more ironic, therefore, that these theorists should also have taken to denouncing formal-structural 'analysis' as an adjunct to the strain of aesthetic ideology which supposedly promotes this complicity with suspect modes of musical experience. After all, until quite recently – in fact, around the time of Kerman's landmark intervention – the main dispute within music criticism was that between 'appreciative' and 'analytic' schools of thought, a dispute going back (as I mentioned at the start of this chapter) to the early days of textual close-reading as a literary-critical method. So it is strange, and a symptom of the currently widespread 'hermeneutics of suspicion', that we should now have a sizeable number of music theorists – something like a new orthodoxy – for whom both approaches must be treated with the utmost caution (or even rejected *tout court*) since they each bear witness to the powerful hold of an aesthetic creed that exerts, in de Man's admonitory phrase, a decisive claim on the 'shape and limits of our freedom'.[73] It seems to me, for reasons argued above, that one unfortunate result of such over-zealous transpositions from one domain (literary theory) to another (music criticism) is to dictate the shape and limits of our musical experience in a way that excludes – or at any rate sternly disapproves – just about everything which gives that experience its ultimate meaning and value.

This is not to deny – far from it – that theory, including those particular strains that I have criticized here, has a proper and legitimate place in musicological discourse. So it does, to be sure, in all areas or disciplines of thought where a refusal to theorize most often betokens either sheer intellectual laziness or (as the deconstructors would claim) an unthinking adherence to received ideologies whose own theoretical content is passed off as straightforward, natural or common-sense wisdom. Besides, it follows from my brief excursion into the field of cognitive psychology that our experience of music can often be affected – significantly changed or enhanced – not only by the reading of perceptive music analyses but also by acquaintance with certain theoretical ideas, among them (quite possibly) those advanced by deconstructive musicologists.[74] Thus, for instance, our understanding/appreciation of Beethoven's late quartets (or the Brahms piano pieces discussed by Alan Street) might well stand to gain through our taking account of those features that hold out against any overly 'organicist' interpretation. Indeed, this idea that musical value may have to do precisely with the conflict or tension between background norms of structural unity and other, more disruptive, foreground elements is one that finds favour even with critics, such as Leonard Meyer, who are often pilloried by the New Musicologists as slavish adherents to the old 'formalist' paradigm.[75] Yet it is hard to see how such an argument could work, or such values apply, were it not for those same normative expect-ations – of structural development, thematic contrast, tonal progression, and so forth – which constitute a point of reference and departure for whatever strikes the well-attuned listener as marking a break with estab-lished modes of compositional practice.

Still less could it work on the curious premise – one shared, be it noted, not only by de Man but also by a high formalist like Kant – that any taint of sensuous experience in our thinking about issues of aesthetic worth or (in the present context) of musical structure and meaning must betoken, as Kant puritanically puts it, a 'pathological' admixture of motives or desires at odds with the properly disinterested character of aesthetic experience or judgement.[76] While the New Musicologists are pretty much united in rejecting Kant's claims for aesthetic disinterest, formal autonomy, 'pure' as opposed to 'impure' modes of judgement, and so forth, they are oddly in accord when it comes to his deep mistrust of that whole dimension of aesthetic experience where the pleasures of sensuous apprehension are closely bound up with those of cognitive understanding and structural grasp. What this gives us, in effect, is the worst of both worlds: an approach whose foregone theoretical commitments enjoin us to renounce (or at any rate to treat with the greatest suspicion) not only the sensuous experience of music but also the heightened pleasure and appreciation that comes of an informed musical understanding. I have suggested that such thinking takes rise from a number of erroneous premises, chief among them the idea that structural analysis must always entail the subscription to some kind of doctrinaire organicist creed, thus revealing the grip of an aesthetic ideology that conflates the realm of linguistic signification with the realm of natural processes or forms. However, this idea is itself the result of a drastic and unwarranted conflation. That is to say, it extrapolates directly from the domain of literary theory – which of course has to do with linguistic texts and where the argument thus has a certain force against the more naïve and perhaps ideologically loaded sorts of naturalistic fallacy – to the domain of music criticism where altogether different considerations apply.

Along with this goes the claim – with its principal source, again, in de Man's writings – that any appeal to the sensory-perceptual experience of music is likewise suspect by reason of that same delusory grounding in those natural phenomena (e.g., the tonal system or overtone-series) that constitute the essence of musical meaning and value. To be sure, such notions if pushed to an extreme have shown themselves amenable to ideological uses, as for instance in Schenker's chauvinist application of them and in kindred claims for the hegemonic status of the 'mainstream', 'classical' (i.e., Austro-German) musical tradition. They are also quite explicit – ironically enough, given his life-history and fervent opposition to any such creed when deployed to overtly nationalist ends – in Schoenberg's idea of the dodecaphonic system as ensuring the continued pre-eminence of that same tradition through its progressive explor-ation of harmonic resources that didn't so much break altogether with tonality as move further out along the overtone-series or circle of fifths.[77] However, it is absurd to suppose that there must always be some deep-laid ideological bias at work whenever critics, analysts or musically informed listeners betray some adherence to the notion of music as gaining much of its expressive power through the affinity that exists between certain tonal or harmonic structures and certain modes of listener-response. Still less can it be warranted to take this as grounds for rejecting the idea that analysis might play a useful, pleasure-enhancing, even (at times) trans-formative role in making the process more readily available to conscious, reflective understanding.

Empson got it right, I suggest, when he remarked in *Seven Types of Ambiguity* that poetic 'appreciation' has nothing to fear from exposure to verbal analysis since good poetry can only benefit from intelligent and perceptive close reading while the pleasures it affords are sufficiently robust to withstand other, less sensitive or tactful approaches.[78] The same is true of musical analysis and moreover – be it said – of music theory just so long as it doesn't invent a whole range of counter-intuitive and misconceived grounds for rejecting what analysis can fairly claim to offer, not only as a matter of formal demonstration but also in terms of heightened appreciative yield. After all, as Empson puts it, 'normal sensibility is a tissue of what has been conscious theory made habitual and returned to the pre-conscious, and, therefore, conscious theory may make an addition to sensibility'.[79] And again: 'the act of knowing is itself an act of sympathising; unless you are enjoying the poetry you cannot create it, as poetry, in your mind'.[80] It seems to me that these claims are strongly borne out by a good deal of recent work in cognitive psychology as well as by the way that a critic like Rosen – one with a wide range of philosophic as well as literary, cultural-historical, and of course music-analytical interests – can provide such a depth of interpretative insight as to render any charge of 'aesthetic ideology' (in his case at least) just a tedious irrelevance. Where theory works to best, most telling effect is not so much by advancing wholesale diagnoses in the deconstructionist mode but rather by promoting a more reflective awareness of how music relates to the various discourses – those of analysis and historiography among them – which undoubtedly inform our perceptual responses yet not to the point of through-and-through ideological conditioning envisaged by some current thinkers. Hence my chief claim in this book: that the best way of promoting and refining that awareness is through a qualified Platonist approach which conserves a sufficiently robust conception of the work, its properties, structure and formal attributes while also respecting the listener's share in the process of its creative–imaginative realization.

Notes

Chapter 1

1   For relevant discussion of realism in logic, mathematics and the formal sciences see William P. Alston, *A Realist Conception of Truth* (Ithaca, NY: Cornell University Press, 1996); Bob Hale, *Abstract Objects* (Oxford: Basil Blackwell, 1987); Jerrold J. Katz, *Realistic Rationalism* (Cambridge, MA: MIT Press, 1998); Scott Soames, *Understanding Truth* (Oxford: Oxford University Press, 1999). From an anti-realist standpoint, see Michael Dummett, *Truth and Other Enigmas* (London: Duckworth, 1978) and *The Logical Basis of Metaphysics* (London: Duckworth, 1991); also Michael Luntley, *Language, Logic and Experience: the case for anti-realism* (London: Duckworth, 1988); Neil Tennant, *The Taming of the True* (Oxford: Oxford University Press, 1997).

2   For further discussion, see Ben Caplan and Carl Matheson, 'Can a Musical Work be Created?', *British Journal of Aesthetics*, 44 (2004): 113–34; Gregory Currie, *An Ontology of Art* (London: Macmillan, 1989); Julian Dodd, 'Musical Works as Eternal Types', *The British Journal of Aesthetics*, 40 (2000): 424–40; 'Defending Musical Platonism', *The British Journal of Aesthetics*, 42 (2002): 380–402; 'Types, Continuants, and the Ontology of Music', *British Journal of Aesthetics*, 44 (2004): 342–60; Peter Kivy, 'Platonism in Music: A kind of defence' and 'Platonism in Music: another kind of defence', in *The Fine Art of Repetition* (Cambridge: Cambridge University Press, 1993), pp. 35–58 and 59–74; Jerrold Levinson, 'What a Musical Work Is' and 'What a Musical Work Is, Again', in *Music, Art and Metaphysics: essays in philosophical aesthetics* (Ithaca, NY: Cornell University Press, 1990), pp. 63–88 and 215–63; Robert A. Sharpe, 'Music, Platonism and Performance: some ontological strains', *British Journal of Aesthetics*, 35 (1995): 38–48; Nicholas Wolterstorff, *Works and Worlds of Art* (Oxford: Clarendon Press, 1980).

3   On response-dependence as a topic in present-day epistemology and philosophy of mind, see for instance Mark Johnston, 'Dispositional

Theories of Value', *Proceedings of the Aristotelian Society*, 63 (1989): 139–74; Philip Pettit, 'Realism and Response Dependence', *Mind*, 100 (1991): 597–626; Mark Powell, 'Realism or Response-Dependence?', *European Review of Philosophy*, 3 (1998): 1–13; Ralph Wedgwood, 'The Essence of Response-Dependence', *European Review of Philosophy*, 3 (1998): 31–54; also – for a critical survey of the field – Christopher Norris, *Truth Matters: realism, anti-realism and response-dependence* (Edinburgh: Edinburgh University Press, 2002).

4   Karl R. Popper, *Unended Quest* (London: Collins/Fontana, 1976).

5   See Note 1, above; also David M. Armstrong, *Universals and Scientific Realism*, 2 vols (Cambridge: Cambridge University Press, 1978); Michael Devitt, *Realism and Truth*, 2nd edn (Oxford: Basil Blackwell, 1986); Jarrett Leplin (ed.), *Scientific Realism* (Berkeley and Los Angeles, CA: University of California Press, 1984); Norris, *Truth Matters* and *Language, Logic and Epistemology: a modal-realist approach* (London: Macmillan, 2004); Karl R. Popper, *Realism and the Aim of Science* (London: Routledge, 1999); Stathis Psillos, *Scientifc Realism: how science tracks truth* (London: Routledge, 1999).

6   See Notes 1 and 3, above; also – from a range of constructivist or anti-realist viewpoints – David Bloor, *Knowledge and Social Imagery* (London: Routledge & Kegan Paul, 1976); Barry Barnes, *Scientific Knowledge and Sociological Theory* (London: Routledge & Kegan Paul, 1974); Steve Fuller, *Social Epistemology* (Bloomington, IN: Indiana University Press, 1988); Richard Rorty, *Contingency, Irony, and Solidarity* (Cambridge: Cambridge University Press, 1989) and *Objectivity, Relativism, and Truth* (Cambridge: Cambridge University Press, 1991); Steve Woolgar, *Science: the very idea* (London: Tavistock Press, 1988). For critical discussion of these and kindred views, see Martin Hollis and Steven Lukes (eds), *Rationality and Relativism* (Oxford: Basil Blackwell, 1982); W. H. Newton-Smith, *The Rationality of Science* (London: Routledge & Kegan Paul, 1981); R. Nola (ed.), *Relativism and Realism in Science* (Dordrecht: Kluwer, 1988); Christopher Norris, *Against Relativism: philosophy of science, deconstruction and critical theory* (Oxford: Basil Blackwell, 1997).

7   See for instance Katherine Bergeron and Philip V. Bohlman (eds), *Disciplining Music: musicology and its canons* (Chicago, IL: University of Chicago Press, 1992); Nicholas Cook and Mark Everist (eds), *Re-Thinking Music* (Oxford: Oxford University Press, 1999); Lydia Goehr, *The Imaginary Museum of Musical Works: an essay in the philosophy of music* (Oxford: Clarendon Press, 1992); Kevin Korsyn, 'Brahms

Research and Aesthetic Ideology', *Music Analysis,* 12 (1993): 89–103; Lawrence Kramer, *Classical Music and Postmodern Knowledge* (Berkeley and Los Angeles, CA: University of California Press, 1995); Judy Lochhead and Joseph Auner (eds), *Postmodern Music/Postmodern Thought* (New York and London: Garland, 2002); Ruth A. Solie (ed.), *Musicology and Difference* (Berkeley and Los Angeles, CA: University of California Press, 1993); also – among the chief sources of this anti-organicist line of thought – Paul de Man, *Aesthetic Ideology,* ed. Andrzej Warminski (Minneapolis, MN: University of Minnesota Press, 1996); Philippe Lacoue-Labarthe and Jean-Luc Nancy, *The Literary Absolute: the theory of literature in German Romanticism,* trans. Philip Barnard and Cheryl Lester (Albany, NY: State University of New York Press, 1988).

8   Friedrich Nietzsche, *The Birth of Tragedy out of the Spirit of Music,* trans. Shaun Whiteside, ed. Michael Tanner (Harmondsworth: Penguin, 1993).

9   Arthur Schopenhauer, *The World as Will and Idea,* 3 vols (London: Routledge & Kegan Paul, 1964).

10 Immanuel Kant, *Critique of Judgement,* trans. J. C. Meredith (Oxford: Clarendon Press, 1978).

11 See especially Kevin Barry, *Language, Music and the Sign* (Cambridge: Cambridge University Press, 1987) and John Neubauer, *The Emancipation of Music from Language: departure from mimesis in eighteenth-century aesthetics* (New Haven, CT: Yale University Press, 1986).

12 See entries under Note 11, above.

13 Barry, *Language, Music and the Sign.*

14 For the classic statement of this *echt*-formalist view, see Eduard Hanslick, *Vom Musikalisch-Schönen* (1891): *The Beautiful in Music,* trans. Gustav Cohen (Indianapolis, IN: Bobbs-Merrill, 1957). For a qualified defence of musical formalism, see also Peter Kivy, *The Corded Shell: reflections on musical expression* (Princeton, NJ: Princeton University Press, 1980) and *The Fine Art of Repetition: essays in the philosophy of music* (Cambridge: Cambridge University Press, 1993).

15 See Note 7.

16 See Pieter C. van den Toorn, *Music, Politics and the Academy* (Berkeley and Los Angeles, CA: University of California Press, 1995); also – in likewise critical but somewhat less hostile vein – Peter Kivy, *New Essays on Musical Understanding* (Oxford: Oxford University Press, 2001) and Christopher Norris, 'The Perceiver's Share (2): deconstructive musicology and cognitive science', in Norris, *Language, Logic and Epistemology,* pp. 185–226.

17 For examples that pretty much cover the range, see Note 6, above; also – at the latter extreme – Susan McClary, *Feminine Endings: music, gender, and sexuality* (Minneapolis, MN: University of Minnesota Press, 1981) and *Conventional Wisdom: the content of musical form* (Berkeley and Los Angeles, CA: University of California Press, 2000); Gary Tomlinson, 'Musical Pasts and Postmodern Musicologies: a response to Lawrence Kramer', *Current Musicology*, 53 (1993): 16–40.

18 See especially Joseph Kerman, 'How We Got into Analysis, and how to get out', *Critical Inquiry*, 7 (1980): 311–31; 'A Few Canonic Variations', *Critical Inquiry*, 10 (1983): 107–25; *Musicology* (London: Fontana, 1985); also Ian Bent and William Drabkin, *Analysis* (Basingstoke: Macmillan, 1987); Scott Burnham, 'A.B. Marx and the Gendering of Sonata Form', in Ian Bent (ed.), *Music Theory in the Age of Romanticism* (Cambridge: Cambridge University Press, 1996), pp. 163–86; Nicholas Cook, 'Music Theory and "Good Comparison": a Viennese perspective', *Journal of Music Theory*, 33 (1989): 117–42 and *A Guide to Musical Analysis* (Oxford: Oxford University Press, 1993); Douglas Dempster and Matthew Brown, 'Evaluating Musical Analyses and Theories: five perspectives', *Journal of Music Theory*, 34 (1990): 247–80; Jonathan Dunsby and Arnold Whittall, *Music Analysis in Theory and Practice* (New Haven, CT: Yale University Press, 1988); Anthony Pople, *Theory, Analysis, and Meaning in Music* (Cambridge: Cambridge University Press, 1994); Ruth A. Solie, 'The Living Work: organicism and musical analysis', *Nineteenth-Century Musicology*, 4 (1980): 147–56.

19 For a range of views on this topic of musical Platonism, see entries under Note 2, above.

20 See Note 3, above.

21 See Notes 1 and 3, above; also Paul Benacerraf, 'What Numbers Could Not Be', in Benacerraf and Hilary Putnam (eds), *The Philosophy of Mathematics: selected essays*, 2nd edn (Cambridge: Cambridge University Press, 1983), pp. 272–94; Hartry Field, *Realism, Mathematics and Modality* (Oxford: Basil Blackwell, 1989); Kurt Gödel, 'What Is Cantor's Continuum Problem?', in Benacerraf and Putnam (eds), *Philosophy of Mathematics*, pp. 470–85; Putnam, *Mathematics, Matter and Method* (Cambridge: Cambridge University Press, 1975).

22 See Norris, *Truth Matters*; also Crispin Wright, 'Moral Values, Projection, and Secondary Qualities', *Proceedings of the Aristotelian Society*, (supplementary vol.) 62 (1988): 1–26.

23 See especially Michael Williams, *Unnatural Doubts: epistemological realism and the basis of scepticism* (Princeton, NJ: Princeton University Press, 1996).

24 See Hilary Putnam, *Reason, Truth and History* (Cambridge: Cambridge University Press, 1981); Crispin Wright, *Truth and Objectivity* (Cambridge, MA: Harvard University Press, 1992); also entries under Note 2, above.

25 Norris, *Truth Matters.*

26 See Note 1.

27 Wright, *Truth and Objectivity*; Plato, *Euthyphro*, in *The Dialogues of Plato*, Vol. 1, trans. R. E. Allen (New Haven, CT: Yale University Press, 1984).

28 Antony Flew, 'Theology and Falsification', in Joel Feinberg (ed.), *Reason and Responsibility: readings in some basic problems of philosophy* (Belmont, CA: Dickenson, 1969), pp. 47–60.

29 From a phenomenological standpoint, see for instance Ernest Ansermet, *Les Fondements de la musique dans la conscience humaine* (Neuchatel: Edition de la Baconnière, 1961); Vladimir Jankélevitch, *Ravel*, trans. Margaret Crosland (New York: Grove Press, 1959) and *Gabriel Fauré: ses mélodies, son esthétique* (Paris: Plon, 1951); Maurice Merleau-Ponty, *The Phenomenology of Perception*, trans. Colin Smith (London: Routledge & Kegan Paul, 1962); *Signs*, trans. Richard C. McCleary (Evanston, IL: Northwestern University Press, 1964); *Sense and Non-Sense*, trans. Hubert L. Dreyfus and Patricia A. Dreyfus (Evanston, IL: Northwestern University Press, 1964); *The Visible and the Invisible*, trans. A. Lingis (Evanston, IL: Northwestern University Press, 1975); also Roman Ingarden, *The Work of Music and the Problem of its Identity*, trans. Adam Czerniawski (London: Macmillan, 1986).

30 See Note 27.

31 See Norris, *Truth Matters*; John Locke, *An Essay Concerning Human Understanding*, ed. A. S. Pringle-Pattison (Oxford: Oxford University Press, 1969), Book II, Ch. 8, Section 15, p. 69.

32 See Note 1, above; also Mark Johnston, 'How to Speak of the Colours', *Philosophical Studies*, 68 (1992): 221–63 and 'Objectivity Refigured: pragmatism without verificationism', in J. Haldane and C. Wright (eds), *Realism, Representation and Projection* (Oxford: Oxford University Press, 1993), pp. 85–130.

33 See J. L. Aronson, 'Testing for Convergent Realism', *British Journal for the Philosophy of Science*, 40 (1989): 255–60; Richard Boyd, 'The Current Status of Scientific Realism', in Jarrett Leplin (ed.), *Scientific Realism* (Berkeley and Los Angeles, CA: University of California Press, 1984), pp. 41–82; Peter Lipton, *Inference to the Best Explanation* (London: Routledge, 1993); Hilary Putnam, *Mind, Language and Reality* (Cambridge: Cambridge University Press, 1975).

34   See Boyd, 'The Current Status of Scientific Realism'.

35   Eugene Wigner, 'The Unreasonable Effectiveness of Mathematics in the Physical Sciences', in *Symmetries and Reflections* (Cambridge, MA: MIT Press, 1960), pp. 222–37; p. 237.

36   See Notes 1 and 21, above.

37   See Dummett, *Truth and Other Enigmas* and *Elements of Intuitionism* (Oxford: Oxford University Press, 1977); Gottlob Frege, 'The Thought', in *The Frege Reader*, ed. Michael Beaney (Oxford: Basil Blackwell, 1997), pp. 181–93; Crispin Wright, *Frege's Conception of Numbers as Objects* (Aberdeen: Aberdeen University Press, 1983).

38   See Notes 1 and 21, above.

39   See John Divers and Alexander Miller, 'Arithmetical Platonism: reliability and judgement-dependence', *Philosophical Studies*, 95 (1999): 277–310 and Miller, 'Rule-Following, Response-Dependence, and McDowell's Debate with Anti-Realism', *European Review of Philosophy*, 3 (1998): 175–97.

40   John McDowell, *Mind and World* (Cambridge, MA: Harvard University Press, 1994).

41   Miller, 'Rule-Following, Response-Dependence, and McDowell's Debate with Anti-Realism', p. 178.

42   McDowell, *Mind and World*; Immanuel Kant, *Critique of Pure Reason*, trans. N. Kemp Smith (London: Macmillan, 1964).

43   McDowell, *Mind and World*, p. 41.

44   Norris, *Truth Matters*.

45   Wilfrid Sellars, *Empiricism and the Philosophy of Mind*, ed. Robert Brandom (Cambridge, MA: Harvard University Press, 1997).

46   Robert B. Brandom, *Making it Explicit: reasoning, representing and discursive commitment* (Cambridge, MA: Harvard University Press, 1994) and *Articulating Reasons: an introduction to inferentialism* (Cambridge, MA: Harvard University Press, 2000).

47   See Notes 7, 18 and 19, above.

48   For a particularly fine example, see Charles Rosen, *The Classical Style*, rev. edn (London: Faber & Faber, 1976).

49   See, for instance, Josef Bleicher, *Contemporary Hermeneutics: hermeneutics as method, philosophy and critique* (London: Routledge & Kegan Paul, 1980); Kurt Müller-Vollmer (ed.), *The Hermeneutics Reader* (New York: Continuum, 1988); Richard E. Palmer, *Hermeneutics: interpretation theory in Schleiermacher, Dilthey, Heidegger, and Gadamer* (Evanston, IL: Northwestern University Press, 1979); Paul Ricoeur, *Hermeneutics and the Human Sciences* (Cambridge: Cambridge University Press, 1981).

50   See Note 6.

51   See especially Pierre Bourdieu, *Distinction: a social critique of the judgement of taste*, trans. R. Nice (Cambridge, MA: Harvard University Press, 1984).

52   See Hanns Eisler, *A Rebel in Music*, ed. Manfred Grabs (London: Kahn & Averill, 2000); also Eric Bentley, *Thirty Years of Treason: excerpts from hearings before the House Committee on Un-American Activities, 1938–1968* (New York: Nation Books, 2002); Albrecht Betz, *Hanns Eisler: political musician* (Cambridge: Cambridge University Press, 1983); David Blake (ed.), *Hanns Eisler: a miscellany* (London: Harwood, 1996); John Willett, *Art and Politics in the Weimar Period* (London: Da Capo Press, 1996). On the methods deployed by US 'security' and intelligence agencies to harass, suborn, cajole and persecute the émigré German intellectual community of 'premature anti-fascists', see Alexander Stephan, *Communazis* (New Haven, CT: Yale University Press, 2001).

53   See Alan Bush and Bertha Stevens (eds), *Bernard Stevens: a symposium* (London: Kahn & Averill, 1986); Duncan Hall, *A Pleasant Change from Politics: music and the British Labour movement between the wars* (London: New Clarion Press, 2001); Christopher Norris (ed.), *Music and the Politics of Culture* (London: Lawrence & Wishart, 1989); also – for a longer historical and sociocultural perspective – Robert Stradling and Meirion Hughes, *The English Musical Renaissance, 1840–1940*, 2nd edn (Manchester: Manchester University Press, 2001).

54   Miller, 'Rule-Following, Response-Dependence, and McDowell's Debate with Anti-Realism', p. 178.

55   Ibid, p. 177.

Chapter 2

1   On the topic of response-dependence, see Mark Johnston, 'How to Speak of the Colours', *Philosophical Studies*, 68 (1992): 221–63, and 'Objectivity Refigured', in J. Haldane and C. Wright (eds), *Realism, Representation and Projection* (Oxford: Oxford University Press, 1993), pp. 85–130; Christopher Norris, *Truth Matters: realism, anti-realism and response-dependence* (Edinburgh: Edinburgh University Press, 2002); Philip Pettit, 'Realism and Response Dependence', *Mind*, 100 (1991): 597–626; Mark Powell, 'Realism or Response-Dependence?', *European Review of Philosophy*, 3 (1998): 1–13; Ralph Wedgwood, 'The Essence of Response-Dependence', *European Review of Philosophy*, 3

(1998): 31–54; Crispin Wright, 'Euthyphronism and the Physicality of Colour', *European Review of Philosophy*, 3 (1998): 15–30 and *Truth and Objectivity* (Cambridge, MA: Harvard University Press, 1992).

2   See especially Peter Railton, 'Red, Bitter, Good', *European Review of Philosophy*, 3 (1998): 67–84 and Crispin Wright, 'Moral Values, Projection, and Secondary Qualities', *Proceedings of the Aristotelian Society*, (supplementary vol.) 62 (1988): 1–26

3   Wright, *Truth and Objectivity*.

4   See Norris, *Truth Matters*; also J. L. Aronson, 'Testing for Convergent Realism', *British Journal for the Philosophy of Science*, 40 (1989): 255–60; J. Aronson, R. Harré and E. Way, *Realism Rescued: how scientific progress is possible* (London: Duckworth, 1994); Richard Boyd, 'The Current Status of Scientific Realism', in Jarrett Leplin (ed.), *Scientific Realism* (Berkeley and Los Angeles, CA: University of California Press, 1984), pp. 41–82; Michael Devitt, *Realism and Truth*, 2nd edn (Oxford: Basil Blackwell, 1986); Gilbert Harman, 'Inference to the Best Explanation', *Philosophical Review*, 74 (1965): 88–95; Peter Lipton, *Inference to the Best Explanation* (London: Routledge, 1993); Stathis Psillos, *Scientific Realism: how science tracks truth* (London: Routledge, 1999); Wesley C. Salmon, *Scientific Explanation and the Causal Structure of the World* (Princeton, NJ: Princeton University Press, 1984).

5   See Notes 1 and 2, above; also Norris, 'Response-Dependence: what's in it for the realist?', in *Epistemology: key concepts in philosophy* (London: Continuum, 2005), pp. 99–128.

6   Plato, *Euthyphro*, in *The Dialogues of Plato*, Vol. 1, trans. R. E. Allen (New Haven, CT: Yale University Press, 1984); also Wright, *Truth and Objectivity*.

7   See Michael Dummett, *Truth and Other Enigmas* (London: Duckworth, 1978), *The Logical Basis of Metaphysics* (London: Duckworth, 1991), and *The Seas of Language* (Oxford: Clarendon Press, 1993); also Michael Luntley, *Language, Logic and Experience: the case for anti-realism* (London: Duckworth, 1988); Neil Tennant, *Anti-Realism and Logic* (Oxford: Clarendon Press, 1987) and *The Taming of the True* (Oxford: Oxford University Press, 1997).

8   For a range of views, see Hartry Field, *Realism, Mathematics and Modality* (Oxford: Basil Blackwell, 1989); Bob Hale, *Abstract Objects* (Oxford: Basil Blackwell, 1987) and 'Is Platonism Epistemologically Bankrupt?', *Philosophical Review*, 103 (1994): 299–325; Jerrold J. Katz, *Realistic Rationalism* (Cambridge, MA.: MIT Press, 1998); Hilary Putnam, *Mathematics, Matter and Method* (Cambridge: Cambridge University Press, 1975); Scott Soames, *Understanding Truth* (Oxford:

Oxford University Press, 1999); Crispin Wright, *Frege's Conception of Numbers as Objects* (Aberdeen: Aberdeen University Press, 1983).

9　For further argument to this effect, see Norris, *Truth Matters*.

10　For a range of views on this issue, see Ben Caplan and Carl Matheson, 'Can a Musical Work be Created?', *British Journal of Aesthetics*, 44 (2004): 113–34; Gregory Currie, *An Ontology of Art* (London: Macmillan, 1989); Julian Dodd, 'Musical Works as Eternal Types', *The British Journal of Aesthetics*, 40 (2000): 424–40; 'Defending Musical Platonism', *The British Journal of Aesthetics*, 42 (2002): 380–402; 'Types, Continuants, and the Ontology of Music', *British Journal of Aesthetics*, 44 (2004): 342–60; Peter Kivy, 'Platonism in Music: a kind of defense' and 'Platonism in Music: another kind of defense', in *The Fine Art of Repetition* (Cambridge: Cambridge University Press, 1993), pp. 35–58 and 59–74; Jerrold Levinson, 'What a Musical Work Is' and 'What a Musical Work Is, Again', in *Music, Art and Metaphysics: essays in philosophical aesthetics* (Ithaca, NY: Cornell University Press, 1990), pp. 63–88 and 215–63; Robert A. Sharpe, 'Music, Platonism and Performance: some ontological strains', *British Journal of Aesthetics*, 35 (1995): 38–48; Nicholas Wolterstorff, *Works and Worlds of Art* (Oxford: Clarendon Press, 1980).

11　T. W. Adorno, 'Bach Defended Against His Devotees', in *Prisms*, trans. Samuel and Shierry Weber (London: Spearman, 1967), pp. 133–46.

12　See Dummett, *Truth and Other Enigmas*; also *Elements of Intuitionism* (Oxford: Oxford University Press, 1977).

13　This debate is taken up by Field, Hale, Katz, Soames and others (see Note 8, above).

14　See Note 4, above.

15　Dummett, *Truth and Other Enigmas*.

16　I take this very apt example from Soames, *Understanding Truth*.

17　For various, more-or-less qualified statements of this view, see Katherine Bergeron and Philip V. Bohlman (eds), *Disciplining Music: musicology and its canons* (Chicago, IL: University of Chicago Press, 1992); Marcia J. Citron, *Gender and the Musical Canon* (Cambridge: Cambridge University Press, 1993); Nicholas Cook and Mark Everist (eds), *Re-Thinking Music* (Oxford: Oxford University Press, 1999); Lydia Goehr, *The Imaginary Museum of Musical Works: an essay in the philosophy of music* (Oxford: Clarendon Press, 1992); Joseph Kerman, 'How We Got into Analysis, and How to Get Out', *Critical Inquiry*, 7 (1980): 311–31; Lawrence Kramer, *Classical Music and Postmodern Knowledge* (Berkeley and Los Angeles, CA: University of California Press, 1995); Judy Lochhead and Joseph Auner (eds),

Postmodern Music/Postmodern Thought (New York and London: Garland, 2002); Susan McClary, *Feminine Endings: music, gender, and sexuality* (Minneapolis, MN: University of Minnesota Press, 1981) and *Conventional Wisdom: the content of musical form* (Berkeley and Los Angeles, CA: University of California Press, 2000); Ruth A. Solie (ed.), *Musicology and Difference* (Berkeley and Los Angeles, CA: University of California Press, 1993); Robert Stradling and Meirion Hughes, *The English Musical Renaissance, 1860–1940: construction and deconstruction*, 2nd edn. (Manchester: Manchester University Press, 2001).

18   See Note 17; also Rose Rosengard Subotnik, *Developing Variations: style and ideology in Western music* (Minneapolis, MN: University of Minnesota Press, 1991) and *Deconstructive Variations: music and reason in Western society* (Minneapolis, MN: University of Minnesota Press, 1996).

19   W. V. O. Quine, 'Two Dogmas of Empiricism', in *From a Logical Point of View*, 2nd edn (Cambridge, MA: Harvard University Press, 1961), pp. 20–46.

20   See especially John McDowell, *Mind and World* (Cambridge, MA: Harvard University Press, 1994).

21   McDowell, *Mind and World*; also Christopher Norris, 'McDowell on Kant: redrawing the bounds of sense' and 'The Limits of Naturalism: further thoughts on McDowell's *Mind and World*', in *Minding the Gap: epistemology and philosophy of science in the two traditions* (Amherst, MA: University of Massachusetts Press, 2000), pp. 172–96 and 197–230.

22   Jacques Derrida, '"Genesis and Structure" and Phenomenology', in *Writing and Difference*, trans. Alan Bass (London: Routledge & Kegan Paul, 1978), pp. 154–68; *Edmund Husserl's 'Origin of Geometry': an introduction*, trans. John P. Leavey (Pittsburgh, PA: Duquesne University Press, 1978); *Le problème de la genèse dans la philosophie de Husserl* (Paris: Presses Universitaires de France, 1990); also *'Speech and Phenomena' and Other Essays on Husserl's Theory of Signs*, trans. David B. Allison (Evanston, IL: Northwestern University Press, 1973).

23   Derrida, *Edmund Husserl's 'Origin of Geometry'*.

24   Derrida, 'Genesis and Structure', pp. 158–9.

25   Ibid., p. 162.

26   See Norris, *Truth Matters*.

27   See Notes 20 and 21, above.

28   See Notes 1, 4, 7 and 8, above.

29   Derrida, 'Structure and Genesis', p. 160.

30   Gottlob Frege, review of Edmund Husserl's *Philosophie der Arithmetik*, trans. by E.-H. W. Kluge, *Mind*, 81 (1972): 321–37; also Gilbert Ryle,

'Phenomenology', 'Review of Martin Farber, *The Foundations of Phenomenology*', and 'Phenomenology versus *The Concept of Mind*', in Ryle, *Collected Papers*, Vol. 1 (London: Hutchinson, 1971), pp. 167–78, 215–24 and 179–96

31 See Dummett, *The Origins of Analytic Philosophy* (London: Duckworth, 1993).

32 Dagfinn Føllesdal, 'Husserl and Frege: a contribution to elucidating the origins of phenomenological philosophy', in Leila Haaparanta (ed.), *Mind, Meaning and Mathematics: essays on the philosophical views of Husserl and Frege* (Dordrecht and Boston: Kluwer, 1994), pp. 3–47; J. N. Mohanty, *Transcendental Phenomenology: an analytic account* (Oxford: Basil Blackwell, 1989); also Johanna Maria Tito, *Logic in the Husserlian Context* (Evanston, IL: Northwestern University Press, 1990).

33 L. E. J. Brouwer, *Collected Works*, Vol. 1, *Philosophy and Foundations of Mathematics*, ed. A. Heyting (Amsterdam: North-Holland, 1975), p. 134.

34 See Notes 7 and 12, above.

35 See Norris, *Truth Matters*; also John Divers and Alexander Miller, 'Arithmetical Platonism: reliability and judgement-dependence', *Philosophical Studies*, 95 (1999): 277–310 and Miller, 'Rule-Following, Response-Dependence, and McDowell's Debate with Anti-Realism', *European Review of Philosophy*, 3 (1998): 175–97.

36 See Note 35, above.

37 See especially J. Alberto Coffa, *The Semantic Tradition from Kant to Carnap: to the Vienna Station* (Cambridge: Cambridge University Press, 1991); also Hilary Putnam, *Realism and Reason* (Cambridge: Cambridge University Press, 1983).

38 See Devitt, *Realism and Truth*, for some strong arguments to this effect.

39 David Lewis, *The Plurality of Worlds* (Oxford: Basil Blackwell, 1986), p. 109.

40 Ibid., p. 109.

41 Eugene Wigner, 'The Unreasonable Effectiveness of Mathematics in the Physical Sciences', in *Symmetries and Reflections* (Cambridge, MA: MIT Press, 1960), pp. 222–37, p. 237.

42 Katz, *Realistic Rationalism*, pp. 36–7.

43 Lewis, *On the Plurality of Worlds*; see also Norris, 'Will the Real Saul Kripke Please Stand Up? Fiction, philosophy and possible worlds', *Textual Practice*, 17, 1 (2003): 225–51.

44 See Raymond Bradley and Norman Swartz, *Possible Worlds: an introduction to logic and its philosophy* (Oxford: Basil Blackwell, 1979);

Jerome S. Bruner, *Actual Minds, Possible Worlds* (Cambridge, MA: Harvard University Press, 1986); Charles S. Chihara, *The Worlds of Possibility: modal realism and the semantics of modal logic* (Oxford: Clarendon Press, 2001); Rod Gierle, *Possible Worlds* (Chesham: Acumen, 2002); M. Loux (ed.), *The Possible and the Actual: readings in the metaphysics of modality* (Ithaca, NY: Cornell University Press, 1979).

45   For further discussion of these issues, see Notes 8 and 35, above; also Paul Benacerraf, 'What Numbers Could Not Be', in Paul Benacerraf and Hilary Putnam (eds), *The Philosophy of Mathematics: selected essays*, 2nd edn (Cambridge: Cambridge University Press, 1983), pp. 272–94; Hartry Field, *Realism, Mathematics and Modality* (Oxford: Basil Blackwell, 1989); Kurt Gödel, 'What Is Cantor's Continuum Problem?', in Benacerraf and Putnam (eds), *Philosophy of Mathematics*, pp. 470–85; Hilary Putnam, *Mathematics, Matter and Method* (Cambridge: Cambridge University Press, 1975).

46   See especially Hilary Putnam, 'Is Semantics Possible?', 'The Meaning of "Meaning"', and 'Language and Reality', in *Mind, Language and Reality* (Cambridge: Cambridge University Press, 1975), pp. 139–52, 215–71 and 272–90.

47   Putnam, *Mind, Language and Reality*; also Saul A. Kripke, *Naming and Necessity* (Oxford: Basil Blackwell, 1980).

48   See Leonard Linsky (ed.), *Reference and Modality* (Oxford: Oxford University Press, 1971); Stephen Schwartz (ed.), *Naming, Necessity, and Natural Kinds* (Ithaca, NY: Cornell University Press, 1977); David Wiggins, *Sameness and Substance* (Oxford: Basil Blackwell, 1980).

49   Katz, *Realistic Rationalism*, p. 37.

50   See Note 35, above.

51   See for instance David Chalmers, *The Conscious Mind* (Oxford: Oxford University Press, 1996); Frank Jackson, 'Epiphenomenal Qualia', *Philosophical Quarterly*, 32 (1982): 127–36); William Lycan, *Consciousness and Experience* (Cambridge, MA: MIT Press, 1996); Lycan (ed.), *Mind and Cognition: a reader* (Oxford: Basil Blackwell, 1990); Thomas Nagel, 'What is it Like to be a Bat?', *Philosophical Review*, 83 (1974): 435–56; J. O'Leary-Hawthorne and M. Michael (eds), *Philosophy of Mind* (Dordrecht: Kluwer Books, 1993); Galen Strawson, *Mental Reality* (Cambridge, MA: MIT Press, 1994).

52   Mark Johnston, 'Are Manifest Qualities Response-Dependent?', *The Monist*, 81 (1998): 3–43; see also Alex Miller, 'The Missing-Explanation Argument Revisited', *Analysis*, 61 (2001): 76–86 and 'More Responses to the Missing-Explanation Argument', *Philosophia*,

25 (1997): 331–49; Peter Menzies and Philip Pettit, 'Found: the
   missing explanation', *Analysis*, 53 (1993): 100–9.

53   See Note 35.

54   For two pioneering essays in this vein, see Allen Forte, 'New
     Approaches to Linear Analysis', *Journal of the American Musicological
     Society*, 41.2 (1988): 315–48 and 'Pitch-Class Set Genera and the
     Origin of the Modern Harmonic Species', *Journal of Music Theory*,
     32.2 (1988): 187–270.

55   Hermann Hesse, *The Glass-Bead Game* (New York: Vintage, 1967).

56   See Note 22, above.

57   Norris, *Minding the Gap*.

58   McDowell, *Mind and World*, p. 41.

59   For further discussion, see Norrris, *Minding the Gap*.

60   See especially T. W. Adorno, *Against Epistemology: a metacritique*,
     trans. Willis Domingo (Cambridge, MA: MIT Press, 1982); also
     Negative Dialectics, trans. E. B. Ashton (London: Routledge & Kegan
     Paul, 1974).

61   Derrida, 'Genesis and Structure', p. 162.

Chapter 3

1   See for instance Malcolm Budd, *Music and the Emotions: the philosophical
    theories* (London: Routledge, 1985); Peter Kivy, *The Corded Shell: reflec-
    tions on musical expression* (Princeton, NJ: Princeton University Press,
    1980) and *The Fine Art of Repetition: essays in the philosophy of music*
    (Cambridge: Cambridge University Press, 1993); Jerrold Levinson,
    Music, Art and Metaphysics (Ithaca, NY: Cornell University Press,
    1990) and *Work and Oeuvre and Other Essays* (Ithaca, NY: Cornell
    University Press, 1996).

2   Jerrold Levinson, *Music in the Moment* (Ithaca, NY: Cornell University
    Press, 1997).

3   Peter Kivy, *New Essays on Musical Understanding* (Oxford: Oxford
    University Press, 2001).

4   See, for instance, T. W. Adorno, *Philosophy of Modern Music*, trans. W.
    Blomster (London: Sheed & Ward, 1973); 'On the Problem of Music
    Analysis', trans. Max Paddison, *Music Analysis*, 1.2 (1982): 170–87;
    Aesthetic Theory, trans. Robert Hullot-Kentnor (London: Athlone
    Press, 1997); *Alban Berg: master of the smallest link*, trans. Juliane
    Brand and Christopher Hailey (Cambridge: Cambridge University
    Press, 1991); *Beethoven: the philosophy of music*, trans. Edmund Jephcott

(Oxford: Polity Press, 1998); *Quasi una Fantasia: essays on modern music*, trans. Rodney Livingstone (London: Verso, 1998).

5 See especially Roman Ingarden, *The Work of Music and the Problem of its Identity*, trans. Adam Czerniawski (London: Macmillan, 1986); also Vladimir Jankélevitch, *Ravel*, trans. Margaret Crosland (New York: Grove Press, 1959) and *Gabriel Fauré: ses mélodies, son esthétique* (Paris: Plon, 1951).

6 John McDowell, *Mind and World* (Cambridge, MA: Harvard University Press, 1994).

7 Christopher Norris, 'McDowell on Kant: redrawing the bounds of sense' and 'The Limits of Naturalism: further thoughts on McDowell's *Mind and World*', in *Minding the Gap: epistemology and philosophy of science in the two traditions* (Amherst, MA: University of Massachusetts Press, 2000), pp. 172–96 and 197–230.

8 For a highly informative and carefully argued treatment of these issues, see Wayne D. Bowman, *Philosophical Perspectives on Music* (New York: Oxford University Press, 1998); also Peter Kivy, *Introduction to a Philosophy of Music* (Oxford: Clarendon Press, 2002); Thomas Christenson (ed.), *The Cambridge History of Western Music Theory* (Cambridge: Cambridge University Press, 2002).

9 See for instance Katherine Bergeron and Philip V. Bohlman (eds), *Disciplining Music: musicology and its canons* (Chicago, IL: University of Chicago Press, 1992); Nicholas Cook and Mark Everist (eds), *Re-Thinking Music* (Oxford: Oxford University Press, 1999); Lawrence Kramer, *Classical Music and Postmodern Knowledge* (Berkeley and Los Angeles, CA: University of California Press, 1995); Judy Lochhead and Joseph Auner (eds), *Postmodern Music/Postmodern Thought* (New York and London: Garland, 2002); Ruth A. Solie (ed.), *Musicology and Difference* (Berkeley and Los Angeles, CA: University of California Press, 1993).

10 T. W. Adorno, *The Culture Industry: selected essays on mass culture*, ed. J. M. Bernstein (London: Routledge, 1991); also Holger Briel and Andreas Kramer (eds), *In Practice: Adorno, critical theory, and cultural studies* (New York: Peter Lang, 2001); Deborah Cook, *The Culture Industry Revisited: Theodor W. Adorno on mass culture* (Lanham, MD: Rowman & Littlefield, 1996); Nigel Gibson and Andrew Rubin (eds), *Adorno: a critical reader* (Oxford: Blackwell, 2002); Max Paddison, *Adorno, Modernism and Mass Culture: essays on critical theory and music* (London: Kahn & Averill, 1996).

11 T. S. Eliot, 'Tradition and the Individual Talent', in *Selected Essays* (London: Faber & Faber, 1949), pp. 13–22.

12   For anti-realist views, see Michael Dummett, *Truth and Other Enigmas*
      (London: Duckworth, 1978), *The Logical Basis of Metaphysics* (London:
      Duckworth, 1991), and *The Seas of Language* (Oxford: Clarendon
      Press, 1993); also Michael Luntley, *Language, Logic and Experience: the
      case for anti-realism* (London: Duckworth, 1988); Neil Tennant, *Anti-
      Realism and Logic* (Oxford: Clarendon Press, 1987) and *The Taming
      of the True* (Oxford: Oxford University Press, 1997). On response-
      dependence – from a range of more-or-less qualified positions – see
      Mark Johnston, 'How to Speak of the Colours', *Philosophical Studies*,
      68 (1992): 221–63, and 'Objectivity Refigured', in J. Haldane and C.
      Wright (eds), *Realism, Representation and Projection* (Oxford: Oxford
      University Press, 1993), pp. 85–130; Christopher Norris, *Truth Matters:
      realism, anti-realism and response-dependence* (Edinburgh: Edinburgh
      University Press, 2002); Philip Pettit, 'Realism and Response
      Dependence', *Mind*, 100 (1991): 597–626; Mark Powell, 'Realism
      or Response-Dependence?', *European Review of Philosophy*, 3 (1998):
      1–13; Ralph Wedgwood, 'The Essence of Response-Dependence',
      European Review of Philosophy, 3 (1998): 31–54; Crispin Wright,
      'Euthyphronism and the Physicality of Colour', *European Review of
      Philosophy*, 3 (1998): 15–30 and *Truth and Objectivity* (Cambridge, MA:
      Harvard University Press, 1992).

13   See especially David Bloor, *Knowledge and Social Imagery* (London:
      Routledge & Kegan Paul, 1976); Barry Barnes, *Scientific Knowledge and
      Sociological Theory* (Routledge & Kegan Paul, 1974); Steve Woolgar,
      Science: the very idea (London: Tavistock Press, 1988). For critical
      views, see Martin Hollis and Steven Lukes (eds), *Rationality and
      Relativism* (Oxford: Basil Blackwell, 1982); W. H. Newton-Smith, *The
      Rationality of Science* (London: Routledge, 1981); Christopher Norris,
      Against Relativism: philosophy of science, deconstruction and critical theory
      (Oxford: Basil Blackwell, 1997).

14   For arguments to this effect, see J. L. Aronson, 'Testing for Convergent
      Realism', *British Journal for the Philosophy of Science*, 40 (1989): 255–60;
      J. Aronson, R. Harré and E. Way, *Realism Rescued: how scientific progress
      is possible* (London: Duckworth, 1994); Richard Boyd, 'The Current
      Status of Scientific Realism', in Jarrett Leplin (ed.), *Scientific Realism*
      (Berkeley and Los Angeles, CA: University of California Press, 1984),
      pp. 41–82; Michael Devitt, *Realism and Truth*, 2nd edn (Oxford: Basil
      Blackwell, 1986); Gilbert Harman, 'Inference to the Best Explanation',
      Philosophical Review, 74 (1965): 88–95; Peter Lipton, *Inference to the
      Best Explanation* (London: Routledge, 1993); Stathis Psillos, *Scientific
      Realism: how science tracks truth* (London: Routledge, 1999).

15 On musical Platonism – from various standpoints – see Ben Caplan and Carl Matheson, 'Can a Musical Work be Created?', *British Journal of Aesthetics*, 44 (2004): 113–34; Gregory Currie, *An Ontology of Art* (London: Macmillan, 1989); Julian Dodd, 'Musical Works as Eternal Types', *The British Journal of Aesthetics*, 40 (2000): 424–40; 'Defending Musical Platonism', *The British Journal of Aesthetics*, 42 (2002): 380–402; 'Types, Continuants, and the Ontology of Music', *British Journal of Aesthetics*, 44 (2004): 342–60; Peter Kivy, 'Platonism in Music: a kind of defense' and 'Platonism in Music: another kind of defense', in *The Fine Art of Repetition* (Cambridge: Cambridge University Press, 1993), pp. 35–58 and 59–74; Jerrold Levinson, 'What a Musical Work Is' and 'What a Musical Work Is, Again', in *Music, Art and Metaphysics: essays in philosophical aesthetics* (Ithaca, NY: Cornell University Press, 1990), pp. 63–88 and 215–63; Robert A. Sharpe, 'Music, Platonism and Performance: some ontological strains', *British Journal of Aesthetics*, 35 (1995): 38–48; Nicholas Wolterstorff, *Works and Worlds of Art* (Oxford: Clarendon Press, 1980).

16 Larry Laudan, 'A Confutation of Convergent Realism', *Philosophy of Science*, 48 (1981): 19–49.

17 See Note 14, above.

18 See especially Stathis Psillos, *Scientific Realism: how science tracks truth* (London: Routledge, 1999); Wesley C. Salmon, *Scientific Explanation and the Causal Structure of the World* (Princeton, NJ: Princeton University Press, 1984).

19 Devitt, *Realism and Truth*, p. 284.

20 See especially Joseph Kerman, 'How We Got into Analysis, and How to Get Out', *Critical Inquiry*, 7 (1980): 311–31; 'A Few Canonic Variations', *Critical Inquiry*, 10 (1983): 107–25; *Musicology* (London: Collins/Fontana, 1985); also Scott Burnham, 'A. B. Marx and the Gendering of Sonata Form', in Ian Bent (ed.), *Music Theory in the Age of Romanticism* (Cambridge: Cambridge University Press, 1996), pp. 163–86; Susan McClary, *Feminine Endings: music, gender, and sexuality* (Minneapolis, MN: University of Minnesota Press, 1981) and *Conventional Wisdom: the content of musical form* (Berkeley and Los Angeles, CA: University of California Press, 2000); Ruth A. Solie, 'The Living Work: organicism and musical analysis', *Nineteenth-Century Musicology*, 4 (1980): 147–56.

21 See, for instance, Lydia Goehr, *The Imaginary Museum of Musical Works: an essay in the philosophy of music* (Oxford: Clarendon Press, 1992); Kevin Korsyn, 'Brahms Research and Aesthetic Ideology', *Music Analysis*, 12 (1993): 89–103; Solie, 'The Living Work'; also –

among the chief sources of this anti-organicist line of thought – Paul de Man, *Aesthetic Ideology*, ed. Andrzej Warminski (Minneapolis, MN: University of Minnesota Press, 1996); Philippe Lacoue-Labarthe and Jean-Luc Nancy, *The Literary Absolute: the theory of literature in German Romanticism*, trans. Philip Barnard and Cheryl Lester (Albany, NY: State University of New York Press, 1988).

22   Goehr, *The Imaginary Museum of Musical Works*.

23   Norris, 'The Perceiver's Share (2): deconstructive musicology and cognitive science', in *Language, Logic and Epistemology: a modal-realist approach* (London: Macmillan, 2004), pp. 185–226.

24   See Note 20, above; also – from a range of (mostly less hostile) viewpoints – Ian Bent and William Drabkin, *Analysis* (Basingstoke: Macmillan, 1987); Nicholas Cook, 'Music Theory and "Good Comparison": a Viennese perspective', *Journal of Music Theory*, 33 (1989): 117–42 and *A Guide to Musical Analysis* (Oxford: Oxford University Press, 1993); Douglas Dempster and Matthew Brown, 'Evaluating Musical Analyses and Theories: five perspectives', *Journal of Music Theory*, 34 (1990): 247–80; Jonathan Dunsby and Arnold Whittall, *Music Analysis in Theory and Practice* (New Haven, CT: Yale University Press, 1988); Anthony Pople, *Theory, Analysis, and Meaning in Music* (Cambridge: Cambridge University Press, 1994).

25   See Note 4, above.

26   See Note 11, above.

27   See Note 2, above.

28   See Heinrich Schenker, *Harmony*, ed. Oswald Jonas, trans. Elisabeth Mann Borgese (Cambridge, MA: MIT Press, 1973) and *Free Composition*, trans. and ed. Ernst Oster (New York: Longman, 1979); also David Beach (ed.), *Aspects of Schenkerian Theory* (New Haven, CT: Yale University Press, 1983); Leslie D. Blasius, *Schenker's Argument and the Claims of Music Theory* (Cambridge: Cambridge University Press, 1996); Allen Forte and Steven E. Gilbert, *Introduction to Schenkerian Analysis* (New York: Norton, 1982); E. Narmour, *Beyond Schenkerism: the need for alternatives in music analysis* (Chicago, IL: University of Chicago Press, 1977); Hedi Siegel (ed.), *Schenker Studies* (Cambridge: Cambridge University Press, 1990); Maury Yeston (ed.), *Readings in Schenker Analysis and other approaches* (New Haven, CT: Yale University Press, 1977).

29   See Note 3, above.

30   See Note 13, above.

31   See Norris, *Truth Matters*; also C. J. Misak, *Verificationism: its history and prospects* (London: Routledge, 1995).

32 Immanuel Kant, *Critique of Pure Reason*, trans. N. Kemp Smith (London: Macmillan, 1964).

33 See Notes 6 and 7, above.

34 See McDowell, *Mind and World*; also Robert B. Brandom, *Making it Explicit: reasoning, representing and discursive commitment* (Cambridge, MA: Harvard University Press, 1994) and *Articulating Reasons: an introduction to inferentialism* (Cambridge, MA: Harvard University Press, 2000).

35 See Note 6, above.

36 See Note 7, above.

37 Jacques Derrida, '"Genesis and Structure" and Phenomenology', in *Writing and Difference*, trans. Alan Bass (London: Routledge & Kegan Paul, 1978), pp. 154–68, p. 160.

38 Ibid., p. 160.

39 Ibid., p. 156.

40 For further discussion of these recent trends, see Norris, *New Idols of the Cave: on the limits of anti-realism* (Manchester: Manchester University Press, 1997); *Resources of Realism: prospects for 'post-analytic' philosophy* (London: Macmillan, 1997); *Against Relativism: philosophy of science, deconstruction and critical theory* (Oxford: Basil Blackwell, 1997).

41 See Note 13, above.

42 Norris, *Truth Matters*.

43 See for instance Roland Barthes, *Image–Music–Text*, trans. Stephen Heath (London: Collins/Fontana, 1977); Jonathan Dunsby, 'Music and Semiotics: the Nattiez phase', *Musical Quarterly*, 69.1 (1983): 27–43; Jean-Jacques Nattiez, *Fondements d'une sémiologie de la musique* (Paris: Union générale d'éditions, 1975); Nicolas Ruwet, *Langage, musique, poésie* (Paris: Seuil, 1972).

44 Ferdinand de Saussure, *Course in General Linguistics*, trans. Roy Harris (London: Duckworth, 1983); also Jonathan Culler, *Structuralist Poetics* (London: Routledge & Kegan Paul, 1975); Terence Hawkes, *Structuralism and Semiotics* (London: Methuen 1977); Michael Lane (ed.), *Structuralism: a reader* (London: Cape, 1970); David Lodge, *The Modes of Modern Writing: metaphor, metonymy and the typology of modern literature* (London: Edward Arnold, 1977).

45 Derrida, 'Genesis and Structure', p. 157.

46 Saussure, *Course in General Linguistics*.

47 Derrida, 'Structure and Genesis'; also *Le problème de la genèse dans la philosophie de Husserl* (Paris: Presses Universitaires de France, 1990).

48 See Note 37, above.

49 See, for instance, Josué V. Harari (ed.), *Textual Strategies: perspectives in post-structuralist criticism* (London: Methuen, 1980); Richard Harland, *Superstructuralism: the philosophy of structuralism and post-structuralism* (London: Routledge, 1987); Robert Young (ed.), *Untying the Text: a post-structuralist reader* (London: Routledge & Kegan Paul, 1981).

50 Derrida, 'Structure, Sign and Play in the Discourse of the Human Sciences', in *Writing and Difference*, pp. 278–93.

51 Derrida, *Of Grammatology*, trans. G. C. Spivak (Baltimore MD: Johns Hopkins University Press, 1976).

52 Cited in Derrida, *Of Grammatology*, p. 199.

53 Ibid., p. 212.

54 Ibid., p. 158.

55 For more detailed discussion, see Norris, 'Deconstruction as Philosophy of Logic: Derrida on Rousseau', in *Language, Logic and Epistemology*, pp. 16–65.

56 Derrida, *Of Grammatology*, p. 158.

57 Ibid., p. 135.

58 Ibid., p. 243.

59 See Notes 37 and 47, above; also Derrida, 'Force and Signification', in *Writing and Difference*, pp. 3–30.

60 See especially Maurice Merleau-Ponty, *Signs*, trans. Richard C. McCleary (Evanston, IL: Northwestern University Press, 1964); *Sense and Non-Sense*, trans. Hubert L. Dreyfus and Patricia A. Dreyfus (Evanston, IL: Northwestern University Press, 1964); *The Visible and the Invisible*, trans. A. Lingis (Evanston, IL: Northwestern University Press, 1975); also M. C. Dillon (ed.), *Ecart et Différance: Merleau-Ponty and Derrida on seeing and writing* (Atlantic Highlands, NJ: Humanities Press, 1997); Galen A. Johnson (ed.), *The Merleau-Ponty Aesthetics Reader* (Evanston, IL: Northwestern University Press, 1993); James Schmidt, *Maurice Merleau-Ponty: between phenomenology and structuralism* (London: Macmillan, 1985).

61 See Norris, *Truth Matters*.

62 See Notes 59 and 60, above.

63 Merleau-Ponty, *The Phenomenology of Perception*, trans. Colin Smith (London: Routledge & Kegan Paul, 1962), p. 389.

64 Roman Jakobson, *Language in Literature*, ed. K. Pomorska and S. Rudy (Cambridge, MA: Harvard University Press, 1987); Derrida, 'Force and Signification', p. 3.

65 See Notes 59 and 60, above.

66 Merleau-Ponty, *Signs*, p. 46.

67 See de Man, *Aesthetic Ideology* and other entries under Note 19, above; also Terry Eagleton, *The Ideology of the Aesthetic* (Oxford: Basil Blackwell, 1989).

68 See especially de Man, 'Aesthetic Formalization in Kleist', in *The Rhetoric of Romanticism* (New York: Columbia University Press, 1984), pp. 263–90.

69 Ibid.; also Friedrich Schiller, *On the Aesthetic Education of Man, in a Series of Letters*, trans. E. M. Wilkinson and L. A. Willoughby (Oxford: Clarendon Press, 1967).

70 Ibid, p. 300.

71 De Man, 'Aesthetic Formalization', p. 265.

72 Ibid., p. 264.

73 Ibid., p. 289.

74 Ibid., p. 289.

75 See Notes 9, 20, 21 and 28, above.

76 See Note 25, above.

77 Hermann Hesse, *The Glass-Bead Game* (New York: Vintage, 1967).

Chapter 4

1 For further discussion of these issues, see Christopher Norris, *Epistemology: key concepts* (London: Continuum, 2005).

2 See especially Michael Dummett, *Truth and Other Enigmas* (London: Duckworth, 1978), *The Logical Basis of Metaphysics* (London: Duckworth, 1991) and *The Seas of Language* (Oxford: Clarendon Press, 1993); also – from a range of viewpoints – Michael Luntley, *Language, Logic and Experience: the case for anti-realism* (London: Duckworth, 1988); Christopher Norris, *Truth Matters: realism, anti-realism and response-dependence* (Edinburgh: Edinburgh University Press, 2002); Neil Tennant, *The Taming of the True* (Oxford: Oxford University Press, 1997).

3 See for instance William P. Alston, *A Realist Conception of Truth* (Ithaca, NY: Cornell University Press, 1996); Bob Hale, *Abstract Objects* (Oxford: Basil Blackwell, 1987); Jerrold J. Katz, *Realistic Rationalism* (Cambridge, MA: MIT Press, 1998); Scott Soames, *Understanding Truth* (Oxford: Oxford University Press, 1999).

4 See Note 3, above.

5 Immanuel Kant, *Critique of Judgement*, trans. J. C. Meredith (Oxford: Clarendon Press, 1978).

6 Kant, *Critique of Pure Reason*, trans. N. Kemp Smith (London: Macmillan, 1964).

7   Kant, *Critique of Judgement.*

8   Alexander Baumgarten, *Aesthetica*, 2 vols (Frankfurt an der Oder, 1750 and 1758); *Reflections on Poetry*, trans. K. Aschenbrenner and W. B. Holther (Berkeley, CA: University of California Press, 1954).

9   Jacques Derrida, 'Parergon', in *The Truth in Painting*, trans. Geoff Bennington and Ian McLeod (Chicago, IL: University of Chicago Press, 1987), pp. 15–147.

10   On this topic, see Mark A. DeBellis, *Music and Conceptualization* (Cambridge: Cambridge University Press, 1995).

11   See Jerry A. Fodor, *The Language of Thought* (Hassocks: Harvester Press, 1976) and *The Modularity of Mind: an essay on faculty psychology* (Cambridge, MA: MIT Press, 1983).

12   Fodor, *The Mind Doesn't Work That Way: the scope and limits of computational psychology* (Cambridge, MA: MIT Press, 2000).

13   See especially Derrida, '"Genesis and Structure" and Phenomenology', in *Writing and Difference*, trans. Alan Bass (London: Routledge & Kegan Paul, 1978), pp. 154–68 and *Le problème de la genèse dans la philosophie de Husserl* (Paris: Presses Universitaires de France, 1990).

14   See Note 13, above.

15   Ludwig Wittgenstein, *Philosophical Investigations*, trans. G. E. M. Anscombe (Oxford: Basil Blackwell, 1953).

16   See Notes 2 and 3, above; also J. Haldane and C. Wright (eds), *Realism, Representation and Projection* (Oxford: Oxford University Press, 1993); Norris, *Truth Matters*; Philip Pettit, *The Common Mind* (Oxford: Oxford University Press, 1992); Crispin Wright, 'Realism, Antirealism, Irrealism, Quasi-Realism', *Midwest Studies in Philosophy*, 12 (1988): 25–49 and *Truth and Objectivity* (Cambridge, MA: Harvard University Press, 1992).

17   For a range of approaches to this question, see Ben Caplan and Carl Matheson, 'Can a Musical Work be Created?', *British Journal of Aesthetics*, 44 (2004): 113–34; Gregory Currie, *An Ontology of Art* (London: Macmillan, 1989); Julian Dodd, 'Musical Works as Eternal Types', *The British Journal of Aesthetics*, 40 (2000): 424–40; 'Defending Musical Platonism', *The British Journal of Aesthetics*, 42 (2002): 380–402; 'Types, Continuants, and the Ontology of Music', *British Journal of Aesthetics*, 44 (2004): 342–60; Peter Kivy, 'Platonism in Music: a kind of defense' and 'Platonism in Music: another kind of defense', in *The Fine Art of Repetition* (Cambridge: Cambridge University Press, 1993), pp. 35–58 and 59–74; Jerrold Levinson, 'What a Musical Work Is' and 'What a Musical Work Is, Again', in *Music, Art and Metaphysics: essays in philosophical aesthetics* (Ithaca, NY: Cornell University Press, 1990),

pp. 63–88 and 215–63; Robert A. Sharpe, 'Music, Platonism and Performance: some ontological strains', *British Journal of Aesthetics*, 35 (1995): 38–48; Nicholas Wolterstorff, *Works and Worlds of Art* (Oxford: Clarendon Press, 1980).

18   See for instance Mark Johnston, 'Dispositional Theories of Value', *Proceedings of the Aristotelian Society*, 63 (1989): 139–74; Philip Pettit, 'Realism and Response Dependence', *Mind*, 100 (1991): 597–626; Mark Powell, 'Realism or Response-Dependence?', *European Review of Philosophy*, 3 (1998): 1–13; Ralph Wedgwood, 'The Essence of Response-Dependence', *European Review of Philosophy*, 3 (1998): 31–54; Crispin Wright, 'Moral Values, Projection, and Secondary Qualities', *Proceedings of the Aristotelian Society*, (supplementary vol.) 62 (1988): 1–26.

19   See, for instance, Malcolm Budd, *Music and the Emotions: the philosophical theories* (London: Routledge, 1985); Peter Kivy, *The Corded Shell: reflections on musical expression* (Princeton, NJ: Princeton University Press, 1980) and *The Fine Art of Repetition: essays in the philosophy of music* (Cambridge: Cambridge University Press, 1993); Jerrold Levinson, *Music, Art and Metaphysics* (Ithaca, NY: Cornell University Press, 1990) and *Work and Oeuvre and Other Essays* (Ithaca, NY: Cornell University Press, 1996).

20   Derrida, 'Genesis and Structure', p. 159.

21   Ibid., p. 157.

22   Derrida, *Writing and Difference*, p. 5.

23   See Hans Reichenbach, *Experience and Prediction* (Berkeley and Los Angeles, CA: University of California Press, 1938).

24   For further discussion of these differences, see Christopher Norris, *Minding the Gap: epistemology and philosophy of science in the two traditions* (Amherst, MA: University of Massachusetts Press, 2000).

25   See Gaston Bachelard, *Le Rationalisme appliqué* (Paris: Presses Universitaires de France, 1949); *The Philosophy of No: a philosophy of the new scientific mind* (New York: Orion, 1968); *The New Scientific Spirit* (Boston, MA: Beacon Press, 1984); also Mary Tiles, *Bachelard: science and objectivity* (Cambridge: Cambridge University Press, 1984).

26   See especially Derrida's commentary on Bachelard in 'White Mythology: metaphor in the text of philosophy', *Margins of Philosophy*, trans. Alan Bass (Chicago, IL: University of Chicago Press, 1982), pp. 207–71; pp. 259–62.

27   See, for instance, Ernest Ansermet, *Les Fondements de la musique dans la conscience humaine* (Edition de la Baconnière, Neuchatel 1961) (German edn, *Die Grundlagen der Musik im menschlichen Bewusstsein*,

trans. H. Leuchtmann and E. Maschat [Munich: Piper Verlag, 1965]; Vladimir Jankélevitch, *Ravel*, trans. Margaret Crosland (New York: Grove Press, 1959) and *Gabriel Fauré: ses mélodies, son esthétique* (Paris: Plon, 1951).

28   Nelson Goodman, *Languages of Art: an approach to a theory of symbols* (Indianapolis, IN: Bobbs-Merrill, 1976).

29   Gottlob Frege, 'The Thought', in *The Frege Reader*, ed. Michael Beaney (Oxford: Basil Blackwell, 1997), pp. 181–93.

30   See Note 13, above.

31   See Note 8, above.

32   See Kevin Barry, *Language, Music and the Sign* (Cambridge: Cambridge University Press, 1987).

33   Philippe Lacoue-Labarthe and Jean-Luc Nancy, *The Literary Absolute: the theory of literature in German Romanticism*, trans. Philip Barnard and Cheryl Lester (Albany, NY: State University of New York Press, 1988); John Neubauer, *The Emancipation of Music from Language: departure from mimesis in eighteenth-century aesthetics* (New Haven, CT: Yale University Press, 1986).

34   See Barry, *Language, Music and the Sign*.

35   For a representative selection of views, see Katherine Bergeron and Philip V. Bohlman (eds), *Disciplining Music: musicology and its canons* (Chicago, IL: University of Chicago Press, 1992); Nicholas Cook and Mark Everist (eds), *Re-Thinking Music* (Oxford: Oxford University Press, 1999); Lawrence Kramer, *Classical Music and Postmodern Knowledge* (Berkeley and Los Angeles, CA: University of California Press, 1995); Judy Lochhead and Joseph Auner (eds), *Postmodern Music/Postmodern Thought* (New York and London: Garland, 2002); Ruth A. Solie (ed.), *Musicology and Difference* (Berkeley and Los Angeles, CA: University of California Press, 1993).

36   Leo Treitler, 'The Historiography of Music: issues of past and present', in Cook and Everist (eds), *Re-Thinking Music*, pp. 356–77; pp. 374–5.

37   See, for instance, Tony Bennett, *Outside Literature* (London: Routledge, 1990).

38   Scott Burnham, 'A.B. Marx and the Gendering of Sonata Form', in Ian Bent (ed.), *Music Theory in the Age of Romanticism* (Cambridge: Cambridge University Press, 1996), pp. 163–86; Lydia Goehr, *The Imaginary Museum of Musical Works: an essay in the philosophy of music* (Oxford: Clarendon Press, 1992); Joseph Kerman, 'How We Got into Analysis, and How to Get Out', *Critical Inquiry*, 7 (1980): 311–31; 'A Few Canonic Variations', *Critical Inquiry*, 10 (1983): 107–25;

Musicology (London: Collins/Fontana, 1985); Kevin Korsyn, 'Brahms Research and Aesthetic Ideology', *Music Analysis*, 12 (1993): 89–103; Ruth A. Solie, 'The Living Work: organicism and musical analysis', *Nineteenth-Century Musicology*, 4 (1980): 147–56; also – in a closely related literary-critical vein – Paul de Man, *Aesthetic Ideology*, ed. Andrzej Warminski (Minneapolis, MN: University of Minnesota Press, 1996); Philippe Lacoue-Labarthe and Jean-Luc Nancy, *The Literary Absolute*.

39 See especially Charles Rosen, *The Classical Style*, rev. edn (London: Faber & Faber 1976).

40 For a highly perceptive survey, see Hans Keller, *The Great Haydn Quartets* (London: Dent, 1986).

41 Jonathan Dunsby, 'The Multi-Piece in Brahms: *Fantasien*, Op. 116', in R. Pascall (ed.), *Brahms: biographical, documentary and analytical studies* (Cambridge: Cambridge University Press, 1983); Alan Street, 'Superior Myths, Dogmatic Allegories: the resistance to musical unity', *Music Analysis*, 8 (1989): 77–123; also Dunsby, *Structural Ambiguity in Brahms: analytical approaches to four works* (Ann Arbor, MI: UMI Research Press, 1981).

42 See de Man, *Aesthetic Ideology*.

43 Treitler, 'The Historiography of Music', p. 369.

44 Ibid., p. 369; Susan McClary, 'A Musical Dialectic from the Enlightenment: Mozart's Piano Concerto in G Major, K.453, Movement 2', *Cultural Critique*, 4 (1986): 129–69; also Lawrence Kramer, '*Carnaval*, Cross-Dressing, and the Woman in the Mirror', in Solie (ed.), *Musicology and Difference*, pp. 305–25.

45 See McClary 'A Musical 'Dialectic', pp. 129–69; Kramer '*Carnaval*', pp. 305–25.

46 See Notes 2, 17 and 18, above.

47 See Notes 17 and 18, above; also Mark Johnston, 'How to Speak of the Colours', *Philosophical Studies*, 68 (1992): 221–63, and 'Objectivity Refigured', in Haldane and Wright (eds), *Realism, Representation and Projection*, pp. 85–130.

48 *Plato's Euthyphro, Apology of Socrates, and Crito*, ed. John Burnet (Oxford: Clarendon Press, 1977); also Crispin Wright, 'Euthyphronism and the Physicality of Colour', *European Review of Philosophy*, 3 (1998): 15–30 and *Truth and Objectivity* (Cambridge, MA: Harvard University Press, 1992).

49 For further argument to this effect, see Norris, *Minding the Gap*.

50 Gilbert Ryle, 'Phenomenology' and 'Phenomenology versus *The Concept of Mind*', in Ryle, *Collected Papers*, Vol. 1 (London: Hutchinson, 1971), pp. 167–78 and 179–96.

51 For some useful pointers in this direction, see Joseph L. DiGiovanna, *Linguistic Phenomenology: philosophical method in J. L. Austin* (New York: Peter Lang, 1989).

52 See Note 3, above.

53 T. S. Eliot, 'Hamlet and his Problems', in *The Sacred Wood: essays on poetry and criticism* (London: Methuen, 1921), pp. 95–103.

54 T. S. Eliot, *Knowledge and Experience in the Philosophy of F.H. Bradley* (London: Faber & Faber, 1964).

55 See Edmund Husserl, *Formal and Transcendental Logic*, trans. Dorion Cairns (The Hague: Nijhoff, 1969); *Logical Investigations*, trans. J. N. Findlay, 2 vols (New York: Humanities Press, 1970); *Ideas: general introduction to pure phenomenology*, trans. W. R. Boyce Gibson (London: Collier Macmillan 1975).

56 Plato, *Meno*, in J. M. Cooper (ed.), *Plato: Complete Works* (Indianapolis, IN: Hackett, 1997).

57 J. Alberto Coffa, *The Semantic Tradition from Kant to Carnap: to the Vienna Station* (Cambridge: Cambridge University Press, 1991).

58 See Note 13, above.

59 T. W. Adorno, 'On the Problem of Musical Analysis', trans. Max Paddison, *Music Analysis*, 1.2 (1982): 170–87, 183.

60 Ibid., p. 185.

61 See also Adorno, *Philosophy of Modern Music*, trans. W. Blomster (London: Sheed & Ward, 1973); *Alban Berg: master of the smallest link*, trans. Juliane Brand and Christopher Hailey (Cambridge: Cambridge University Press, 1991); *In Search of Wagner*, trans. Rodney Livingstone (London: Verso, 1991); *Aesthetic Theory*, trans. Robert Hullot-Kentnor (London: Athlone Press, 1997); *Quasi una Fantasia: essays on modern music*, trans. Rodney Livingstone (London: Verso, 1998); *Beethoven: the philosophy of music*, trans. Edmund Jephcott (Oxford: Polity Press, 1998).

62 See especially Adorno, *Aesthetic Theory* and *Negative Dialectics*, trans. E. B. Ashton (London: Routledge & Kegan Paul, 1974).

63 Adorno, 'On the Problem of Musical Analysis', p. 186.

64 See Note 61, above.

65 Derrida, *Of Grammatology*, trans. G. C. Spivak (Baltimore, MD: Johns Hopkins University Press, 1976).

66 Ibid., p. 200.

67 Christopher Norris, 'Derrida on Rousseau: deconstruction as philosophy of logic', in Norris, *Language, Logic and Epistemology: a modal-realist approach* (London: Macmillan, 2004), pp. 16–65.

68 See Note 19, above.

69 See Note 38, above.

Chapter 5

1   William Empson, *Seven Types of Ambiguity* (London: Chatto & Windus, 1930).

2   See for instance Rosamond Tuve, *A Reading of George Herbert* (London: Faber & Faber, 1952).

3   Empson, 'O Miselle Passer', in *Argufying: essays on literature and culture*, ed. John Haffenden (London: Chatto & Windus, 1987), pp. 193–202; also John Sparrow, 'Practical Criticism: a reply to Mr. Empson', *Oxford Outlook*, 10 (November 1930): 598–607.

4   See various of the articles and reviews collected in Empson, *Argufying* for further arguments to this effect.

5   See Jacques Derrida, *Of Grammatology*, trans. G. C. Spivak (Baltimore, MD: Johns Hopkins University Press, 1976) and 'Structure, Sign and Play in the Discourse of the Human Sciences', in *Writing and Difference*, trans. Alan Bass (London: Routledge & Kegan Paul, 1978), pp. 278–93.

6   Roland Barthes, *The Pleasure of the Text*, trans. Richard Miller (London: Jonathan Cape, 1976).

7   For further striking examples see Barthes, *S/Z*, trans. Richard Miller (London: Cape, 1975); *Image–Music–Text*, trans. and ed. Stephen Heath (London: Collins/Fontana, 1977); *Roland Barthes by Roland Barthes*, trans. Richard Howard (London: Macmillan, 1977).

8   See Empson, *Argufying*, for some of his repeated fallings-out with 'theory' in its various forms.

9   See, for instance, Charles Rosen, *Arnold Schoenberg* (New York: Viking Press, 1975), *The Classical Style*, rev. edn (London: Faber & Faber 1976), *The Romantic Generation* (London: HarperCollins, 1996), and *Critical Entertainments: music old and new* (Cambridge, MA: Harvard University Press, 2000).

10   For discussion of these and related topics, see 'Charles Rosen in Conversation with Christopher Norris', *Music and Musicians*, 25 (1977): 30–32 and 34.

11   See, for instance, James M. Baker, David W. Beach and Jonathan W. Bernard (eds), *Music Theory in Concept and Practice* (Rochester, NY: University of Rochester Press, 1977); Katherine Bergeron and Philip V. Bohlman (eds), *Disciplining Music: musicology and its canons* (Chicago, IL: University of Chicago Press, 1992); Nicholas Cook and Mark Everist (eds), *Re-Thinking Music* (Oxford: Oxford University Press, 1999); Lawrence Kramer, *Classical Music and Postmodern Knowledge* (Berkeley and Los Angeles, CA: University of California

Press, 1995); Judy Lochhead and Joseph Auner (eds), *Postmodern Music/Postmodern Thought* (New York and London: Garland, 2002); Ruth A. Solie (ed.), *Musicology and Difference* (Berkeley and Los Angeles, CA: University of California Press, 1993).

12 Eduard Hanslick, *On the Musically Beautiful: a contribution towards the revision of the aesthetics of music*, trans. Geoffrey Payzant (Indianapolis, IN: Hackett, 1986).

13 See Joseph Kerman, 'How We Got into Analysis, and how to get out', *Critical Inquiry*, 7 (1980): 311–31; 'A Few Canonic Variations', *Critical Inquiry*, 10 (1983): 107–25; *Musicology* (London: Collins/Fontana, 1985); also Scott Burnham, 'A.B. Marx and the Gendering of Sonata Form', in Ian Bent (ed.), *Music Theory in the Age of Romanticism* (Cambridge: Cambridge University Press, 1996), pp. 163–86; Ruth A. Solie, 'The Living Work: organicism and musical analysis', *Nineteenth-Century Musicology*, 4 (1980): 147–56.

14 See Heinrich Schenker, *Harmony*, ed. Oswald Jonas, trans. Elisabeth Mann Borgese (Cambridge, MA: MIT Press, 1973) and *Free Composition*, trans. and ed. Ernst Oster (New York: Longman, 1979); also David Beach (ed.), *Aspects of Schenkerian Theory* (New Haven, CT: Yale University Press, 1983); Leslie D. Blasius, *Schenker's Argument and the Claims of Music Theory* (Cambridge: Cambridge University Press, 1996); Allen Forte and Steven E. Gilbert, *Introduction to Schenkerian Analysis* (New York: Norton, 1982); E. Narmour, *Beyond Schenkerism: the need for alternatives in music analysis* (Chicago, IL: University of Chicago Press, 1977); Hedi Siegel (ed.), *Schenker Studies* (Cambridge: Cambridge University Press, 1990); Leo Treitler, 'Music Analysis in a Historical Context', in *Music and the Historical Imagination* (Cambridge, MA: Harvard University Press, 1989), pp. 67–78; Maury Yeston (ed.), *Readings in Schenker Analysis and Other Approaches* (New Haven, CT: Yale University Press, 1977).

15 See various entries under Notes 11, 13 and 14, above.

16 See for instance Lydia Goehr, *The Imaginary Museum of Musical Works: an essay in the philosophy of music* (Oxford: Clarendon Press, 1992); Kevin Korsyn, 'Brahms Research and Aesthetic Ideology', *Music Analysis*, 12 (1993): 89–103; Solie, 'The Living Work'; also – in a closely related vein – Paul de Man, *Aesthetic Ideology*, ed. Andrzej Warminski (Minneapolis, MN: University of Minnesota Press, 1996); Philippe Lacoue-Labarthe and Jean-Luc Nancy, *The Literary Absolute: the theory of literature in German Romanticism*, trans. Philip Barnard and Cheryl Lester (Albany, NY: State University of New York Press, 1988).

17 Lacoue-Labarthe and Nancy, *The Literary Absolute.*

18   Notes 11, 13 and 14, above.

19   For a range of views on musical analysis, its scope and limits, see Ian
      Bent and William Drabkin, *Analysis* (Basingstoke: Macmillan, 1987);
      Nicholas Cook, 'Music Theory and "Good Comparison": a Viennese
      perspective', *Journal of Music Theory*, 33 (1989): 117–42, *A Guide to
      Musical Analysis* (Oxford: Oxford University Press, 1993) and *Analysis
      through Composition* (Oxford: Oxford University Press, 1996); Douglas
      Dempster and Matthew Brown, 'Evaluating Musical Analyses and
      Theories: five perspectives', *Journal of Music Theory*, 34 (1990):
      247–80; Jonathan Dunsby and Arnold Whittall, *Music Analysis in
      Theory and Practice* (New Haven, CT: Yale University Press, 1988);
      Anthony Pople, *Theory, Analysis, and Meaning in Music* (Cambridge:
      Cambridge University Press, 1994).

20   See especially Theodor W. Adorno, *Philosophy of Modern Music*, trans.
      W. Blomster (London: Sheed & Ward, 1973); 'On the Problem of
      Music Analysis', trans. Max Paddison, *Music Analysis*, 1.2 (1982):
      170–87; *Aesthetic Theory*, trans. Robert Hullot-Kentnor (London:
      Athlone Press, 1997); *Quasi una Fantasia: essays on modern music*,
      trans. Rodney Livingstone (London: Verso, 1998).

21   Adorno, *The Culture Industry: selected essays on mass culture*, ed. J. M.
      Bernstein (London: Routledge, 1991).

22   See Holger Briel and Andreas Kramer (eds), *In Practice: Adorno,
      critical theory, and cultural studies* (New York: Peter Lang, 2001);
      Deborah Cook, *The Culture Industry Revisited: Theodor W. Adorno
      on mass culture* (Lanham, MD: Rowman & Littlefield, 1996); Nigel
      Gibson and Andrew Rubin (eds), *Adorno: a critical reader* (Oxford:
      Basil Blackwell, 2002); Max Paddison, *Adorno, Modernism and Mass
      Culture: essays on critical theory and music* (London: Kahn & Averill,
      1996).

23   Rose Rosengard Subotnik, *Deconstructive Variations: music and reason in
      Western society* (Minneapolis, MN: University of Minnesota Press, 1996).

24   Adorno, *The Culture Industry*.

25   Subotnik, *Developing Variations: style and ideology in Western music*
      (Minneapolis, MN: University of Minnesota Press, 1991).

26   Adorno, *Alban Berg: master of the smallest link*, trans. Juliane Brand
      and Christopher Hailey (Cambridge: Cambridge University Press,
      1991); *In Search of Wagner*, trans. Rodney Livingstone (London:
      Verso, 1991); *Beethoven: the philosophy of music*, trans. Edmund Jephcott
      (Oxford: Polity Press, 1998).

27   See Adorno, *Aesthetic Theory* and *Negative Dialectics*, trans. E. B.
      Ashton (London: Routledge & Kegan Paul, 1974).

28 See various entries under Notes 11, 13, 14 and 16, above; also Pierre Bourdieu, *Distinction: a social critique of the judgement of taste*, trans. R. Nice (Cambridge, MA: Harvard University Press, 1984).

29 See especially Hans Reichenbach, *Experience and Prediction* (Chicago, IL: University of Chicago Press, 1938).

30 Kerman, 'How We Got into Analysis'.

31 See Notes 13 and 16, above.

32 See, for instance, Kerman, *The Elizabethan Madrigal: a comparative study* (New York: American Musicological Society, 1962), *The Beethoven Quartets* (Oxford: Oxford University Press, 1967) and *The Masses and Motets of William Byrd* (London: Faber & Faber, 1981).

33 See de Man, *Aesthetic Ideology*; also *Blindness and Insight: essays in the rhetoric of contemporary criticism* (London: Methuen, 1983), *The Rhetoric of Romanticism* (New York: Columbia University Press, 1984) and *The Resistance to Theory* (Manchester: Manchester University Press. 1986).

34 See Notes 11, 13 and 16, above.

35 Jonathan Dunsby, 'The Multi-Piece in Brahms: *Fantasien*, Op. 116', in R. Pascall (ed.), *Brahms: biographical, documentary and analytical studies* (Cambridge: Cambridge University Press, 1983); also Dunsby, *Structural Ambiguity in Brahms: analytical approaches to four works* (Ann Arbor, MI: UMI Research Press, 1981).

36 Alan Street, 'Superior Myths, Dogmatic Allegories: the resistance to musical unity', *Music Analysis*, 8 (1989): 77–123.

37 De Man, *The Resistance to Theory*, p. 11.

38 See entries under Note 33, above.

39 See especially Cleanth Brooks, *The Well Wrought Urn: studies in the structure of poetry* (New York: Harcourt Brace, 1947) and W. K. Wimsatt, *The Verbal Icon: studies in the meaning of poetry* (Lexington, KY: University of Kentucky Press, 1954).

40 De Man, *Blindness and Insight*.

41 See de Man, 'The Rhetoric of Temporality', ibid., pp. 187–208; also *Allegories of Reading: figural language in Rousseau, Nietzsche, Rilke, and Proust* (New Haven, CT: Yale University Press, 1979).

42 De Man, *Allegories of Reading* and entries under Note 30, above; also Rodolphe Gasché, *The Wild Card of Reading: on Paul de Man* (Cambridge, MA: Harvard University Press, 1998) and Christopher Norris, *Paul de Man: deconstruction and the critique of aesthetic ideology* (New York: Routledge, 1988).

43 De Man, *The Resistance to Theory*, p. 11.

44 Ferdinand de Saussure, *Course in General Linguistics*, trans. Wade Baskin (London: Collins/Fontana, 1974).

45   De Man, *The Resistance to Theory*, p. 10.

46   Ibid., p. 11.

47   Fred Lerdahl and Ray Jackendoff, *A Generative Theory of Tonal Music* (Cambridge, MA: MIT Press, 1983).

48   Jerrold Levinson, *Music in the Moment* (Ithaca, NY: Cornell University Press, 1997).

49   Peter Kivy, *New Essays on Musical Understanding* (Oxford: Oxford University Press, 2001).

50   See Susan McClary, *Feminine Endings: music, gender, and sexuality* (Minneapolis, MN: University of Minnesota Press, 1981); also *Conventional Wisdom: the content of musical form* (Berkeley and Los Angeles, CA: University of California Press, 2000).

51   McClary, *Feminine Endings*.

52   Kivy, *New Essays on Musical Understanding.*

53   See Notes 20, 21, 26 and 27, above.

54   See Notes 9 and 10, above.

55   Vladimir Jankélevitch, *Ravel*, trans. Margaret Crosland (New York: Grove Press, 1959); also *Gabriel Fauré: ses mélodies, son esthétique* (Paris: Plon, 1951).

56   Rosen, 'Music à la Mode', *The New York Review of Books*, 41.12 (June, 1994).

57   See especially David Lodge, *The Modes of Modern Writing: metaphor, metonymy, and the typology of modern literature* (London: Edward Arnold, 1977).

58   Roland Barthes, *Mythologies*, trans. Anette Lavers (New York: Hill & Wang, 1984), p. 186.

60   Jerry A. Fodor, *The Language of Thought* (Hassocks: Harvester Press, 1976), *The Modularity of Mind: an essay on faculty psychology* (Cambridge, MA: MIT Press, 1983) and *A Theory of Content and other essays* (Cambridge, MA: MIT Press, 1989).

61   Fodor, *The Mind Doesn't Work That Way: the scope and limits of computational psychology* (Cambridge, MA: MIT Press, 2000).

62   Mark A. DeBellis, *Music and Conceptualization* (Cambridge: Cambridge University Press, 1995).

63   Jacques Derrida, 'Parergon', in *The Truth in Painting*, trans. Geoff Bennington and Ian McLeod (Chicago, IL: University of Chicago Press, 1987), pp. 15–147.

64   Immanuel Kant, *Critique of Judgement*, trans. J. C. Meredith (Oxford: Clarendon Press, 1978).

65   See Derrida, *The Truth in Painting*; *Of Grammatology*; *Dissemination*, trans. Barbara Johnson (London: Athlone Press, 1980); *Margins of*

Philosophy, trans. Alan Bass (Chicago, IL: University of Chicago Press, 1982); *Limited Inc*, ed. Gerald Graff (Evanston, IL: Northwestern University Press, 1989); also Christopher Norris, 'Derrida on Rousseau : deconstruction as philosophy of logic', in Norris and David Roden (eds), *Jacques Derrida*, 4 vols (London: Sage, 2003), Vol. 2, pp. 70–124.

66   See especially Bourdieu, *Distinction: a critique of the judgement of taste*; also – for some arguments to contrary or at any rate more philosophically nuanced effect – Terry Eagleton, *The Ideology of the Aesthetic* (Oxford: Basil Blackwell, 1989) and Norris, *Deconstruction and the 'Unfinished Project of Modernity'* (London: Athlone Press, 2000).

67   In this connection, see Jacques Derrida, 'The Principle of Reason: the university in the eyes of its pupils', *Diacritics*, 19 (1983): 3–20; 'Mochlos, or the Conflict of the Faculties', in Richard Rand (ed.), *Logomachia* (Lincoln and Nebraska, NB: University of Nebraska Press, 1992), pp. 3–34; 'Of an Apocalyptic Tone Newly Adopted in Philosophy', in Harold Coward and Toby Foshay (eds), *Derrida and Negative Theology* (Albany, NY: State University of New York Press, 1992), pp. 24–71; also Norris, *Deconstruction and the 'Unfinished Project of Modernity'* and 'Kant Disfigured: ethics, deconstruction, and the textual sublime', in *The Truth about Postmodernism* (Oxford: Basil Blackwell, 1993), pp. 182–256.

68   Jean-François Lyotard, *The Postmodern Condition: a report on knowledge*, trans. Geoff Bennington and Brian Massumi (Manchester: Manchester University Press, 1984).

69   See Kant, *The Conflict of the Faculties*, trans. Mary J. Gregor (New York: Abaris Books, 1979) and *Political Writings*, ed. Hans Reiss (Cambridge: Cambridge University Press, 1976).

70   See especially Jacques Derrida, 'Force and Signification', in *Writing and Difference*, trans. Alan Bass (London: Routledge & Kegan Paul, 1978), pp. 3–30.

71   For further discussion, see Norris, *Minding the Gap: epistemology and philosophy of science in the two traditions* (Amherst, MA: University of Massachusetts Press, 2000).

72   De Man, *The Resistance to Theory*.

73   See especially de Man, 'Aesthetic Formalization in Kleist', in *The Rhetoric of Romanticism*, pp. 263–90.

74   On this topic more generally, see Rita Aiello and John Sloboda (eds), *Musical Perceptions* (New York: Oxford University Press, 1993); Dane Deutsch (ed.), *The Psychology of Music* (San Diego, CA: Academic Press, 1999); W. J. Dowling and Diane L. Harwood, *Music Cognition*

(San Diego, CA: Academic Press, 1986); John Sloboda, *The Musical Mind: the cognitive psychology of music* (Oxford: Oxford University Press, 1985).

75   See for instance Leonard B. Meyer, *Music, the Arts, and Ideas* (Chicago, IL: University of Chicago Press, 1965).

76   Kant, *Critique of Judgement*.

77   Arnold Schoenberg, *Style and Idea: selected writings of Arnold Schoenberg*, trans. Leo Black (London: Faber & Faber 1984) and *The Musical Idea and the logic, technique, and art of its presentation*, trans. Patricia Carpenter and Severine Neff (New York: Columbia University Press, 1995).

78   Empson, *Seven Types of Ambiguity*.

79   Ibid., p. 254.

80   Ibid., p. 253.

Index of Names